Teaching

Teaching Latin
Contexts, Theories, Practices

Steven Hunt

BLOOMSBURY ACADEMIC
LONDON • NEW YORK • OXFORD • NEW DELHI • SYDNEY

BLOOMSBURY ACADEMIC
Bloomsbury Publishing Plc
50 Bedford Square, London, WC1B 3DP, UK
1385 Broadway, New York, NY 10018, USA
29 Earlsfort Terrace, Dublin 2, Ireland

BLOOMSBURY, BLOOMSBURY ACADEMIC and the Diana logo are trademarks
of Bloomsbury Publishing Plc

First published in Great Britain 2022

Cover image: Iordache Laurentiu / 500px via Getty

A catalogue record for this book is available from the British Library.

A catalog record for this book is available from the Library of Congress.

ISBN: HB: 978-1-3501-6138-2
      PB: 978-1-3501-6137-5
      ePDF: 978-1-3501-6139-9
      eBook: 978-1-3501-6140-5

Typeset by RefineCatch Limited, Bungay, Suffolk
Printed and bound in Great Britain

To find out more about our authors and books visit www.bloomsbury.com
and sign up for our newsletters.

Contents

The references to the *Cambridge Latin Course* on pp. 66–7 and 171–4 are with permission of CSCP.

Acknowledgements

This book is lovingly dedicated to my father John Hunt (1933–2020). I have been lucky enough to have made a career of sorts out of teaching Classics to students in schools and, more recently, to trainee teachers. After university, I had one year in the 'real world', decided I did not like it, and went back to school. Following training, I started as a school teacher in 1987 in a non-selective state-maintained boys' school in the eastern suburbs of London, teaching Latin, Greek, Ancient History and Classical Civilization. Today, it feels like it must have been a dream – to teach all four subjects at the same school. It did not last, of course: a new headteacher pruned the department and I left to go to another school in North London. I became an examiner for A level Ancient History with OCR, and then for Classical Civilization for AQA, and became a member of the Joint Association of Classical Teachers (JACT) Council as subject representative for Classical Civilization. I moved shortly after to a small town in Hertfordshire, where the local school had a more enlightened headteacher, and Latin, Greek and Classical Civilization were back on the menu (as were annual trips to Greece and Italy and seemingly more music and drama in the school than in the West End).

It was there that I became involved with the Faculty of Education at the University of Cambridge as a mentor for teacher trainees in Classics and helped Bob Lister's team at the Cambridge School Classics Project (CSCP) develop digital resources for the *Cambridge Latin Course*. When Bob retired from the Faculty in 2008, I was lucky enough to be appointed the Subject Lecturer for Initial Teacher Education (ITE) in Classics on the Postgraduate Certificate of Education (PGCE) programme. I continued to work a little at my local school in Cambridge, teaching Latin part-time. I had a minor part in developing the WJEC Latin examinations and also in the soon-to-be-released version of the International Baccalaureate Latin examination. I became Editor of the *Journal of Classics Teaching* (*JCT*). I also became a consultant and teacher-trainer for the charity Classics for All, whose aim is to support the introduction of classical subjects into state-maintained schools in the UK. With them, I helped set up ITE courses at Liverpool Hope University and for the Harris Academies Trust. I was President of the Association for Latin Teaching (ARLT) and directed a summer school at Uppingham School. I helped with the new Latin course *Suburani*.

On the way, I have had the great fortune to be involved in numerous classics-related organizations and initiatives, and to have met and talked Classics with many great people: at CSCP with Pat Story, Bob Lister and Will Griffiths (now at *Suburani*); with ITE colleagues Aisha Khan-Evans at King's College London, Rowley Darby at the University of Sussex, and with Pantelis Iacovou at Harris Academies and Alice Case and Joanne Mcnamara at Liverpool College; with US colleagues (via the American Classical League) Peter Howard, Kenneth Kitchell, Ronnie Ancona, Benjamin Joffe, Bartolo Natoli and Justin Scwhamm; with ARLT friends; with ACE team Edith Hall and Arlene Holmes-Henderson; with Oxford colleagues Mai Musié and Cressida Ryan; with Cambridge colleagues Frances Foster, David Butterfield, Mary Beard, James Clackson and Rosanna Omitowoju; with the 'Latin-Speaking Group' Mair Lloyd, Fergus Walsh, Rachel Plummer, Clive Letchford and Laura Manning; with Barbara Bell, Caroline Lawrence, Evelien Bracke, John Bulwer, Emily Matters, Terence Tunberg, Sara Aguilar, Gill Mead, Steve Llewellyn, Simon Trafford, John Collett, Gratus Avitus, Hilary Hodgson and many others from universities and schools across the world. I must also thank Alice Wright and Lily Mac Mahon at Bloomsbury Publishing for encouraging me to continue writing and for the anonymous reviewers who gave help and advice in earlier versions of the manuscript. Having around twenty new teacher trainees each year, I get to 'see' inside classrooms across the range of schools and try out new ideas as well as refine old practices; and they produce a glorious set of mini-research projects each year – some of which find their way into *JCT* and help inform present and future teachers. A virtuous circle. If I go back a little, I must also thank my own instructors when I undertook initial teacher training: Richard Woff and John Muir. Their clever ideas and kind support saw me through that difficult period of training when you realize that not everyone in the classroom is as obsessed with ancient languages as you are.

Introduction

This book is for teachers who want to teach the Latin as a language, involving listening to, reading, speaking and writing Latin. By developing students' skills in using the language, rather than merely training them to describe it, second-language research suggests they will develop proficiency efficiently, effectively and joyfully – and provide the necessary knowledge and skills for examinations. The aim is to bring together examples of current practice, underpinned by research, for beginning and more experienced teachers and to encourage them to explore teaching approaches that they have perhaps not yet tried. Teachers on Latin/Classics Initial Teacher Education (ITE) programmes and for non-specialists who are asked to bring Latin into schools where there has been none before will find this book essential reading.

In the UK, for nearly fifty years, Kenneth Baker's National Curriculum, an entitlement for all students in state-maintained schools, has made little room for Latin. During that period, support from government in helping the subject community develop a curriculum which is suitable for the conditions in which school students might learn it has been minimal, sporadic and inconsistent. Baker's reforms nearly killed Latin off in state-maintained schools. More recently, however, perhaps out of remorse, there has been a change of heart: the education reforms of 2010–14 promoted Latin by allowing it to be one of the compulsory languages for 7-to-11-year-old students in primary school, and by counting it among the recommended GCSE subjects of the English Baccalaureate, a school accountability measure which acts as a prompt to school leaders to encourage students to aspire to higher education in research-intensive universities. There is greater interest now in putting Latin into school curricula than has existed for a long time. Simultaneous with the demand for more Latin has come an attack on teacher training: placements are relatively few, and many teachers come to teach Latin with only a GCSE or A level or nothing at all in Latin. Similar difficulties in the provision of specialist training for Latin teaching exist in the US. My first book, *Starting to Teach Latin* (2016), was designed to appeal to beginners in Latin teaching, and to show them how to approach such important issues as vocabulary learning, differentiation (now called adaptive teaching in the UK) and reading comprehension. This book builds on that one.

For a subject which has been around in schools and universities perhaps longer than most, there has been precious little research carried out in Anglophone countries about the practice of Latin teaching. Readers of this book from other subject areas, especially those from Modern Foreign Languages (MFL) will no doubt be surprised; but the fact is that, since the 1990s, the subject communities have spent most of their time fighting for survival in a period when the subject has been marginalized from the curriculum in both the UK and the US. Energy has been – and continues to be – put into the development of suitable resources, training and advocacy work.

A small number of books have been published on teaching Latin. They are all very well worth reading. From the US perspective, Rick LaFleur's *Latin for the 21st Century: From Concept to Classroom*, although dating from 1998, still contains useful chapters on teaching Latin texts, grammar and vocabulary at the school levels. John Gruber-Miller's *When Dead Tongues Speak: Teaching Beginning Latin and Greek* (2006) also contains excellent practical advice for the classroom. From the UK comes Bob Lister's *Meeting the Challenge: International Perspectives on the Teaching of Latin* (2008), with many chapters of a pedagogic nature. Less specific, James Morwood's *The Teaching of Classics* (2003) provides an overview of conditions in school teaching and Lister's *Changing Classics in Schools* (2007) details the development of the *Cambridge Latin Course* digital resources and that author's War with Troy materials for younger students. More recently, my own *Forward with Classics* (2018), co-edited with Arlene Holmes-Henderson and Mai Musié, elaborated on some of the institutional barriers to setting up Latin in schools and how to overcome them. My book *Teaching Classics with Technology* (2019), co-edited with Bartolo Natoli, showcased some exciting developments in using educational technology in bringing the world of classics – and teaching it – alive for the twenty-first-century classroom. My book *Communicative Approaches for Ancient Languages* (2021), co-edited with Mair Lloyd, explores recent initiatives at the school and university level to bring living Latin back to the classroom. All three are designed to be of practical use, containing examples of classroom practices that any teacher can try out.

There has, however, been almost no large-scale research into how modern students learn Latin, at least in English, outside occasional doctoral theses,[1] let alone how to improve it. But classroom practice has evolved way beyond the traditional Present-Practice-Feedback routines of traditional practices, and in the last ten years the subject communities' professional journals on both sides of the Atlantic have improved in quality and extent and provide multiple snapshots of classroom practice, as well as being increasingly grounded in language-learning theories.

For the US, *The Classical Outlook* and *Teaching Classical Languages* always contain articles of real pedagogic value. For the UK, the *Journal of Classics Teaching* (disclaimer alert – I am the editor!) publishes many small-scale examples of practitioner research, often carried out by teachers on initial teacher training programmes in the UK and from the rest of Europe. There are many good non-English professional journals about the teaching of Latin, drawn from the experiences of teachers across Europe and further afield: for the monolingual teacher, *Google Translate* has potential in making many of these accessible; the *Euroclassica* website has interest for teachers in mainland Europe, as does John Bulwer's book *Classics Teaching in Europe* (Bulwer 2006).[2] Though sometimes methodologically uneven, these articles enable us to glimpse valuable and practical ideas, underpinned by theory and often drawing on research in Second Language Development (SLD). Many Latin teachers are now beginning to investigate SLD research themselves, in the belief that it may have value for Latin teaching, even if the ultimate aims of MFL and Latin teaching may be different. Students might not have to communicate in Latin as their MFL colleagues are aiming to do; nor are they assessed in their ability to listen, speak, read and write as students of MFL. Nevertheless, it would not be sensible to discount the findings of some fifty years of research into SLD if at least some of it would help students' learning in Latin. Particularly useful readings in this regard have been Jacqui Carlon's 'The Implications of SLA Research for Latin Pedagogy: Modernizing Latin Instruction and Securing its Place in Curricula' (2013), and Alan van den Arend's 'Something Old, Something New: Marrying Early Modern Latin Pedagogy and Second Language Acquisition (SLA) Theory' (2018). The *Journal of Classics Teaching*, issue 39 (2019), also contains several good contributors' articles edited by Keith Rogers on the subject of teaching Latin with Comprehensible Input. As a teacher trainer for Classics, I always start by telling my trainees that I want them to accomplish two things: to learn how to do the job as it is, and how to do it differently – perhaps better! In the same vein, this book aims to get the reader started on fresh adventures.

There are no 'best ways' of teaching, let alone teaching Latin. Instead, there are many different ways which work for individual teachers, for different students, and in different classrooms and schools from one place to the next, one time to the next. How many times have teachers noted the differences in which a class behaves in the afternoon compared to the way it behaves in the morning, or after lunch or after sports? But some methods *do* work better than others and it would be foolish to censure the students for their lack of learning if it was the method that was the cause of the blame. And teachers, too, change. As a beginning teacher, I admit I was more interested in developing my own teaching style and securing my own subject knowledge to worry too much about whom I was teaching: survival in the classroom and 'delivery' of the curriculum were paramount. Anxiety about my own and my students' performance (this, in the days of teachers and schools being held to account for their students' national examination results) meant many late nights translating ahead, preparing questions and turning out resources. The Banda machine and then the photocopier became my closest friends. The advent of educational technology at the beginning of the twenty-first century meant everything had to be done again, turned from paper into digital masterworks that were attractive and (merely by being digitized) guaranteed to be engaging and motivating.

I started off as a grammar enthusiast, then transformed into an aficionado of the reading-comprehension method. As I became older and more established, I realized that there is only a certain length of time that the ablative absolute can hold interest (I'd give it about six years), and as I became more interested in my students, the way they worked (or not), the way they listened (or not), the way they acted on my advice (or not), the more I realized that Latin teaching – at least *my* Latin teaching – had become a little dull, a little stale, a little predictable: read the passage, answer the questions, translate the passage, move on. That was all the examinations required. Why do anything else? Because other methods might be worth a try? It was attending the Institute of the American Classical League (ACL) for the first time in Memphis in 2013 that I discovered a world unexplored: unencumbered by the UK's national examinations system (although the AP and the National Latin Examination have their own challenges), US Latin teachers seemed to have so much more interesting things to say about pedagogy than the UK's obsessions with preparation for an examination that seemed set in a 1950s paradigm. I have since attended more of the ACL Institutes, at Williamsburg, Storrs, Grand Rapids and New York, sometimes as a member of the CSCP team, more recently as a presenter in my own right. Of course, traditional grammar-translation approaches are still common in the US, as well as reading-comprehension, and there were presentations and subcommittees and resources for all them. But the groups interested in teaching Latin by communicative means was – for a UK teacher, at least – much more unusual.

I followed it up with a Living Latin conference at Fordham College in New York to help me gain further insights into communicative approaches to learning Latin. I still do not think there is one best way to teach or learn Latin: what suits a younger learner might not suit an older one; what is right for teaching six 18-year-old students who have chosen to be in the Latin class will not be appropriate for thirty-one 13-year-olds who are wondering if they can drop it. A good teacher will try to do the best by their students – all of them. Therefore, I would probably advocate an eclectic approach: you cannot do Latin without vocabulary and grammar; nor can it be done without plentiful input – listening and reading. Speaking Latin can be engaging and motivational, under the right circumstances. Free writing has its place, perhaps with older, more experienced students. Two things, though. As a teacher, I have come to realize I am more interested in seeing the Latin lesson as a place to learn how to use Latin – to hear it, to speak it, to read it and to write it – rather than as a study of linguistic phenomena. They can do that at home. And I am actually more interested in how my students learn it than I am in the language itself.

With this in mind, therefore, I group the chapters of this book broadly under the four main skills of listening, reading, speaking and writing. This does not follow the approach of most coursebooks, which set out Latin as a series of grammar points to be digested and ticked off one after the other. Instead, these four skills MFL teachers will easily recognize as being the means by which students learn languages. Indeed, there was a brief flourishing of treating Latin in the same way – as a language rather than as a language study – at the beginning of the twentieth century, under the influence of W. H. D. Rouse and the Direct Method of Latin teaching (Stray 1992, 2003).[3] But the Direct Method was marginalized in Latin teaching in favour of language *study*, assessed by translation and comprehension exercises, rather than language *use*. In many countries, including the UK, this was precipitated by the transformation of Latin teaching at schools into a means of assessing students' worthiness for entry into the most selective schools and universities: Latin as proxy IQ test (Hunt 2016; Forrest 1996).[4] Despite the removal of this requirement in the UK in the 1960s, the association of Latin with testing for high intellectual ability and therefore suitable only for the most academically talented continues to be a compelling narrative. Movement towards other approaches has been steady, however, partly in response to more egalitarian views about education. Besides, if Latin should survive in the competitive marketplace of the school curriculum, it cannot afford to reject students

In the UK, the development of reading-comprehension courses in the 1970s started a trend towards reading continuous narratives rather than translating isolated words and sentences (Story 2003; Tristram 2003; Sebesta 1998): Latin was about the Romans, what they said and what they did. In the last twenty years in the US, where traditional approaches continue to have a strong following among teachers, interest in Krashen's Comprehensible Input theory have widened discussion about making Latin teaching more accessible (Patrick 2015, 2019). Communicative methods have also been slowly returning to the classroom (LLoyd and Hunt 2021; Hunt 2018; Rasmussen 2015; Abbott 1998). It is clear there is perhaps no 'best way' to teach. Nevertheless, proven strategies which work both for modern and ancient languages do exist – because language development in humans always follows the same path. Comprehensible input matters first of all. The human brain is hardwired for sound first. With it comes reading – another form of input. After this, output. Speaking (probably not very well in the initial stages and, accordingly, unforced) and finally personal writing. It is curious how much traditional Latin teaching starts at the wrong end of this sequence and misrepresents traslation into Latin for writing and translation from Latin for reading. Instead, teachers should consider making a start with living Latin approaches. This is not just a call to put to bed the myth that Latin is a dead language. It is how humans learn languages, all of them, dead or alive. We know that institutional demands and external examinations squeeze new approaches in favour of tradition and teachers are anxious to change. But perhaps there is now real change in the air. Why? Because, in the last few years, social media and online digital conferences have enabled teachers to break out of their classroom-silos, to share new ideas with one another and consider experimentation. Professional learning communities provide a semi-anonymous safe place to think aloud, to provide professional feedback, a helping hand and access to resources. In my co-edited book with Lloyd, *Communicative Approaches for Ancient Languages* (2021), I described communicative approaches as 'the fourth transformation' in modern Latin teaching, and the catalyst for this has been the internet. Teachers cannot just read about Latin being taught, they can observe lessons and participate more easily than ever before, in spoken Latin, too, if they want. There is an explosion of ideas in Latin teaching which the institutionalized examination systems and the coursebooks that feed them can barely contain.

I have tried to interweave research and the lived experiences of teachers and of students in the classroom, drawn from my own observations of lessons, of talking to teachers, and of keenly following social media and conferences. Inevitably, I have had to make some choices, and they may have been determined by personal preference and interest. I have focused on narrative writing rather than poetry (which needs an entire book of its own), as it aligns with the sort of materials which most students use in the beginning and intermediate stages of learning Latin. There will inevitably be gaps. I hope the reader will forgive me for the occasions when my own interpretations and reflections come through: teaching is quite a personal endeavour and it is hard to be completely dispassionate about something one cares about so much to have given their whole school and professional life over to it, as I have done. Thus, some sections are practical, some observational and reflective, some downright fanciful. The chapter on writing, for example, contains a long, rather historical section on how prose composition has developed in the UK, and there are occasional shout-outs towards the eccentric, such as writing fan fiction. The reader must forgive the personal choices. I do think it interesting in itself to have drawn on such a wide selection of resources, including blogs, YouTube videos, Facebook, Twitter, websites and digital materials of all kinds, as well as published academic literature: social media reveals Latin teaching to be as alive and full of new ideas and practices as any modern language. It is difficult to keep up. But the ultimate aim of this book is to draw out some common and perhaps not-so-common themes and threads and I hope that they will inspire further investigation, classroom experimentation and research. And if you are a teacher with a good idea (or even one who has learnt from a bad one!), I advise that you write to one of the journals and share the experience!

Chapter 1 is about **approaches to teaching Latin** in the classroom. I include brief descriptions of the three main approaches – grammar-translation, reading-comprehension and active Latin, with some recommendations for practice in each case. I follow with sections on teaching grammar, vocabulary, translation and comprehension – the four stalwarts of most Latin lessons. I finish with some observations on the Duolingo app for Latin – an assessment of the app as a means of learning that could be applicable in other situations. Chapter 2 is about the importance of **listening** for language acquisiton and learning. After an overview of the theory of the phonological loop and its role in memory, I provide practical examples of listening activities for Latin, inlcuding different types of dictation, Total Physical Response, and various forms of comprehensible input. I also consider music and singing. Chapter 3 is about **reading Latin**. After a comparison of reading and translating, I discuss cognitive and social forms of learning how to read Latin, with examples. I go on to examine tiered readings, and other ways to make Latin texts more comprehensible through read-alouds, think-alouds and text manipulation. From here I move to Narrow Reading and Linear Reading and end with an extended discussion about Free Voluntary Reading and Latin novellas, a subject of much current interest. In Chapter 4, I turn to **speaking Latin**. First, an exploration why, next a number of practical examples, followed by a section on corrective feedback. The chapter ends with suggestions for professional development in speaking Latin. Chapter 5 brings us to **writing Latin**. First, I discuss the historical and continuing practice of Latin prose composition (or English into Latin translation) still common in UK schools and universities. I follow with free Latin composition itself, with examples of current practice, and consider the benefits and pitfalls of the writing of fanfiction as a learning tool. Chapter 6 touches on current interests in **access, diversity and inclusion** in the teaching of Latin and asks, inter alia, whether currently available teaching resources and common pedagogical practices are now fit for purpose. Chapter 7 looks into the crystal ball and asks: **The future: Is it digital?** This chapter considers a number of aspects which digital technology potentially offers: the impact of crisis online teaching in 2020–1 on teaching practice; new developments in media, such as augmented and virtual reality, videogames and online Latin resources; and its use in reaching out to new audiences. The Appendices contain a glossary and resources list. The companion website to this book www.stevenhuntclassics.com contains further details of resources, including a growing list of relevant websites and links to the journal articles and books mentioned in this one.

Notes

1. See Lloyd's PhD thesis, Living Latin (2017); and Luger's PhD thesis, Lost in Latin Translation (2020).
2. For a more recent account of changing priorities in Classics teaching in schools in Europe, see Bulwer (2018).
3. For Rouse on the Direct Method, see the Association for Latin Teaching website at: www.arlt.co.uk. Occasional second-hand copies of *Latin by the Direct Method* (Rouse and Appleton 1925) can be found. The June 1967 edition of *Latin Teaching* provides a number of snapshots, including Rouse's famous admonitions:

   1 Languages can be learnt only through sentences, not through isolated words.
   2 Nature teaches phrases, pedants teach words, especially isolated nouns.
   3 The study of literature can be pursued only after the language of practical life has been acquired.

4 Grammatical rules teach only the science of language, not language itself.
5 Learn to think in the language.
6 Nothing can be done well unless it is done subconsciously.

Rouse 1950/1967: 92

4. The authors of *The Teaching of Classics* (Incorporated Association of Assistant Masters in Secondary Schools 1954) make the following observations, which illustrate well the then sentiment behind what sort of person was 'suited' to the study of Latin:

> At the end of the second year there will be in most schools a sorting-out of pupils. Already they will have demonstrated the degree to which they are capable of going on with Latin. Ultimately there will be four classes of pupils, the degree of precision with which these classes can be determined usually depending on the number of pupils from whom the selection can be made. There will be –
>
> a) Boys likely to pursue Latin to Advanced and Scholarship standard.
> b) Boys likely to take Latin as one of a group of Modern Subjects.
> c) Boys of mediocre ability in Latin, who would benefit by continuing Latin on less formal lines.
> d) Boys who would be better advised to drop Latin altogether.
>
> Incorporated Association of Assistant Masters in Secondary Schools 1954: 32

Note not just the absence of the mention of girls, but also that of differentiation/adaptive teaching for all students. Latin had become the 'sorting hat' of the 1950s UK classroom (with apologies to J. K. Rowling).

References

Abbott, M. (1998). Trends in Language Education: Latin in the Mainstream. In R. LaFleur, *Latin for the 21st Century: From Concept to Classroom* (pp. 36–43). Glenview, IL: Scott Foresman-Addison Wesley.

Bulwer, J. (2006). *Classics Teaching in Europe*. Bristol: Bristol Classical Press.

Bulwer, J. (2018). Changing Priorities in Classics Education in Mainland Europe. In A. Holmes-Henderson, S. Hunt and M. Musié, *Forward with Classics: Classical Languages in Schools and Communities* (pp. 67–88). London: Bloomsbury Academic.

Carlon, J. (2013). The Implications of SLA Research for Latin Pedagogy: Modernizing Latin Instruction and Securing Its Place in Curricula. *Teaching Classical Languages*, Spring: 106–22.

Forrest, M. (1996). *Modernising the Classics: A Study in Curriculum Development*. Exeter: University of Exeter Press.

Gruber-Miller, J. (2006). *When Dead Tongues Speak: Teaching Beginning Greek and Latin*. Oxford: Oxford University Press.

Holmes-Henderson, A., S. Hunt and M. Musié (2018). *Forward with Classics: Classical Languages in Schools and Communities*. London: Bloomsbury Academic.

Hunt, S. (2016). *Starting to Teach Latin*. London: Bloomsbury Academic.

Hunt, S. (2018). Latin is Not Dead: The Rise of Communicative Approaches to the Teaching of Latin in the United States. In A. Holmes-Henderson, S. Hunt and M. Musié, *Forward with Classics: Classical Languages in Schools and Communities* (pp. 89–108). London: Bloomsbury Academic.

Incorporated Association of Assistant Masters in Secondary Schools (1954). *The Teaching of Classics*. Cambridge: Cambridge University Press.

Lister, B. (2007). *Changing Classics in Schools*. Cambridge: Cambridge University Press.

Lister, B. (2008). *Meeting the Challenge: International Perspectives on the Teaching of Latin*. Cambridge: Cambridge University Press.

Lloyd, M. (2017). Living Latin: Exploring a Communicative Approach to Latin Teaching through a Sociocultural Perspective on Language Learning. PhD thesis, The Open University. Available at: http://oro.open.ac.uk/48886.

LLoyd, M. and S. Hunt (2021). *Communicative Approaches for Ancient Languages*. London: Bloomsbury Academic.

Luger, S. (2020). Lost in Latin Translation: Teaching Students to Produce Coherent Target Texts. PhD thesis, University of Amsterdam.

Morwood, J. (2003). *The Teaching of Classics*. Cambridge: Cambridge University Press.

Natoli, B. and S. Hunt (2019). *Teaching Classics with Technology*. London: Bloomsbury Academic.

Patrick, R. (2015). Making Sense of Comprehensible Input in the Latin Classroom. *Teaching Classical Langauges*, Spring: 108–36.

Patrick, R. (2019). Comprehensible Input and Krashen's Theory. *Journal of Classics Teaching*, 39: 37–44.

Rasmussen, S. (2015). Why Oral Latin? *Teaching Classical Langauges*, Spring: 37–45. Available at: https://tcl.camws.org/sites/default/files/TCL%20Spring%202015%20Rasmussen_0.pdf.

Rouse, W. (1950/1967). What's the Use of Latin? *Latin Teaching*, 32 (4): 188–93.

Rouse, W. and R. Appleton (1925). *Latin on the Direct Method*. London: University of London Press.

Sebesta, J. (1998). *Aliquid Semper Novi*: New Challenges, New Approaches. In R. LaFleur, *Latin for the 21st Century: From Concept to Classroom* (pp. 15–24). Glenview, IL: Scott Foresman-Addison Wesley.

Story, P. (2003). The Development of the Cambridge Latin Course. In J. Morwood, *The Teaching of Classics* (pp. 85–91). Cambridge: Cambridge University Press.

Stray, C. (1992). *The Living Word. W. H. D. Rouse and the Crisis of Classics in Edwardian England*. Bristol: Bristol Classical Press.

Stray, C. (2003). Classics in the Curriculum up to the 1960s. In J. Morwood, *The Teaching of Classics* (pp. 1–5). Cambridge: Cambridge University Press.

Tristram, D. (2003). Classics in the Curriculum from the 1960s to the 1990s. In J. Morwood, *The Teaching of Classics* (pp. 6–19). Cambridge: Cambridge University Press.

van den Arend, A. (2018). Something Old, Something New: Marrying Early Modern Latin Pedagogy and Second Language Acquisition (SLA) Theory. *Teaching Classical Languages*, 10 (1): 1–32.

Latin Language Teaching and Learning

Teaching methods

Most teachers probably use a mixed-methods approach, pulled as they are in different directions by their own learning experiences, teaching preferences and the institutional demands that are made on them. They also pay attention to the needs of their students. A brief resume of the more common methods used in Latin teaching today is given below, but the next four chapters in this book are designed to introduce further ideas for teachers to interweave into practice. Some of them are uncommon; others, such as speaking, are gaining significant interest in the modern classroom; others I present as more provocative. It is a remarkable and encouraging notion that teachers maintain a passionately lively discussion about teaching and learning a supposedly dead language.

Deductive methods: 'Grammar-translation'

In deductive methods, the method usually conforms to the Presentation-Practice-Feedback paradigm. Course materials are generally presented sequentially: (1) the student is presented with a description in English about the new grammar feature and a list of new Latin vocabulary, which they are often told to memorize; (2) they translate a series of practice sentences from Latin to English (and sometimes English to Latin); (3) they translate a more extended Latin passage into English (and sometimes one from English into Latin). This Latin passage often has an explanatory title and introduction in English, a vocabulary gloss, and sometimes an illustration. The passage may act as a summative assessment of the previously learnt grammar and vocabulary, and as a kind of reward for the effort of all the previous practice. It is usually of a length that allows completion in the classroom, and contains no unfamiliar words (or at least, nothing that cannot be intuited) or unfamiliar grammar. Teachers use their judgement whether to allow students access to dictionaries or grammar supplements. Feedback usually takes place on completion of the translations, either immediately after completion or, more often, after it has been taken in and marked by the teacher. For further details of grammar-translation activities, see Singh (1998) for the high-school and May (1998) for university-level.

The traditional grammar-translation method of teaching Latin places explicit grammar instruction at the heart, in the belief that knowing about the grammatical features of the language will transfer to being able to comprehend it elsewhere in continuous and previously unseen texts. The evidence for the effectiveness of this is not good. Skehan (1996) points out there is no research to show that it delivers reading and speaking fluency. In a review of research, Lichtman and VanPatten point out (their Italics) that '*explicit teaching, learning, and testing of textbook grammar rules and grammatical forms should be minimized*, as it does not lead directly or even indirectly to the development of mental representation that underlies language use' (2021: 17). Ellis, Basturkmen and Loewen (2002) note that explicit grammar instruction only helps students perform well on discrete-point grammar tests. So, while the grammar-translation method might help students learn grammar, there is no research evidence that it might lead them easily to comprehend a language, let alone translate it. There are those, myself included, who will say that the grammar-translation method served us well. But it has to be said that we might be the exceptions which prove the rule; aside from which, although we perhaps know Latin grammar very well and can rattle through our charts and tables, we could not at the time and probably still cannot just read and comprehend unadapted Latin very easily. Kitchell (2000) lays the blame for this lack of ability to do the thing that we are supposedly teaching the student to do on their lack of cultural knowledge which they might use as a support for making rational deductions about a text. I think it is more than this. Grammar-translation is fixated on morphology rather than meaning, and often comprises (I am looking at several of the commonly used grammar-translation coursebooks here – *Wheelock's Latin, de Romanis, Latin to GCSE*), lists of vocabulary, charts, isolated words and phrases, short, disconnected sentences, and passages 'for translation' made clunky by the constrictions placed on them by the need for testing the newly introduced grammar. None of these are conducive to helping students how to read fluently, because *the very point of them prevents it*. Indeed, it is more likely that those of us who were taught by this method gained the ability to read and comprehend Latin through long exposure to Latin texts as university students and Latin teachers long after we left the classroom. To me, it seems odd to ignore the decades of research into second-language development and despite the evidence continue to use a method which 'has no theory' (Richards and Rodgers 2009: 7) and which does not easily and quickly lead to proficiency for most participating students. Yet, grammar-translation remains popular amongst Latin teachers, most likely because of its predominance in university-level courses.[1] This method is the one often privileged by university language teachers and seems to wash back into the school system and exert a disproportionate influence over the type of teaching of the vast majority of students who never, in fact, get there.[2]

Inductive method: 'Reading-comprehension'

In more inductive methods, such as those of reading-compression coursebooks,[3] there is usually more flexibility. Extended Latin passages make up the bulk of each section, usually with glossed vocabulary, supplementary grammar notes and often with supporting images and historical/cultural notes. The teacher uses their professional judgement on how to use the passage with the students.[4] Reading of the passages is carried out in the classroom, with considerable teacher guidance and support and/or peer collaboration. The teacher models the process of reading, while checking and supporting the students' language development, developing their cultural knowledge and providing feedback en route, as much as possible with reference to the original Latin. Most frequently, the language of the discussion takes place in English, although Latin may be used. Grammar and vocabulary are dealt with as the need arises: so-called 'pop-up' grammar should focus on one thing at a time. The vast majority of teachers use the students' first language for discussion, although this does not preclude the use of Latin if the teacher is confident. Written translation, as in the deductive model above, may also be set as part of the process of study, provided that the passage set is short enough for everyone to complete in the time allocated. Feedback usually takes place immediately. The teacher should use their professional judgement as to the type and quantity of support needed for differentiation. For further details of reading-comprehension activities (US-based), see Perry (1998) for high-school and Gruber-Miller (1998), and (UK-based) Hunt (2016).

Both grammar-translation and, to an extent, reading-comprehension methods employ a fixed text as the central element for teaching and learning. It is assumed that the text is sufficiently interesting both narratively (to hold the student's attention) and grammatically (to test student mastery in the former or to teach new material in the latter). Teachers need to use the passages common in both methods as intended by the writers of the coursebooks in which they are found. Providing students with extraneous activities such as crosswords, word searches or vocabulary games encourage the superficial learning of discrete lexical or morphological items at the expense of learning how to pick up on the hints and cues which a continuous narrative provides, to understand how the words in a sentence are linked together and how one sentence links with another. Treating a reading-comprehension passage as a translation exercise will often result in disengagement: the wealth of new material – vocabulary, grammar and cultural content – can be indigestible. Teaching should be adaptive to the resource rather than the other way round. It should be used as intended: a 'conversation piece' shared with and explored by students and teacher together, not as a competitive exercise done 'against the clock'. Worse, rewriting a passage designed for reading-comprehension or transforming it into a cloze exercise defeats the purpose: students need to learn how to read the passage as it is, not be provided with the sort of help or hindrances that they will not receive elsewhere.

Active Latin approaches

There are too many different approaches to discuss here, in what is a developing field of Latin pedagogy. Some people think of active Latin as being only speaking and are frightened off by it or think it serves no purpose; after all, the aim of learning Latin is to read original literature (Nesbit 2021). Suffice to say, communication is the method of instruction, gained through listening, reading, speaking and writing.

Many of these practices are dealt with in the following chapters and many teachers feel that they develop students' ability to read original literature just as well if not better than more traditional ways. I will briefly address the idea of speaking here. Its advocates tend to point out that the purpose of speaking Latin is to learn it better rather than that they are learning to speak Latin from scratch. For MFL, teachers should talk *with* their students, not *at* them, by 'engag[ing] learners in the content of meaning-making along the way' (Lichtman and VanPatten 2021); in Latin, of course, the approach is highly dependent on the teacher's proficiency. This can be a restraint on practice initially, but can sometimes become an incentive to improve (Urbanski 2021; Affleck 2021). Remember, too, that speaking simple, conversational Latin is not the same as that of speaking the sorts of literary Latin that is the subject of advanced study. Advocates note the opportunity to create a very personalized learning experience for students, since communicative interaction between teacher and students and with each other is driven by the personal nature of the subject matter (Bailey 2021; Lloyd 2021; Ash 2019; Patrick 2011). Others advocate the use of neo-Latin for conversation, gleaned from extensive reading of more easily comprehensible texts on subject matter that is easier to grasp than that provided in the traditional canon of Latin texts (Leite 2021; Minkova and Tunberg 2021).

Simple, spoken Latin has the potential to be quicker and more efficient at delivering input than other methods. The fact that the input has to be comprehended in real time means that the input should be comprehensible at all times: clear messages, understandable by the students is key. It can also be fun. Active Latin can also be partially inserted into reading-comprehension activities. I have seen some teachers use simple or even quite complex Latin to elicit responses from students about the passage under consideration; however, on occasions, the use of the students' first language can clearly be more efficient and current debates about the use of the target language in MFL lessons similarly fluctuate on the use of the target language at all times.[5] Digital media can also be used for the input, including readings of texts, stories and video presentations, where the images and actions support comprehension. Whether and when students should be expected or required to produce spoken output is debatable, but advocates note greater motivation for personal engagement with the language if students are given opportunities to use it conversationally. In a related study of older students learning ancient Hebrew at a theological college, Overland (2004) suggested that communicative practices speeded up development of the students' literacy. He recommended four strategies:

1 Teach to the learning styles of the students, making use of experiential and visual modes.
2 Use interactive digital media and music.
3 Devise oral presentations to consolidate learning.
4 Create small group projects and games to foster camaraderie and relaxation.

After Overland, 2004

Personalization is often at the heart of active Latin teaching. Studies have shown that simple communicative activities such as games, storytelling, question-and-answer, music, drama strongly engage and motivate students by making them participants in their own language learning rather than recipients of someone else's knowledge (see Bailey 2021; Letchford 2021; Domagala, Loch and Ochman 2021; Hunt, Letchford, Lloyd, Manning and Plummer, 2018). For more interactive approaches for acquiring Latin, through discussion and conversations, see Lloyd (2021). There is a difference of opinion as to how much interaction is necessary for language acquisition to take place. Long (1981) places interaction at the centre of language acquisition, where individuals' negotiation of meaning drives the improvement of language proficiency. By contrast, Krashen (1998) argues that while interaction can be useful as a means of language acquisition, it is not absolutely necessary: language may still be acquired without the necessity of output.[6]

Teaching grammar

Research and theory show that significant amounts of comprehensible, meaningful, interesting and compelling input through listening to speech and reading text in the target language is needed for students to develop language proficiency. In MFL, debate continues over the relative importance of implicit or explicit approaches to teaching grammar. Some believe that drawing attention to grammar explicitly, if succinctly, can be beneficial and can enhance implicit learning (Macaro 2003). Explicit learning, they say, leads to declarative knowledge – the ability of a student to be able to explain the rules of grammar. This type of knowledge is often highly prized in traditional approaches to Latin teaching, where the ability of a student to be able to 'show their working' by analysing the constituent grammatical parts of a Latin sentence is reminiscent of them working through a mathematical puzzle.[7] Current examinations in the UK and in the US require students to show their knowledge of formal grammar.[8] This requirement washes back into much teaching at earlier stages in a Latin programme and often constitutes much of the learning there, when it could perhaps be spent on more productive, creative and engaging tasks. For a student of MFL, of course, declarative knowledge is of less use when it comes to speaking and listening input, which must take place in real time: automatization is the key to fluency. Research in SLD has resulted in three positions about whether knowledge gained by explicit instruction can become implicit:

1 The non-interface position holds that explicit instruction cannot become implicit (Krashen 1993).
2 The weak interface position holds that explicit knowledge serves to heighten students' awareness of language features which they add to their knowledge when ready (Schmidt 2001; Ellis 2001).
3 The strong interface position holds that implicit knowledge derives from the proceduralization and practice of explicit knowledge (DeKeyser 2001).

According to Pachler, Evans, Redondo and Fisher (2014), research currently supports the arguments of both of the weak and strong interfaces. Nassaji (2017) suggests that there *is* a need for formal instruction for students to attain a high degree of accuracy. More recently, however, in their review of the available literature on language acquisition and language learning, Lichtman and VanPatten argue otherwise: 'The explicit learning of surface features and rules of language leads to explicit knowledge of the same, but [...] this explicit knowledge plays little or no role in language acquisition as normally defined' (2021: 17). Conversely, they note that if teachers *want to test* students' explicit knowledge of grammar, they will clearly *need to teach* it explicitly 'if the intention is to develop explicit knowledge as a paramount goal and [the teacher] doesn't care about other goals such as fluency. Then and only then might explicit instruction play a central role' (2021:17). For MFL, Lichtman and VanPatten argue against all this: for teachers to try to '"implicitly" teach textbook vocabulary and grammar through input-based approaches is as doomed to failure as is explicitly teaching and practice of the same' (2021:17). How do we apply this to Latin? For most Latin teachers, the aim is to develop their students' proficiency in reading original texts and strict adherence to the grammar-translation method is less common than it used to be – indeed, most Latin teachers have long adopted reading-comprehension as the main alternative (Forrest 1996; LaFleur 1998; Morwood 2003; Gruber-Miller 2006; Lister 2007, 2008). Still, all the reading-comprehension coursebooks continue to follow a traditional sequence based on grammar-focused approaches and using and assessing students' proficiency by means of written texts. Lichtman and VanPatten (2021) would suggest (I suspect) that trying to teach a Latin coursebook using input-based approaches is a non-starter. The logical step if acquistion is desired is that the Latin coursebook must be thrown out and a teaching programme of spoken and reading input which enable it must be devised.[9]

Whatever approach(es) Latin teachers do use, I feel they should be cognizant of the research which SLD does provide about explicit grammar instruction. Nassaji and Fotos (2004) report that formal instruction is necessary: the student needs to notice target forms in input, otherwise they process purely for meaning and do not attend to the forms. The type of instruction matters, inevitably. Long (1991) distinguishes between a focus on forms approach and a focus on form approach (note the absence of the letter 's'). Focus on forms is explicit, point-by-point explanation of grammar, taught in isolation. This is typical of the Presentation-Practice-Feedback model of grammar-translation teaching, still common in Latin teaching. The problem is that excessive time can be spent explaining so many or all of the forms in detail (and there are a lot of forms possible in Latin) at the expense of language practice through listening, reading, speaking and writing. I have seen many classes which have been taken up with a teacher's lengthy explanations of grammar, but no Latin has actually been read. A modification is focus on form teaching (note the absence of the letter 's'). This is when the teacher provides a grammar explanation at the point in the reading or communicative interaction when it occurs – sometimes colloquially referred to as 'pop-up' grammar. Ellis et al. (2002) and Nassaji and Fotos (2004) suggest that focus on form (without the 's') is more effective, following Long (2000) who advises that this approach is effective for teaching grammar since it is learner-centred. If a focus on form approach is used, Batstone and Ellis (2009) provide a set of principles that should guide the selection of instruction:

1 Given-to-new principle: Making new form/function connections with students' prior knowledge, rather than in isolation.
2 Awareness principle: Making students aware of how meaning is encoded by a grammatical form.

3 Real-operating conditions principle: Making students use grammar as a communicative tool.

In the case of learning Latin, the following precepts are worth considering:

- Keep the cognitive steps simple and few.
- Model examples, lots of them.
- Make sure that form-to-meaning is easy to recognize.
- Focus on regular forms first, irregular once the principle has been established.
- Make sure the focus is on the grammar – the student need not have to concern themselves with having to cope with new or unfamiliar vocabulary or a meaning which is obscure.
- Ensure that the grammatical feature is made salient. If done aurally, choose forms which are aurally salient; if done through writing, use colours/highlighters/annotations.
- Show grammatical parallels, where such exist, between Latin and English sentences. It is best to write the English directly below the Latin so that students can see the correspondence between words easily:

  o mercator **uxori** anulum **tradidit**.
  o The merchant **handed** the ring over **to his wife**.
     [highlights the dependency of the dative form of uxor on the verb to express the indirect object]

  o mulier ad forum contendit || **ut** pompam **spectaret**.
  o The woman hurried to the forum   **to see** the procession.
     *[highlights the separation of the subordinate purpose/final clause from the main clause, the significance of the word **ut** and its dependent subjunctive verb]*

Three simple steps:

1 Start with concrete examples – perhaps drawn from the textbook – and use abstract terminology very little at first. What can the students hear or see that makes them notice the new form?
2 What is the effect of the new form on the meaning? Repeat with further examples until the student understands what to look for and what effect it has on the meaning.
3 What do we call this new form? Bring in the terminology at this point.

Two more steps:

1 Manipulate grammar on the board, using previously worked examples, such as by changing singular to plural, masculine to feminine, direct to indirect.
2 Encourage students to predict changes, as above.

Increasingly I train my teachers old-fashioned board-work, where the Latin sentence is written out and annotated as the teacher speaks. Such things as subject-verb complement or adjectival agreement is rendered visible on the board as the teacher 'thinks aloud' and models the thought-process in real time (in my view, PowerPoint slides have limited functionality for classroom responsiveness).

If in doubt, don't just tell students – *show* them.

Vocabulary learning

I have discussed some vocabulary learning and acquisition strategies before in *Starting to Teach Latin* (Hunt 2016). I append some further thoughts here.

Groot (2000) suggests that there are three stages of vocabulary acquisition:

1 Noticing the properties of the new word, morphological, phonological, semantic, syntactic, stylistic, collocational, etc.
2 Storage in the internal lexicon in networks of relationships that correspond to the properties in (1).
3 Consolidation of the storage in (2) by further exposure to the word in a variety of contexts which illustrate its properties.

Groot 2000: 46

It is likely therefore that it is better for students to meet vocabulary in meaningful contexts rather than in isolation. Having to intuit the word from the context means that the student may have to work harder at recalling the word. This is dependent, however, on the student being familiar with the context in which the word appears.

Research on vocabulary learning distinguishes between incidental and intentional learning. Incidental learning is a by-product of extensive reading and other language activities; intentional learning is systematic. There is consensus that both are needed, especially in language learning contexts where there is limited use of the target language, such as the school classroom (Pachler et al. 2014).

Incidental learning of vocabulary can be haphazard. To compensate Bruton, Lopez and Mesa (2011) suggest that the teacher can give added saliency to particular words as they are met in reading or listening activities. Hulstijn (2001) suggests that both intentional and incidental learning of vocabulary should be promoted. Read (2004) urges the need for regular rehearsal of words, rote learning, word recognition tasks: students should feel that they need to learn a word, that they should search for the meaning of the word, and work out how the information helped them understand the word's use.

For pleasure reading, research suggests that 95–98 per cent of the words need to be known (Nation 2001). There are implications for providing the right sort of reading material (e.g. for extensive reading) or supplementary vocabulary. The skills of listening and reading require more vocabulary to be known than for speaking and writing, where the student can choose their own words (Macaro 2003). Students should compile lists of vocabulary which they are learning.

There are different criteria for what it means to know a word (Macaro 2003). The student:

1 Does not recognize the word.
2 Recognizes the word, but not its meaning.
3 Gives the meaning of the word.
4 Understands the use of the word in a sentence.
5 Understands the use of the word's grammatical form in the sentence.

After Macaro 2003

These have implications as to the sort of support a student needs in the classroom, especially with regard to teacher–student questions when carrying our oral translation activities.

McCarten (2007) suggests that a student needs to have the following information about a word before they can be said to know it:

- The meaning(s) of the word.
- Its spoken and written forms.
- The word parts it has – such as suffix, prefix and root form.
- Its grammatical behaviour (noun/verb/adjective, etc., and the way it fits into particular word patterns).
- Its collocations.
- Its register.
- Its associations with other words (synonyms, antonyms).
- Its connotations.
- Its frequency.

After McCarten 2007

The implications for all of this are that words need to be presented frequently, repeatedly and in context, and the meaning must be clear and obvious so that the student makes an easy association of the meaning with the word (Ellis 2001). Vocabulary learning with the grammar-translation approach to teaching Latin is problematic, as words are generally not introduced in meaningful contexts or in sufficient frequency or variety of forms within the same passage or exercises. Attention is deliberately diverted towards the endings of words rather than their meanings. Time may be spent on endings at the expense of beginnings. Separate vocabulary-learning activities are therefore often required – games, quizzes and tests. Reading comprehension approaches provide sufficient contextual variety, but students are not always able to intuit new or unfamiliar forms within a text:

they need to be taught how to use the supporting vocabulary and to develop understanding of the context of the passage. There has been very little research on how students use Latin dictionaries. Bartelds (2021) notes that Latin and Greek students' use of the dictionary is a part of the reason for their 'mechanical approach to translation, which typically produces awkward and incoherent translations' (Bartelds 2021: 2). He observes five common dictionary mistakes for classical languages:

1 Excessive use – students look up almost every word, from left to right, without prioritizing.
2 Not arriving at the correct lemma – students do not perform morphological analysis.
3 Navigating with semantic tunnel vision – without a lemma, students direct their attention solely to semantic information, ignoring other information and often choosing the word which best fits their own preconceived translation.
4 Wrongly sticking to a choice – students do not consult the dictionary again, even if they have difficulties formulating a coherent translation as a result of their wrong choices.
5 Creating a 'bridge-language' – students replace all the Greek or Latin words in a sentence, one by one, with their respective translations from the dictionary. The garbled collection of words in the target language, rather than the (moprho) syntactic features of the source language, forms the groundwork from which the students build up their translation.

After Bartelds 2021

My own observations show similar student behaviours and no doubt readers of this book recognize the same. The students' errors derive from the haphazard way in which they are not reading the passage logically. They do not seem to be seeing the connections between words, but rather trying to concoct meaning by taking each word as it comes, piece by piece with no clear strategic thinking about the whole sentence and the morphosyntactic connections between them: 'I write down the words that we translated and then I just put them in order, in the way that they make sense' (Year 9 girl to teacher, author's own transcript). Not only have they atomized the passage into a series of words which they must fit together as their own sense suits, the strategies which they do use which would be helpful are not consistently applied or shared (such as checking the spelling of individual words when searching for them in the dictionary; missing out a word and coming back to it; reading through the whole sentence; using their understanding of the narrative and the characters within it to help follow the line of the story). Bartelds (2021) notes Bogaards' (1993) iterative dictionary-use model in which students make use of a 'feedback loop', whereby they 'loop between text and dictionary, engaging in a constant verification process … Often multiple words are unknown and closely connected, resulting in several parallel searches: the decision-making process for one word is often embedded in the decision-making process for other words' (Bartelds 2021: 3). For many students, he suggests, this practice does not come naturally and the high cognitive demand may be too challenging. Bartelds (2021) recommends a three-pronged approach:

1 Teachers should explicitly model how to use dictionary-style entries, even at the early stages where students use vocabulary lists, so that students make informed searches.
2 Students should keep a thumb or bookmark in the dictionary to help them revisit the entries as they loop back and forth between dictionary and text.
3 Students should monitor their approach and be able to articulate their choices.

After Bartelds 2021

For my part, I consider the first point to be the most important: teachers should frequently – especially in the early stages – model how students should read a sentence which contains unfamiliar vocabulary, step by step, using 'think-alouds' while demonstrating the process visually on the board.

Communicative approaches give the teacher an opportunity to provide many repetitions of individual words (speaking is far quicker than reading), in messages that, by their very nature, must be readily understood by the students. The teacher needs to ensure that the students' phonological memory of the words is transferred to written forms if reading Latin is the aim. In all approaches, practising vocabulary through reading and exercises based on the reading should always be the follow-up. Retrieval practice, games, quizzes and crosswords can be motivational and engaging, but they do not encourage the *elaboration* of vocabulary knowledge that seeing it in context provides.

There has been little research in Latin vocabulary acquisition. For an excellent overview on the role of working memory on language acquisition, especially vocabulary, written from a Latinist's perspective, see Carlon (2016). Again, very small-scale, methodologically uneven practitioner research reveals a few glimpses of practice. Warwicker (2019) questioned her students on their preferred methods and found that the traditional 'look, cover, check' and computer-assisted methods were prevalent. Following trials of three methods new to the class, she found that the students preferred more active approaches to be helpful for learning (making a presentation of new vocabulary to the class) to more cognitive methods (keyword method, sentence completion method). Stehle (2020) found that students' use of flashcards and the length of time spent learning discreet items correlated to an improved retention of vocabulary. Veysey (2014), in a study about student perceptions of the value of English derivatives as a means of helping to learn Latin vocabulary, found that students had mixed feelings of their efficacy. Walker

(2015) noted a positive impact on student engagement and motivation of using the app Memrise, which led to improved retention. Bungard (2020) found that vocabulary with images self-selected by students seemed well retained. Ash (2017) provides some suggested activities for using a movie-talk to acquire vocabulary, including the writing of scripts.

In general, vocabulary met in context is more difficult to recognize and so to learn, but seems to be better remembered. Greater usage seems to improve acquisition. Chapter 3 of Nation's *Learning Vocabulary in Another Language* (2008) is perhaps the best place to look for examples of how to teach vocabulary.

Some recommendations from practising Latin teachers are gathered here:

- Dual coding (picture + word)
- Use of Total Physical Response (TPR)
- Use of gesture and intonation (sometime comic)
- Use of manipulatives, puppets
- Circling/repetition of words in spoken context
- Language-learning/testing apps such as Quizlet, Kahoot, etc.
- Word walls
- Word-of-the day/week
- Cutting words up (e.g. *festinavimus > festina-v-imus [we hurried > we hurri-ed]*)
- Showing word 'families' (e.g. *multus/multitudo; pulcher/pulchritudo [much/a crowd; beautiful/beauty]*)
- Playing with prefixes (e.g. *mitto, admitto, dimitto, emitto, permitto, remitto, amitto [send, send to, send away, send out/throw, allow, send back, lose]*)
- Association of different words with a character or scene in a story rather than *in vacuo* (e.g. recalling the words used to describe someone in the text)
- Frequent retrieval practice[10]
- Pre-teaching vocabulary for use in a text
- Semantic mapping

Many teachers consider the use of English (or other language) cognates or derivations are of use in helping students recall Latin vocabulary. Problems arise, however, when the cognate is pronounced differently from the Latin (and is not displayed on the board in writing when used by the teacher); the derivation is obscure; or the derivation is unknown to the student. The teacher needs to decide whether it is easier telling the student the meaning of the word rather than asking them to second-guess. Also, some Latin words, while superficially similar to English derivatives, are not, in fact, etymologically connected.

Computer-aided testing apps can be effective. However, the best of these are the ones which promote frequent spaced-interval retrieval practice, and which have easy-to-recognize visual prompts. Those which encourage some kind of competition either between students or so as to attain a 'personal best' seem, anecdotally, to be popular. The creation of the material for these apps can be time-consuming, however: rather than the teacher spending too much time and energy creating the resources, the responsibility should be entrusted to the students. Several of the more well-known Latin coursebooks have their own ready-made online vocabulary testers.[11]

Verbs and (especially) concrete nouns appear to be more easily remembered than other forms of vocabulary. Other words, such as adjectives and adverbs, are often ignored during translation and sometimes a special effort needs to be made to check understanding. Connectives are often dismissed as relatively unimportant, but they serve to shape the narrative or rhetoric of a passage and are of greater significance for reading more generally. When teaching new cohesive features, it is a good idea to prime students' understanding not just of the meaning of the connective but also of its function in the discourse of the text:

> 'pastor anxius erat, [Why?] quod leo eum agitabat.' [The shepherd was anxious, [Why?] because the lion was chasing him.]
> 'milites ad forum contenderunt, [Reason?] ut imperatorem audirent.' [The soldiers hurried to the forum, [Reason?] to hear the general.]

The many inflections of Latin words are often confusing for beginners, who expect to find the exact forms in the dictionary and who seem perplexed by the appearance of so many apparently new words. Teachers will be reassured that this tends to wear off after a few weeks. Seeing the forms in continuous text helps students not just notice that the words have different endings, but helps them consolidate the idea that the form has an effect on the meaning of the word. This is difficult to achieve when the word is on its own, devoid of context.

Many demonstratives are routinely ignored by students. Try replacing the words with their proper or concrete noun equivalents to show their importance and to help the student consider their meaning and function within the narrative.

When teaching a Latin word, it helps to give the Latin first many times, with the student expected to tell the meaning of it in their own language. Teachers should not be tempted to switch round from English to Latin too early, before the meaning of the Latin form itself has been adequately assimilated.

Crossword puzzles and word searches are ineffective means of learning vocabulary as they provide the wrong sorts of clues – the overlap of common letters.

Knowledge of Latin grammar and vocabulary are not in themselves sufficient for students to make good progress in Latin. Sparks and Wegenhart (2011) point out that students who are not proficient in their own language also tend not to be proficient in the second language. The two are dependent on each other. Students who have not been taught the phonology, orthography and grammar of their own language, have difficulty with their second. They recommend that the Latin teacher should not assume that students enrolled in Latin are proficient in their own language, and they should also call attention to how Latin orthography and sound-symbol correspondences in Latin differ from those in English.

Translation

For the MFL teaching community, translation has something of a mixed press, particularly in regard to communicative approaches to language teaching. Positively, it can draw students' close attention to vocabulary, the structure of sentences and their interconnectedness and 'sensitize them to differences between the two languages' (Allford 1999: 231). It can also be stimulating, exciting and creative (Cook 2018). Both of these can seem to apply to the teaching of Latin. Negatively, the process of translation slows down the ability to use the language automatically – the aim of MFL teaching itself. While this is clearly less of an issue for learners of Latin, translation can be a slow and laborious process, which is sometimes obscured by the use of a complex metalanguage, and which can serve to demotivate students.

Translation is most often used summatively. The national Latin examinations in the UK require students to translate an unseen ('at sight') passage of Latin (made-up at GCSE and from an original Roman author at A level) into standard, written English. Set texts at GCSE and A level routinely ask students to translate a few lines or a short section of the original author. The examination necessitates translation, which tends to dominate classroom practice for students aged between 14 and 19, and often washes back into the earlier stages – making students 'exam-ready' at the expense of other forms of language learning which may be more beneficial at that time.

Luger (2020) explores some of the reasons why translation as an assignment is problematic. The translation is for a fictional intended reader and it must be as literal as possible and as free as necessary: the student needs to make an almost impossible judgement about what is appropriate as they go about translating. It is used as a test to assess students' linguistic knowledge of Latin in final exams: the teacher who provides the assignment is more proficient in the source language than the student. The learner is much younger and less proficient than the recipient: there are dynamics of power at play. The teacher-recipient does not actually need the translation: there is a mismatch between intention (translate for a recipient) and function (as linguistic test). It is under this set of circumstances that we can see why the student struggles.

In the end, the aim of the translation itself as a means of providing the students with practice to improve their language proficiency is problematic because the students know that any errors they make do not really matter and will be corrected by the teacher: '[The words] don't always have to make sense' (Year 10 boy to co-student, author's own transcript). In contrast to learning a modern language, where the ability to communicate in real time is a major desired outcome, students know for real that accurate intake (of listening and reading input) and output (in speaking and writing) matters. In Latin class, translation practice does not have the same communicative necessity or immediacy. In the world of the classroom errors do not matter – teacher will correct you. The risk is that, without immediate feedback, errors in vocabulary and grammar knowledge may be reinforced and internalized. Often assessment takes place *post eventum* and is returned later – the salience of immediate feedback gone. If the teacher does 'go over' the passage in English in class, the process tends to be crammed into the end of the lesson and the students' focus on correcting their English translation rather than looking at the original Latin. Worse, if some students have not reached the end of the story, the sense arises that finishing is unimportant, or even that the story was not worth beginning. Such students fail to develop an understanding of how the narrative structure of a passage helps them develop reading skills, and those who most need the practice do not receive it.

If it is done well, translation can provide the teacher with a ready check on students' progress and the levels of their knowledge and understanding of vocabulary, accidence and syntax.

I make a number of recommendations for teaching translation below:

- More questions than answers – translation in lessons is a way of learning about language as an encoder of meaning, not just as assessment of language knowledge.
- Model how to translate – the steps taken from consideration of the meaning of words, how to recall them or look them up from a word list or a dictionary, how to use morphosyntactic knowledge to check meaning (otherwise students will guess purely from lexical knowledge), how phrases and sentences relate to one another in the creation of narrative cohesion, and how to check and refine meaning. Use 'think-alouds' and board writing and annotation.
- Prioritize the process of translation rather than the outcome. Encourage students to ask questions about how to create meaning. Build a relationship with students that is based on cooperation rather than competition.
- Finding formative assessment and/or diagnostic methods which gather information from all students in the class, rather than relying on one or two who always 'get it right' and assuming they speak for the whole class.
- In the very early stages, it seems better to be consistent in association of a Latin word with its meaning, even if it sounds a little 'clunky'. When students show secure recall of vocabulary, allow more flexibility to suit the context.
- Be judicious in the choice of metalanguage. Consider what is essential 'shorthand' and in common usage to facilitate explanations and discussion. Be

consistent. Over-complex or obscure metalanguage can be as difficult to learn as Latin vocabulary itself.

- Explain to students how the coursebook 'works': show them the 'shape' of the course and how to look up information, such as vocabulary. Help students understand the terminology of the textbook or commentary, as appropriate. Be consistent with the books that they are using.
- Work with the students, not against them. Translation can be an exploratory activity, not a competitive one. Consider different student groupings: work in pairs, groups or individually all have their benefits and disadvantages.
- Be clear with whether you want students to write translations in idiomatic, fluent English or whether you want some form of translation which reflects the Latin language structures. There may be a case for either at different points.
- Gap-fill exercises for 'speeding through' a translation barely give the teacher any indication of proficiency. Too much can be intuited by the format of the exercise.

Translation can also enhance a students' use of their own language. Many people, who were good at it, fondly remember how much they learnt about their own language from practising Latin unseen translation. For students whose mastery of their own tongue or whose language is different to that into which the Latin is to be translated might find have a different opinion. Over seventy years ago, Latin teachers were complaining: 'The truth is that in the early stages the pupils' English is usually so poor that the result of translation is merely translationese, and a bad translation spoils rather than improves the English' (Incorportaed Association of Assistant Masters in Secondary Schools 1954: 78). How applicable can such a statement be for novice students in the non-selective, multilingual classroom of today?[12] While it is clearly not a binary choice between using translation to improve a student's Latin or their English, over-reliance on translation brings its own set of problems: what does it *really* show the teacher about a student's performance in Latin?

Comprehension questions

Twenty ways to comprehend a Latin passage:

Too often in the past, although possessing a vast reservoir, rich in the finest subject material, we have been content to offer little more than the dry bones from a grammarian's provender.

Karsten 1971

David Karsten's observations more than fifty years ago are as valid today. I have updated his original suggestions, and added in others. In particular, I would point out that many of these comprehension questions are more demanding than one would perhaps ask of students in a written examination. At the GCSE level, a teacher would most likely employ straightforward factual questions (Who? What? Where? When? Why?), which can be answered by direct reference to understanding the meaning of the Latin text. Multiple-choice questions can also be quite simple, and they can also act as a useful bridge to more open-ended, interpretative questions, as they potentially provide models of how to engage with the text.

The following passage of Livy (*ab urbe condita I, 54*) illustrates the different sorts of comprehension questions that can be asked. Of course, a simpler text can also be used – even made-up Latin can provide plenty of possibilities. You must forgive my attempt at a translation.

inde in consilia publica adhiberi. ubi cum de aliis rebus adsentire se veteribus Gabinis diceret quibus eae notiores essent, ipse identidem belli auctor esse et in eo sibi praecipuam prudentiam adsumere quod utriusque populi vires nosset, sciretque invisam profecto superbiam regiam civibus esse quam ferre ne liberi quidem potuissent. ita cum sensim ad rebellandum primores Gabinorum incitaret, ipse promptissimis iuvenum praedatum atque in expeditiones iret et dictis factisque omnibus ad fallendum instructis vana adcresceret fides, dux ad ultimum belli legitur. ibi cum inscia multitudine quid ageretur, proelia parva inter Romam Gabiosque fierent quibus plerumque Gabina res superior esset, tum certatim summi infimique Gabinorum Sex. Tarquinium dono deum sibi missum ducem credere. apud milites vero obeundo pericula ac labores pariter, praedam munifice largiendo tanta caritate esse ut non pater Tarquinius potentior Romae quam filius Gabiis esset. itaque postquam satis virium conlectum ad omnes conatus videbat, tum ex suis unum sciscitatum Romam ad patrem mittit quidnam se facere vellet, quando quidem ut omnia unus publice Gabiis posset ei di dedissent. huic nuntio, quia, credo, dubiae fidei videbatur, nihil voce responsum est; rex velut deliberabundus in hortum aedium transit sequente nuntio filii; ibi inambulans tacitus summa papaverum capita dicitur baculo decussisse. interrogando exspectandoque responsum nuntius fessus, ut re imperfecta, redit Gabios; quae dixerit ipse quaeque viderit refert; seu ira seu odio seu superbia insita ingenio nullam eum vocem emisisse. Sexto ubi quid vellet parens quidve praeciperet tacitis ambagibus patuit, primores civitatis criminando alios apud populum, alios sua ipsos invidia opportunos interemit. multi palam, quidam in quibus minus speciosa criminatio erat futura clam interfecti. patuit quibusdam volentibus fuga, aut in exsilium acti sunt, absentiumque bona iuxta atque interemptorum divisui fuere. largitiones inde praedaeque; et dulcedine privati commodi sensus malorum publicorum adimi, donec orba consilio auxilioque Gabina res regi Romano sine ulla dimicatione in manum traditur. (Livy, *ab urbe condita* I, 54)

Next, he applied himself to the councils of state. Then, after saying that he agreed with the elders of Gabii on all the other matters with which they were more familiar, he said again and again that he himself was a supporter of war and that he possessed a special understanding about it because he knew the strength of both peoples, and he knew that the pride of the king was hated by the citizens for sure, as not even his own children had been able to bear it. In this way little by little he encouraged the leaders of Gabii to start the war again; he himself used to go out with the boldest of the young men to plunder and on raids, and, using all his words and deeds to deceive them, their groundless trust in him increased; finally, he was chosen their commander. Then, while the people were still ignorant of what was happening, there were some little battles between Rome and Gabii, in which for the most part the Gabini were more successful; that was the point when the highest and lowest citizens of Gabii believed for certain that their commander Sextus Tarquinius had been sent to them as a gift of the gods. He was equal in sharing the soldiers' dangers and hardships, generous in dividing up the plunder, and he became so loved by them that the father Tarquinius was no more powerful in Rome than the son was in Gabii. Therefore, after he saw that he had gained enough strength for every endeavour, he sent one of his followers to Rome to his father to find out what he wanted him to do, now that the gods had granted that one man should possess all state powers in Gabii. To this messenger, because, I believe, he was not to be trusted, no spoken response was given; the king went into the palace garden as if to deliberate, with his son's messenger following; there, walking up and down silently, it is said that he knocked off the heads of the tallest poppies with his stick. Tired of asking and waiting for a reply, the messenger returned to Gabii, not having completed his mission; he reported what he had said and what he had seen; whether due to anger or hatred or because of his natural arrogance, he had not said anything. It was obvious to Sextus what his father wanted and what he was telling him with his silent suggestions; he did away with the leading citizens of Gabii by accusing some before the people and accusing others who had made themselves conveniently hated. Many were openly killed; some, for whom an accusation would not look too good, were killed in secret. Some were allowed to flee, or they were driven into exile, and the property of the ones who had left or who had been put to death was auctioned. From there came largesse and spoils; and, with the sweetness of private gain, the feeling that the state was evil was taken away, until, deprived of good counsel and support, the state of Gabii was handed over to the king of Rome, without a fight.

Author's own translation

1 Straight translation from the passage:

   a) *Sentence*: Translate: '*interrogando exspectandoque responsum nuntius fessus, ut re imperfecta, redit Gabios*' (lines 15–16).

   b) *Phrase*: Translate: '*ad omnes conatus*' (line 11).

   c) *Word*: Translate: '*voce*' (line 13).

2 Comprehension: translation through a variety of questions:

   a) Direct question: 'Whom did Sextus Tarquinius address in Gabii first of all? How did he win them over?'

   b) Less direct question: 'How do we know that the messenger did not understand the instructions which the king had given him?'

   c) Comparative question: 'How did Sextus Tarquinius treat the leaders in Gabii differently? Give a reason to explain your answer.'

   d) Unknown word question: 'What do you think '*largitiones*' (line 21) might consist of?

3 Idiomatic versions and translation:

   a) Give the (i) literal meaning and (ii) idiomatic version in English of '*patuit quibusdam volentibus fuga*' (lines 19–20).

   b) Put '*ut re imperfecta*' (line 15) into good English.

4 Multiple-choice questions:

   a) Does '*ex suis unum*' (line 10) mean:

      (i)   A man on his own.

      (ii) One man from them.

      (iii) One of his men.

      (iv) His own man.

   b) Which of these is the best translation for '*proelia parva*' (line 7)?

      (i)   Small battles.

      (ii) Light battles.

      (iii) Small wars.

      (iv) Skirmishes.

5 Alternative meanings:

   a) Give a meaning other than 'empty' for '*vana*' (line 6).

6 Short paraphrase or general meaning:

   a) Explain in about 40 words how Sextus Tarquinius won over the soldiers of Gabii.

   b) Give a short synopsis of this passage.

   c) Paraphrase in English '*ibi . . . esset*' (lines 7–10).

7 Deduction and filling in gaps in the story:

  a) '*ipse promptissimis iuvenum praedatum atque in expeditiones iret*' (lines 4–5). Why do you think Sextus Tarquinius chose these men in particular to fight with him?

  b) What do you think the messenger was feeling when he reported back to Sextus Tarquinius? Explain your answer.

  c) Do you think the initial successes of the Gabinian army were entirely due to the skill of their commander?

8 General historica/social background knowledge:

  a) Where was Gabii? Was it far from Rome? Why was it advantageous for Rome to conquer it?

  b) What do you know about the Roman army at this time? How was it superior to other armies?

  c) What do you know about the stability of the monarchy in Rome at this time?

9 Relationship with today's world:

  a) How might someone like Sextus Tarquinius appeal to the people today?

  b) Do leaders promote wars today to further their own or their country's ambitions?

10 Identification from the Latin passage of an English translation or paraphrase:

  a) How does Livy say 'because of his natural arrogance'?

  b) What is the Latin in this passage for: 'The feeling that the state was evil was taken away'?

11 Explanation:

  a) '*dono deum sibi missum ducem credere*' (line 8). Explain fully what had led the Gabii to believe this.

  b) '*largitiones inde praedaeque*' (line 21). Explore the role these played in this and earlier parts of Sextus Tarquinius' rise to power.

  c) '*dubiae fidei videbatur*' (line 13) Explain more fully what you think Livy means by this phrase.

12 General character/tone/mood of the passage:

  a) Is Livy pro-Rome or pro-Gabii in this passage?

  b) How does Livy present the Gabinians? Are we meant to feel any sympathy for them? How do our emotions change through the passage?

  c) What words could best describe this passage: emotive; reliable; narrative; condescending; ambiguous; frightening; dramatic; trite; factual; forceful; tense; ridiculous.

13 The character of the participants:

   a) How are Sextus Tarquinius and his father portrayed? Are they similar in character? Are they believable? Is there anything to commend Sextus' behaviour?

   b) Are the Gabii merely gullible? Do you have any sympathy for their behaviour?

14 Diagrams, maps and drawings from the text:

   a) Make a drawing to represent '*ibi inambulans tacitus summa papaverum capita dicitur baculo decussisse*' (lines 14–15).

   b) Sketch a map to show the relative positions of Gabii and Rome.

   c) Design a graphic to represent the sequence of events by which the Tarquinii deceived the Gabinians.

15 Derivations:

   a) Straight: Give five English words from Latin words in the first sentence.

   b) Looking further into words: '*potentior*' (line 10). What does this word mean in Latin? What is the connection between this word and the Latin word 'possum'? How does it relate to the English word 'potential'?

   c) Compound words and their form: '*imperfecta*' (line 15). How does this word mean 'not finished'? What English word do we take from the Latin?

16 Words and their use:

   a) Which words in lines 1–4 show that Sextus Tarquinius' actions increased in frequency?

   b) Pick out a pair of words in line 19 which have the opposite meanings.

   c) Why do you think Livy refers to the elder Tarquinius sometimes as '*rex*', sometimes as '*pater*'?

   d) What is a synonym for '*dux*' (line 6); or '*palam*' (line 19)?

   e) How many words in this passage refer to deception, bribery or corruption? What is the effect of these words on the tone of the whole passage?

   f) Why do you think Livy has put the phrase '*sequente nuntio filii*' (line 14) at the end of the line?

   g) '*dulcedine*' (line 21). Why do you think Livy has chosen to emphasize this word by positioning it at the start of the sentence?

17 Style:

   a) Compare this passage with any of Caesar, Cicero or Tacitus. What would you say are the main differences in style?

   b) Pick out a sentence where Livy has not followed standard prose order. Why do you think he has done this?

   c) Is Livy writing history, do you think? Would it stand up to scrutiny today for its historical authenticity?

18 Grammar and syntax:

   a) Example from the text. 'Find (i) a gerund, (ii) a result (consecutive) clause.'
   b) Why? 'Why is '*vellet*' (line 12) subjunctive?
   c) False friends. What is '*virium*' (line 10) often confused with?
   d) Alternative construction. Put '*ad rebellandum*' (line 4) into another way in Latin.
   e) Indirect speech into direct speech. '*nullam eum vocem emisisse*' (lines 17). What were the original words of the messenger?

19 Dates, numbers and names in full:

   a) What is '*Sex.*' an abbreviation for? What other abbreviations for names can you find (in this and other passages)?

20 Identification of pronouns, relatives, etc.:

   a) To whom do '*ipse*' (line 2) and '*ipse*' (line 16) refer?
   b) To what happening does '*quid*' (line 17) refer?
   c) '*eum*' (line 17). Who is this?

While I was compiling these comprehension questions, I did, of course, have to refresh my memory of the passage itself. I had studied the text many years, and several times, before. Having read it so many times, I realized that I could barely translate it (as you can see from the attempt I made for this book), but that I understood what it meant and could appreciate the way Livy encoded meaning in it. Furthermore, I enjoyed and delighted in reading it – almost as if meeting an old friend again – and found new ways to understand the meaning of it, even as I read it for the second or third time in preparation. It struck me, once again, how blunt and blind translation is as a means of understanding a text in another language: if we cannot just 'read' the text, thoughtful and wide-ranging comprehension questions, such as the above, are perhaps a better way for students to get a deeper understanding of the meanings of the text.

Duolingo: A new way to learn Latin?

Duolingo is an American website and app for language learning. The basic app is free. Latin is one of thirty-eight languages currently available. The approach uses spaced repetition and the interleaving of language skills, consisting primarily of translation into and out of the target language, speaking, and listening to dictation. It provides a variety of activities, including recognizing and recalling images, writing, multiple choice and text noting. There is a discussion area for participants. Each day, the app reminds learners to carry out a small number of exercises, thematically based, which increase in language complexity. Learners are rewarded for successful completion of the tasks. There is a gamification aspect, with rewards and incentives to continue using the app. Most of the activities can be broadly described as translation-based. Krashen (2014) has questioned its effectiveness because it privileges language *learning* over language *acquisition*. However, others maintain translation is an important component of second language development (Cook 2018; Hall and Cook 2012). This may suggest that Duolingo can have a part to play.

The Latin Duolingo app does not at present extend beyond simple phrases, although I am informed by the developers that further stages are in the process of being written. There is something of a tension between, on the one hand, an emphasis on word-for-word recognition and translation, and, on the other, a structuring of material by themes such as the family, routines, and the gods. The first perhaps aligns more with a traditional approach to teaching Latin (but not MFL), while the latter aligns more with teaching MFL (but not Latin). The app uses simple images to aid comprehension of vocabulary when it is introduced. The activities themselves are enlivened by animations, providing a small ludic element. These are not used as a support for developing an understanding of the language, however, but rather as motivational aids to completing the tasks. The inclusion of an aural element is a welcome innovation, however, especially for Latin: the learner hears a recording of the sentences and individual words as they are introduced and when words are clicked; a click repeats the recording; some of the activities are dictations in the original language, for which the student has to select the appropriate vocabulary from a list. Studies by Rahimi (2008) and Kuo (2010) suggest that dictation helps students perform better in tests of language listening comprehension (not without its use even for Latin); but Nation and Newton (2009) go further, saying that dictation makes leaners focus on the language form of phrase and clause level constructions. Research by Jensen and Vinther (2003) showed that the repetition of dictated words and phrases led to improvements in comprehension, phonological decoding strategies and grammatical accuracy.

There are some teething problems: a click sometimes curtails the recording; the sentences, made up of several individual recorded elements, are sometimes disjointed. Nevertheless, if learners could be persuaded to listen to and repeat the words, the app would have more value to a learner than if they merely clicked their way through the exercises in silence.

What Duolingo does have, of course, is infinite 'patience', and provides the learner with access anywhere and at any time. Its effectiveness is inevitably tempered by the learner's motivation. Research carried out on behalf of Duolingo found that some learners had difficulty in keeping up with the daily requirements (Vesselinov and Grego 2012); and Garcia Botero, Questier and Zhu (2019), in their study of university students, found that they needed direction and to be allocated time to practise. More positive outcomes are also noted: Munday (2016) reported most students in a Spanish school said they enjoyed the app, with up to 10 per cent reporting continued use afterwards; and Rachels and Rockinson-Szapkiw (2018) reported that Spanish schools students found learning by the app as effective as face-to-face learning after a twelve week course. The gamification aspects ('lingot' rewards and advancement to higher tiers) encourage learners to stay the course and personalized feedback has an immediacy that more formal learning methods lack. However, from a second-language development perspective where communication is the desired outcome, it is clear that the app has a long way to go. In the case of Latin, however, where communication is not a primary aim, *Duolingo* might have a supplementary role in vocabulary development.

There are currently three tiers. Tier 1 comprises greetings, parents, school and two more grammar-aligned: 'plurals' and 'where'. Tier 2 comprises market, travels, work, routines, emotions, food, time, 'plurals 2'. Tier 3 comprises language, home, gods, shop, activities, nature, feast. One has to admire Duolingo for aligning the language thematically, as is common with the way teachers teach modern languages. However, traditionally minded Latin teachers might find this problematic. Similarly, the vocabulary of choice is more reflective of contemporary feelings, situations and interests. Teachers might find the references to drunken parrots and poo disconcerting – although they may excite the interest of their students. There is a further concern, however, in that the app promotes intuition and repetition for success, rather than making explicit the grammar of the language. The following sentences are early in the course:

- *bene me habeo – I feel well.*
- *male me habeo – I feel poorly.*
- *Livia se bene habet – Livia feels well.*

None of these statements explain or mention the use of the reflexive pronouns *me [me]* and *se [her]*; nor, indeed, does it reveal the rather more common use of the verb *habere [to have]*. Some teachers might find such a lexico-grammatical approach hard to take.

These things aside, the app is easy to use, attractive and fun. It is worth considering as a supplement for students in the early stages of learning and any concerns teachers might hold about the choice and use of vocabulary might have to form 'teachable moments' in class.

Notes

1. See, e.g., Lloyd and Robson's (2018) survey of *ab initio* Latin teaching at British universities, in which the predominant courses are orientated towards grammar-translation methods.
2. For a discussion about the effects on languages teaching of the lack of expertise of language instructors in MFL in US higher education, see VanPatten (2015). UK

university courses in Latin reflect similar challenges, although some have recently started to offer supplementary communicative courses (see Letchford 2021 and Lloyd 2021).

3. No commonly used coursebook for Latin is purely inductive (providing no grammar notes at all). The closest example to the pure inductive model is *Lingua Latina Per Se Illustrata* (Ørberg 2011), but even that has supplementary materials published in parallel books in the series. The *Cambridge Latin Course* (CSCP 2007), *Ecce Romani* (Scottish Classics Group 1971), *Oxford Latin Course* (Balme and Morwood 2003) and *Suburani* (Hands-Up Education 2020) all contain supplementary grammar notes and practice exercises.

4. Any of the reading-comprehension courses which use continuous narratives will, of course, require the teacher to follow the order in which they are presented in the book. The *Cambridge Latin Course* (CSCP 2007) is unusual in that it has a carefully worked-out scheme based on a particular sequence of activities (model sentences – narratives – language explanations and practice).

5. For an historical precedent:

> Sometimes English is essential, particularly when dealing with abstract ideas. There must be no hesitation about using English, prefaced by 'Anglice', if time really can, on a long-term view, be saved. Usually, however, the time is well spent, since Latin is being used all the time and the pupils are hearing and using more Latin for themselves. Moreover, a grammatical point can often be fixed in the pupils' minds for ever by a good explanation or example.
> Incorportaed Association of Assistant Masters in Secondary Schools 1954: 77–8

For MFL, Macaro (2000) discusses the use of the target language extensively.

6. For useful books on SLD, see Richards and Rodgers (2009) and VanPatten and Benati (2015).

7. E.g., the Editor of Quinquennium, an online blog for early-career Classics teachers, states: 'The value of learning an inflected language, in part, has to be the way it trains your brain to triangulate, scrutinizing grammatical units and solving the puzzle with a careful method' ('Dom' 2020).

8. E.g., the UK specifications for Latin at GCSE (Eduqas 2019: 22–3; OCR 2020a: 20–2), and at A level (OCR 2020b: 23–4) state that students will be tested explicitly on grammar terminology. The US syllabus for the National Latin Exam (ACL/NJCL 2021), and the sample questions from the Advanced Placement Exam (College Board/AP 2020: 157–61) also indicate that students will be asked explicit grammar questions. Research carried out by Lloyd and Robson in 2018 showed that most of the *ab initio* Latin courses at UK universities assessed grammar questions explicitly (Lloyd and Robson 2018).

9. Such a radical approach is becoming increasingly common in the US, where teachers have more freedom of choice over pedagogical preferences as they are not bound by national assessments. See, e.g., Ash (2019).

10. A recent metasurvey of some 50 classroom-based examples of research into the effectiveness of retrieval practice suggested that it was beneficial for learning

(Agarwal, Nunes and Blunt 2021). However, the authors note that only four of the studies related to spelling and vocabulary, and that the 'results indicate that more applied research is needed in non-science areas, particularly in skills-based learning, mathematics, the humanities, and foreign language learning' (Agarwal, Nunes and Blunt 2021:13). Until more evidence is forthcoming, perhaps one should guard against too much time spent on retrieval practice of discrete lexical and morphological items at the expense of actual usage and experience of connected Latin. For examples of retrieval practice types, see Jones (2019).

11. For example, *Cambridge Latin Course* and *Suburani* both have their own online vocabulary testers; *de Romanis* has online vocabulary quizzes. Many of the more commonly used vocabulary testing apps have Latin vocabulary collections made by individual teachers which align with the vocabulary in coursebooks. Some advanced users recommend *The Bridge*, an app which generates customizable vocabulary lists from a database of Latin texts, available at: https://bridge.haverford.edu/.

12. The idea of the teaching of Latin vocabulary and English derivations as a means for improving students' English has a long history (for a detailed and positive look at the US programmes of the late twentieth century, see Polsky 1998; for a more cautionary approach for the UK, see Lister 2007). Bracke and Bradshaw's (2017) review of the available evidence suggested that so-called Latin for Literacy programmes had a significant impact on the development of students' English vocabulary. Crosson, McKeown, Lei, Zhao, Li, Patrick, Brown and Shan's (2021) research indicates the value of morphological analysis through Latin roots as a help for multilingual students' reading comprehension. Quigley (2018) argues in his book for UK English teachers, *Closing the Vocabulary Gap*, for the teaching of greater 'word depth' in the classroom, particularly with regard to academic vocabulary, much of which is derived from Graeco-Latinate origins: 'When students begin, either consciously or subconsciously, to make connections between words, to see word parts and roots emerging within words as they listen or read, they begin to unlock a powerful armoury of tools for reading independently' (Quigley 2018: 52). Quigley's book has been very influential in the UK. While the presentation of Latin vocabulary decontextualized from its cultural background might not be as appealing to students as teachers might like to think (Bracke 2016), Latin for Literacy programmes, such as those promoted by organizations such as Classics for All with its *Maximum Classics* programme and The Paideia Institute with *Aequora* continue to be attractive to school leaders as a means of improving literacy rates among younger students, especially in areas of social-economic and cultural deprivation (see Holmes-Henderson, Hunt and Musié 2018). In Germany, Kipf and Frings (2021) note:

> Das Lateinische soll als Refl exionssprache einen spezifi schen Beitrag zur Entwicklung sprachlicher Fähigkeiten leisten, und zwar als „Modell von Sprache", um ein grundsätzliches Bewusstsein dafür zu schaff en, wie eine Sprache funktioniert. Da die meisten europäischen Sprachen einen hohen Anteil an lateinischen Ursprüngen aufweisen, bietet der Lateinunterricht ebenfalls gute Anknüpfungs- und

Vertiefungspunkte zu den modernen Fremdsprachen und kann als Transferbasis zur Förderung einer refl exionsbasierten Mehrsprachigkeit beitragen.

Kipf and Frings 2021

[As a language for reflection, Latin is intended to make a specific contribution to develop language skills, namely as a model of language to get a basic awareness of how a language works. As most of the European languages have a high proportion of words of Latin origin, Latin lessons also provide good points of contact and consolidation in modern foreign languages and can be used as a transfer base to promote reflection-based multilingual contributions.]

In consequence, Kipf and Frings (2021) argue for Latin as an ideal bridging language between German and Turkish, seeing it as a 'neutrales Vergleichsmedium [neutral comparative medium]' between the first and second languages and an important way to promote greater understanding of academic German and linguistic terminology for Turkish immigrant students in German high schools.

References

ACL/NJCL (2021). *National Latin Examination Syllabus*. Retrieved from National Latin Examination. Available at: https://www.nle.org/Portals/0/PDF/NLE%20Syllabus%20 for%202022%20(Revised%202021%20for%20COVID-19).pdf?ver=8iunMyhDY3IRl 1NfDVHC0A%3d%3d.

Affleck, J. (2021). Live Latin: Global Experiments in Shakespeare's Classom. In M. Lloyd and S. Hunt, *Communicative Approaches for Ancient Languages* (pp. 25–32). London: Bloomsbury Academic.

Agarwal, P., L. Nunes and J. Blunt. (2021). Retrieval Practice Consistently Benefits Student Learning: A Systematic Review of Applied Research in Schools and Classrooms. *Educational Psychology Review*. Available a: https://doi.org/10.1007/ s10648-021-09595-9.

Allford, D. (1999). Translation in the Communicative Classroom. In N. Pachler, *Teaching Modern Foreign Languages at A Level* (pp. 230–50). London: Routledge.

Ash, R. (2017). The MovieTalk: A Practical Application of Comprehensible Input theory. *Teaching Classical Languages*, 8 (2): 70–84.

Ash, R. (2019). Untextbooking for the CI Latin Class: Why and How to Begin. *Journal of Classics Teaching*, 39: 65–70.

Bailey, J. (2021). Communication in All Modes as Efficient Preparation for Reading a Text. In M. Lloyd and S. Hunt, *Communicative Approaches for Ancient Languages* (pp. 33–46). London: Bloomsbury Academic.

Balme, M. and J. Morwood (2003). The Oxford Latin Course. In J. Morwood, *The Teaching of Classics* (pp. 92–4). Cambridge: Cambridge University Press.

Bartelds, D. (2021). How to Stay in the Loop: A Think-Aloud Study on Dictionary Use by Excellent Secondary-School Students of Ancient Greek. *International Journal of Lexicography*, 1–19.

Batstone, R. and R. Ellis (2009). Pricnipled Grammar Teaching. *System*, 37: 194–204.

Bogaards, P. (1993). Models of Dictionary Use. *Toegepaste Taalwetenschap in Artikelen*, 46–7: 17–28.

Bracke, E. (2016). *Is Learning Latin Beneficial for School Pupils?* Retrieved from British Academy Review. Available at: https://www.thebritishacademy.ac.uk/documents/868/BAR28-05-Bracke.pdf.

Bracke, E. and C. Bradshaw (2017). The Impact of Learning Latin on School Pupils: A Review of Existing Data. *Language Learning Journal*, 48 (2): 226–36.

Bruton, A., M. Lopez and R. Mesa (2011). Incidental L2 Vocabulary Learning: An Impracticable Term? *TESOL Quartely*, 45 (4): 759–68.

Bungard, C. (2020). Visuaising Vocabulary: Student-Driven Visual Vocabularies. *Teaching Classical Languages*, 11 (1): 51–87.

Carlon, J. (2016). *Quomodo Dicitur?* The Importance of Memory in Language Learning. *Teaching Classical Languages*, 7 (2): 109–35.

College Board/AP (2020). *AP Latin Course and Exam Description.* Retrieved from College Board/Advanced Placement. Available at: https://apcentral.collegeboard.org/pdf/ap-latin-course-and-exam-description-0.pdf?course=ap-latin.

Cook, G. (2018). *Translation in Language Teaching.* Oxford: Oxford University Press.

Crosson, A., M. McKeown, P. Lei, H. Zhao, X. Li, K. Patrick, K. Brown and Y. Shen (2021). Morphological Analysis Skill and Academic Vocabulary Knowledge are Malleable through Intervention and May Contribute to Reading Comprehension for Multilingual Adolescents. *Journal of Research in Reading*, 44 (1): 154–74.

DeKeyser, R. (2001). Automaticity and Automatization. In P. Robinson, *Cognition and Second Language Instruction* (pp. 125–51). Cambridge: Cambridge Univeristy Press.

'Dom' (2020, 15 Dec.). *Can You Imagine Year 7 Latin without* Caecilius in horto? Retrieved from Quinquennium. Available at: http://www.quinquennium.com/can-you-imagine-year-7-latin-without-caecilius-in-horto/.

Domagala, S., M. Loch and K. Ochman (2021). Latin Teaching in Poland: A New Renaissance with Communicative Approaches? In M. Lloyd and S. Hunt, *Communicative Approaches for Ancient Langauges* (pp. 161–78). London: Bloomsbury Academic.

Eduqas (2019, 2 Jan.). *WJEC Eduqas GCSE (9–1) in Latin.* Retrieved from Eduqas. Available at: https://www.eduqas.co.uk/media/rtxlja0x/eduqas-gcse-latin-spec-from-2016.pdf.

Ellis, N. (2001). Memory for Language. In P. Robinson, *Cognition and Second Language Instruction* (pp. 33–68). Cambridge: Cambridge University Press.

Ellis, R., H. Basturkmen and S. Loewen (2002). Doing Focus-on-Form. *System*, 30: 419–32.

Forrest, M. (1996). *Modernising the Classics.* Exeter: Exeter University Press.

Garcia Botero, G., F. Questier and C. Zhu (2019). Self-directed language learning in a mobile-assisted, out-of-class context: Do students walk the talk? *Computer Assisted Language Learning*, 32, 71–97.

Groot, P. (2000). Computer Assisted Second Language Acqusition. *Language Learning & Technology*, 4 (1): 60–81.

Gruber-Miller, J. (1998). Toward Fluency and Accuracy: A Reading Approach to College Latin. In R. LaFleur, *Latin for the 21st Century: From Concept to Classroom* (pp. 162–75). Glenview, IL: Scott Foresman-Addison Wesley.

Gruber-Miller, J. (2006). *When Dead Tongues Speak: Teaching Beginning Greek and Latin.* Oxford: Oxford University Press.

Hall, G. and G. Cook (2012). Own-Language Use in Language Teaching and Learning: State of the Art. *Language Teaching,* 45 (3): 271–308.

Holmes-Henderson, A., S. Hunt and M. Musié (2018). *Forward with Classics: Classical Languages in Schools and Communities.* London: Bloomsbury Academic.

Hulstijn, J. (2001). Intentional and Incidental Second Language Vocabulary Learning: A Reappraisal of Elaboration, Rehearsal and Automaticity. In P. Robinson, *Cognition and Second Language Instruction* (pp. 258–86). Cambridge: Cambridge University Press.

Hunt, S. (2016). *Starting to Teach Latin.* London: Bloomsbury Academic.

Hunt, S., C. Letchford, M. Lloyd, L. Manning and R. Plummer (2018). The Virtue of Variety: Opening the Doors to Wider Pedagogical Practices in UK Schools and Universities. *Journal of Classics Teaching,* 19 (38): 53–60.

Incorporated Association of Assistant Masters in Secondary Schools (1954). *The Teaching of Classics.* Cambridge: Cambridge University Press.

Jensen, E. and T. Vinther (2003). Exact Repetition as Input Enhancement in Second Language Acquisition. *Language Learning,* 53 (3): 373–428.

Jones, K. (2019). *Retrieval Practice: Research and Resources for Every Classroom.* Woodbridge: John Catt Educational.

Karsten, D. (1971). Teaching Comprehension. *Didaskalos,* 3 (3): 492–506.

Kipf, S. and K. Frings (2021). Latein als Brückensprache. In S. Kipf, *Integration durch Sprache: Schüler nichtdeutscher Herkunftssprache lernen Latein* (pp. 22–42). Heidleberg: Propylaeum.

Kitchell, K. (2000). *Latin III's Dirty Little Secret: Why Johnny Can't Read.* Retrieved from *New England Classical Journal.* Available at: http://www.ascaniusyci.org/workshops/Roman%20and%20Greek%20Culture/Documents/IV%20-%20Culture%20in%20the%20Literature%20Classroom/Kitchell%20-%20Cultural%20Literacy.pdf.

Krashen, S. (1993). The Effect of Formal Grammar Study Still Peripheral. *TESOL Quarterly,* 27: 722–5.

Krashen, S. (1998). Comprehensibe Output Hypothesis and the Interaction Hypothesis. *System,* 26: 175–82.

Krashen, S. (2014). Does Duolingo 'Trump' University-Level Language Learning? *International Journal of Foreign Langauge Teaching,* 9 (1): 13–15.

Kuo, Y. (2010). Using Partial Dictation of an English Teaching Radio Program to Enhance EFL Learners' Listening Comprehension. *Asian EFL Journal Professional Teaching Articles,* 47: 4–29.

LaFleur, R. (1998). *Latin for the 21st Century: From Concept to Classroom.* Glenview, IL: Scott Foresman-Addison Wesley.

Leite, L. (2021). Active Latin in the Tropics: An Experience with Neo-Latin in Brazil. In M. Lloyd and S. Hunt, *Communicative Approaches for Ancient Languages* (pp. 91–100). London: Bloomsbury Academic.

Letchford, C. (2021). Communicative Latin for All in a UK University. In M. Lloyd and S. Hunt, *Communicative Approaches for Ancient Languages* (pp. 81–90). London: Bloomsbury Academic.

Lichtman, K. and B. VanPatten (2021). Was Krashen Right? Forty Years Later. *Foreign Language Annals*, 54 (2): 1–23.

Lister, B. (2007). *Changing Classics in Schools.* Cambridge: Cambridge University Press.

Lister, B. (2008). *Meeting the Challenge: International Perspectives on the Teaching of Latin.* Cambridge: Cambridge University Press.

Lloyd, M. (2021). Exploring Communicative Approaches for Beginners. In M. Lloyd and S. Hunt, *Communicative Approaches for Ancient Languages* (pp. 67–80). London: Bloomsbury Academic.

Lloyd, M. and S. Hunt (2021). *Communicative Approaches for Ancient Languages.* London: Bloomsbury Academic.

Lloyd, M. and J. Robson (2018). A Survey of Beginner's Language Teaching in UK Classics Departments: Latin. Retrieved from *CUCD Bulletin, 47.* Available at: https://cucd.blogs. sas.ac.uk/files/2018/05/LLOYD-ROBSON-CUCD-Latin-Survey.pdf.

Long, M. (1981). Input, Interaction, and Second Language Acquisition. *Annals of the New York Academy of Sciences*, 379: 259–78.

Long, M. (1991). Focus on Form: A Design Feature in Language Teaching Methodology. In K. DeBot, R. Ginsberg and C. Kramsch, *Foreign Language Research in Cross-Cultural Perspective* (pp. 39–52). Amsterdam: Benjamins.

Long, M. (2000). Focus on Form in Task-Based Language Teaching. In R. Lambert and E. Shohamy, *Language Policy and Pedagogy: Essays in Honor of A. Ronald Walton* (pp. 179–92). Philadelphia, PA: Benjamins.

Luger, S. (2020). Lost in Latin Translation: Teaching Students to Produce Coherent Target Texts. PhD thesis, University of Amsterdam.

Macaro, E. (2000). Issues in Target Language Teaching. In K. Field, *Issues in Modern Foreign Languages Teaching* (pp. 171–89). London: Routledge Falmer.

Macaro, E. (2003). *Teaching and Learning a Second Language: A Guide to Recent Research and Its Applications.* London: Continuum.

May, J. (1998). The Grammar-Translation Approach to College Latin. In R. LaFleur, *Latin for the 21st Century: From Concept to Classroom* (pp. 148–61). Glenview, IL: Scott Foresman-Addison Wesley.

McCarten, J. (2007). *Teaching Vocabulary: Lessons from the Corpus: Lessons for the Classroom.* Cambridge: Cambridge University Press.

Minkova, M. and T. Tunberg (2021). Global Latin, Active Latin: Kentucky and Beyond. In M. Lloyd and S. Hunt, *Communicative Approaches for Ancient Langauges* (pp. 125–32). London: Bloomsbury Academic.

Morwood, J. (2003). *The Teaching of Classics.* Cambridge: Cambridge University Press.

Munday, P. (2016). The Case for Using Duolingo as Part of the Language Classroom Experience. *Revista Iberoamericana de Educacion a Distancia*, 19 (1): 83–101.

Nassaji, H. (2017). Grammar Acquistion. In S. Loewen and M. Sato, *The Routledge Handbook of Second Language Acquisition* (pp. 205–23). London: Routledge.

Nassaji, H. and S. Fotos (2004). Current Developments in Research on the Teaching of Grammar. *Annual Review of Applied Linguistics*, 24: 126–45.

Nation, I. (2001). *Teaching and Learning Vocabulary.* New York: Newbury House.

Nation, I. (2008). *Learning Vocabulary in Another Langauge.* Cambridge: Cambridge University Press.

Nation, I. and J. Newton (2009). *Teaching ESL/EFL Listening and Speaking.* New York: Routledge.

Nesbit, J. (2021, 16 September). ubi est piscina? Teaching Ancient and Modern Languages. Retrieved from *Antigone Journal.* Available at https://antigonejournal.com/2021/09/teaching-ancient-modern-languages/.

OCR (2020a, June). *OCR GCSE (9–1) Latin Specification.* Retrieved from OCR GCSE Latin. Available at: https://www.ocr.org.uk/Images/220702-specification-accredited-gcse-latin-j282.pdf.

OCR (2020b, June). *OCR A Level Latin Specification.* Retrieved from OCR Latin. Available at: https://www.ocr.org.uk/Images/220734-specification-accredited-a-level-gce-latin-h443.pdf.

Ørberg, H. (2011). *Lingua Latina Per Se Illustrata. Familia Romana.* London: Hackett Publishing.

Overland, P. (2004). Can Communicative Methods Enhance Ancient Language Acquisition? *Teaching Theology and Religion*, 7: 51–7.

Pachler, N., M. Evans, A. Redondo and L. Fisher (2014). *Learning to Teach Foreign Languages in the Secondary School.* London: Routledge.

Patrick, R. (2011). TPRS & Latin in the Classroom: Experiences of a US Latin Teacher. *Journal of Classics Teaching*, 22: 8–10.

Perry, D. (1998). Using the Reading Approach in Secondary Schools. In R. LaFleur, *Latin for the 21st Century: From Concept to Classroom* (pp. 105–16). Glenview, IL: Scott Foresman-Addison Wesley.

Polsky, M. (1998). Latin in the Elementary Schools. In R. LaFleur, *Latin for the 21st Century: From Concept to Classroom* (pp. 59–69). Glenview, IL: Scott Foresman-Addison Wesley.

Quigley, A. (2018). *Closing the Vocabulary Gap.* London: Routledge.

Rachels, J. and A. Rockinson-Szapkiw (2018). The Effects of a Mobile Gamification App on Elementary Students' Spanish Achievment and Self-Efficacy. *Computer Assisted Language Learning*, 31: 72–89.

Rahimi, M. (2008). Using Dictation to Improve Language Proficiency. *Asian EFL Journal*, 10 (1): 33–47.

Read, J. (2004). Research in Teaching Vocabulary. *Annual Review of Applied Linguistics*, 24: 146–61.

Richards, J. and T. Rodgers (2009). *Approaches and Methods in Languages Teaching.* Cambridge: Cambridge University Press.

Schmidt, R. (2001). Attention. In P. Robinson, *Cognition and Second Language Instruction* (pp. 3–32). Cambridge: Cambridge University Press.

Singh, K. (1998). Grammar-Translation and High-School Latin. In R. LaFleur, *Latin for the 21st Century: From Concept to Classroom* (pp. 90–104). Glenview, IL: Scott Foresman-Addison Wesley.

Skehan, P. (1996). Second Language Acquisition Research and Task-Based Instruction. In J. Willis and D. Willis, *Challenge and Change in Language Teaching* (pp. 17–30). Oxford: Heinemann.

Sparks, R. and T. Wegenhart (2011). Is Learning to Read Latin Similar to Learning to Read English? *The Classical Outlook*, 88 (2): 40–7.

Stehle, A. (2020). The Role of Study Time and Method on Vocabulary Learning and Retention: An Action Research Study. *The Classical Outlook*, 88 (1): 18–21.

Urbanski, D. (2021). Active Latin Promotes Open-Mindedness in Language-Learning. In M. Lloyd and S. Hunt, *Communicative Approaches for Ancient Langauges* (pp. 17–24). London: Bloomsbury Academic.

VanPatten, B. (2015). 'Hispania' White Paper: Where are the Experts? *Hispania*, 98 (1): 2–13.

VanPatten, B. and A. Benati (2015). *Key Terms in Second Language Acquisition.* London: Bloomsbury Academic.

Vesselinov, R. and J. Grego (2012). *Duolingo Effectiveness Study.* Retrieved from Duolingo. Available at: http://static.duolingo.com/s3/DuolingoReport_Final.pdf.

Veysey, J. (2014). An Investigation into Teachers' and Pupils' Perceptions of the Value of Teaching and Learning Latin Derivations at GCSE. *Journal of Classics Teaching*, 30: 13–22.

Walker, L. (2015). The Impact of Using Memrise on Student Perceptions of Learning Latin Vocabulary and on Long-Term Memory of Words. *Journal of Classics Teaching*, 32: 14–20.

Warwicker, H. (2019). An Investigation into the Effects of Vocabulary Learning Strategies on the Retention of Latin Vocabulary in a Year 7 Class. *Jounral of Classics Teaching*, 40: 4–13.

2

Listening

Hearing Latin is easy

Listening to the language (with the teacher speaking extempore or reading aloud from a book or prepared transcript) provides masses of input relatively efficiently. The student also becomes aware of Latin as a language rather than a mere series of words on a page. Students enjoy repeating what has been heard to the teacher. Choral repetition allows shy students to take part but not feel exposed (Rivers 1981). With practice, students can also read aloud to each other: one reads, the other listens, they swap. Digital resources are available for most of the commonly used textbooks, enabling students to hear Latin as they read.[1] But listening is more than just a pleasure. Even though the student is unlikely to need or want to listen to Latin outside the classroom, listening is an essential part of language development.

The phonological loop and its role in memory

When a student learns a new word, it needs to be repeated for the sound to be assigned to the word, a process which allows the word find its way into long-term memory

(Gibson and England 2008). If students are not given the chance to say a word or phrase several times, they may assign the wrong sound to the word before it is transferred to long-term memory (Woo and Price 2015). Milton, Wade and Hopkins (2010) note that when readers recall a word, they recall the sound of it rather than the spelling. Reading aloud, too, helps the retention of vocabulary (Forrin and MacLeod 2018; Hipfner-Boucher, Lam and Chen 2014).

The phonological short-term memory (reflected in the ability to repeat words accurately, that is, being a good mimic) correlates with future second-language learning performance (Service 2011). Reading aloud helps promote oral fluency by training the articulators (Seo 2014). While the Latin teacher might not think that being able to listen to Latin in order to help speak it is an important skill, being able to articulate the language promotes better interaction between teacher and students in the classroom. Articulating words, phrases and sentences can boost motivation to talk and provides a less threatening opportunity to do so (Shonozuka, Shibata and Mizusawa 2017). This applies just as much to Latin as it does to modern foreign languages, even though the aim is not in itself to communicate.

Reading aloud by the teacher raises student awareness of rhythms, stresses and intonations by using connected texts rather than decontextualized vocabulary items (Gibson and England 2008). The teacher should model how to say new words whenever they meet them or if they cause particular challenges. They should be as consistent as they can be. There is some variation in how modern teachers pronounce Latin, depending on their own training and preferences, but a consistent pronunciation in the classroom should be the aim. There is not enough space to go into how Latin ought to be pronounced here. Suffice to say that most textbooks have detailed pronunciation guides and that there are many examples of Latin pronunciation on the internet. If a teacher is unsure how to pronounce Latin, they should listen to a colleague and/or listen to recordings of Latin from digital resources which accompany the coursebook which they are using, if such is available.[2] The great thing about Latin, unless you want to take a rarefied view on this, is that its pronunciation is consistent, every vowel and consonant is spoken, there are no 'silent letters' and – best of all! – there are no Romans to correct you.

The value of the teaching of phonics as a means of improving early years students' English reading comprehension is contested (Gibson and England 2008). However, there may be more value in second-languages teaching in order to train students to notice morphology that perhaps has significance in the second language but can easily not be noticed by beginners as being significant. The Latin alphabet being orthographically familiar to most students and its pronunciation being phonologically consistent, one might feel that spending much time on the pronunciation of the individual components of a Latin word is not worth the effort. However, experience has shown me that teaching which draws emphasis to the listening and spoken aspect of the parts of a Latin word is advantageous. Noticing new forms, as Schmidt

(1990) pointed out, is highly important and aural as well as visual clues can play a significant part. A teacher reading aloud carefully helps students identify particular features of morphology which raises their grammatical awareness and comprehension accuracy.

Example 1: Reading nouns

The plural endings of 1st and 2nd declension nouns, e.g.:

puella [girl]   *puellae [girls]*
puer [boy]   *pueri [boys]*

The Anglicized pronunciation of the *-ae* and *-i* endings may sound similar, unless modelled correctly by the teacher. Remember that we are asking students to notice the difference in pronunciation of the plural forms by hearing them as well as by seeing them. If they just see them, they may assign an incorrect sound into the long-term memory: it is common, for example, for students to pronounce *-i* and *-ae* the same, unless corrected. Two problems might arise: first, that the student might be inconsistent in themselves; second, that the assigning might be inconsistent with that of the teacher. In both cases, retrieval of the vocabulary and matching with the teacher's pronunciation might prove difficult and make future comprehension more challenging.

Example 2: Reading verbs

Verbs convey much information: the meaning, tense, mood, person. Careful attention to the pronunciation of the verb will help draw students' attention to the individual components and accustom them to thinking accurately about their meaning. The verbs should be written so that students can see as well as hear. We should not be too worried that we put an emphasis on a part of the word which the Romans themselves would not have: the pedagogical use of emphasis is initially necessary so that students notice what element has changed.

The emphasis can be more moderate once the students have assimilated the significance of the change in meaning that the form indicates. The teacher should control only one small part of the verb so that it is easy to spot. Irregularities should be avoided in the early stages until the principal changes have been assimilated correctly.

ambulabas [you were walking]   *ambulabis [you will walk]*
ambulamus [we are walking]   *ambulemus [let us walk]*
volunt [they want]   *volebant [they were wanting]*
voluerunt [they have wanted]   *voluerant [they had wanted]*

One of the things to remember is that most Latin verbs follow a similar pattern: the person inflections and the tense markers are usually easy to spot. Make it easy to spot in the initial stages: compare the same persons across tenses or compare the same case terminations across different declensions. It is not advisable to mix and match too much in the early stages. The more cognitive dissonance one brings in with different persons and different tenses in any order, for example, the more challenging it is for many students to focus on the one component that is being controlled. To provide students with masses of disembodied examples and expect them to play some kind of game of 'spot the tense' is not effective. Provide frequent and tightly controlled examples.

Here are some suggestions to get started with pronouncing Latin:

1   Draw attention to the sounds – make it memorable:

> For example, draw attention to the appearance of the infinitive forms of the verb by an exaggeration of the -re sound, and also ensure that the infinitive is seen as collocated with the verb *possum* by phrasing together *videre non potest [he is not able to see]* and *pugnare non possum [I am not able to fight]*, etc. Note, in particular, that it is always best to focus on the meaning of *possum* as 'able to' rather than 'can', as this encourages students to link the verb with the preceding infinitive.

2   Use your mouth to exaggerate the sound:

> For example, the comparative and superlative terminations -*ior [more . . .]* and -*issiumus [very . . .]* can be made especially memorable with the rounded opening of the mouth and a hissing sound.

3   Use gesture to show the change in sound:

> For example, verb forms for the 1st and 2nd person singular present tense can be given added salience with a gesture by the teacher to themselves or to the students, as appropriate.

4   Get students to gesture when they hear a particular sound:

> For example, in the story *pugna [The fight]*, Cambridge Latin Course 1, Stage 6, p. 72, there is a mix of imperfect and perfect tense verbs. As the teacher reads the story aloud, students are instructed to gesture or call out when they hear the letter 'b' or 'v', which signifies the tense modifier.

5   Give whole-class feedback when you hear a student mispronounce a word.

The practice of rote-learning charts of forms is often still found in Latin teaching, because those teachers who practise it feel that helps students recall the forms of what is a heavily inflected language. The value of memorizing paradigms by rote is contested: many adult learners, and those who themselves learnt through grammar-translation methods, approve (Lightbown and Spada 2017). However, evidence for the success of rote learning as a means of developing language skills among younger students in the classroom, perhaps less dedicated to language study, suggests their inefficacy (Wong and Van Patten 2003). Lightbown and Spada (2017) report studies that show that:

> an almost exclusive focus on accuracy and practice of particular grammatical forms does not mean that learners will be able to use the forms correctly outside the classroom drill setting, nor that they will continue to use them correctly once other forms are introduced.
>
> Lightbown and Spada 2017: 158

However, the exaggerated emphasis of individual endings can be helpful for beginning students of Latin where (unlike for MFL teaching) authentic pronunciation is not the aim, and can draw students' attention to the significance of the form and thus the meaning of the endings of nouns, verbs and adjectives. My first Latin lesson in 1975, traditionally given, was the memorization of the terminations of the 1st conjugation verb *amo [I love]* and the 1st declension noun *mensa [a table]*[3] in full. More modern practice would ask students to memorize across rather than down a noun or verb paradigm: noticing that the accusative forms of all 1st–3rd declension nouns end in *-m* or that (in the active voice) all 3rd person singular verbs end in *-t* and 3rd person plural verbs end in *-nt* (for example). This can reduce the cognitive load for the student and more clearly helps them associate the form with its function within a sentence. Indeed, more modern coursebooks all introduce new cases or verb endings in this way.[4]

Dictation activities

In the teaching of MFL, dictation helps students understand the grapheme-phoneme correspondence of the language in order to distinguish between words in spoken discourse. I have to admit to being initially sceptical of the value of this, until I watched Terence Tunberg at a Classical Association conference demonstrate different types of dictation to delegates and realized how useful a tool for beginning students of Latin it could be. For those teachers who are interested in using spoken Latin in the classroom, dictation would clearly be very helpful in the initial stages of learning. Even if spoken Latin was not the aim, dictation still forces students to identify the component parts of individual Latin words – essential in a language as morphologically varied as Latin is. But it also supports vocabulary learning as the students hold the words in their heads when they repeat them back or while they write them down.

Simple dictation

1 The teacher says a long, complex word, which the students repeat back or write down.

2 The teacher says a phrase or sentence which students repeat back to them.

3 The same, except the students write it down, for checking afterwards with the teacher for accuracy.

4 The same, except the checking takes place with another student or group of students (this depends on the length of the sentence or the number of sentences).

5 The teacher says a sentence which a student or the whole class repeats. The teacher repeats the sentence, but adds another sentence to the first, which the students repeat. The teacher adds a further sentence, and so on, until the students cannot remember any more.

6 The teacher records a transcript aloud, which the students later read aloud for themselves, tracking the teacher's rhythm, intonation and pronunciation. A variation on this – called 'ghost time' – requires students to read along in a whisper, which accentuates pronunciation, especially of small morphological changes.

Running dictation

A set of sentences introducing new vocabulary or morphology is written on pieces of paper which are stuck to the classroom wall. A scribe sits at the desk and their partner goes to read and memorize the first sentence, returning back to the scribe. They tell the scribe what the first sentence was, with the scribe writing it down. The partner checks for spelling, returning to the wall if necessary. The process is repeated until all the sentences are completed. The activity can be set to a timer to increase motivation. By this activity, both students receive multiple exposures to vocabulary at word and sentence level, checking for pronunciation, spelling and punctuation, by both aural and written means.

Delayed dictation

The teacher reads the sentence. Students wait for 10 seconds, before transcribing it. This means the student is running the words through in their head, perhaps several times – the more times the words or phrases are repeated in the short-term memory, the more likely it is they will enter the long-term memory and be accessible at a later date.

Smith (2019) suggests some variations, which I have adapted for Latin:

1 The teacher reads a sentence, waits 10 seconds, and then the students write it down.

2 The teacher reads a sentence with a gap which students fill in with a suitable word or phrase of their own. For example, the teacher says *'multi milites per vias . . . .'* [*'Many soldiers . . . . through the streets'*]. Students may choose *ambulabant [were walking]* or *festinabant [were hurrying]* or anything else suitable (rather a challenge!). Perhaps easier to use simple phrases in which students could 'slot' individual words, such as places or people.

3 As 1, but the teacher uses an audio or video source (many textbooks have recordings to use, or the teacher could record their own for present and future use).

4 The teacher displays a sentence without reading it aloud, removes the sentence, waits for 10 seconds, and then the students write it down, with or without support.

5 The teacher and students together chorally read aloud a displayed sentence.

6 The teacher sings the sentence so that students have to retain both the language and tune. This helps memorability.

7 'How much can you remember?' The teacher reads a longer sentence, or even more than one. The students try to retain as much as they can before writing them down. Pairs of students may help one another.

After Smith 2019

Listening for comprehensible input

A number of approaches which involve listening have been influenced by Krashen's principle of comprehensible input. Activities which involve circling/personalized questions and answers (PQA) techniques require extensive listening on the part of the students. The teacher uses multiple spoken repetitions, clarifications and personalizes the subject matter to fit the students' own interests, thereby contributing to making the input comprehensible and compelling. Speaking and listening is faster and more efficient than reading and writing and a great deal may be achieved in a short period of time. The effectiveness of the techniques has been much described elsewhere (see Bracey 2019; Bailey 2016; and Patrick 2011, 2015).

Total Physical Response (TPR)

Asher's (2012) Total Physical Response (TPR) method has been shown to be effective for helping students to acquire vocabulary. The teacher says a word or phrase, and students re-enact the meaning of it physically. The method is more easily applied with verbs, but some nouns and some adverbial phrases are also possible to be acted out. I suspect TPR would be possible with the students listening to a recording, but some of the success of the activity is probably derived from the social aspect itself. The following steps seem to be most effective:

Step 1: The teacher says the target word and models an appropriate action: *laborat [works]*/action of digging. Repeats. The students mimic the action.

Step 2: The teacher repeats the word and action; the students say the word and mimic the action (it could be argued that the students do not need to say the word – but I have found that it is helpful).

Steps 1–2 are repeated with a number of words. In practice, I have found ten words are sufficient before students begin to tire.

Variations:

1 After practice, the teacher says the word (without an action) and the students act it out.
2 After practice, the teacher acts out the word (but does not say it) and the students mimic the action and say the word.
3 The students practise with each other in pairs or small groups, using any of the above approaches.
4 The teacher 'makes a mistake' by acting out the wrong meaning – students notice and correct the teacher.
5 Rather than single verbs, the teacher uses adverbial phrases (humour allowed): *currit [runs]; lente currit [runs slowly]; celeriter currit [runs quickly]*. Note that TPR typically uses imperative forms of the verb, but there is no reason why other forms should not be used – the emphasis should, however, not be on the grammar so much as the meaning of the word or phrase. TPR is a means to acquire vocabulary rather than grammar.
6 It is also possible to enact certain nouns (e.g. animals) and adjectives (size, height, etc). These, however, have more limited or obvious actions.
7 I have found varying and emphasizing the intonation of words is also helpful.

Teaching Proficiency through Reading and Storytelling (TPRS) and Story-asking

TPR is effective for learning concrete vocabulary which can be easily expressed through gestures and movements. It is less effective for abstract vocabulary or ideas that are more personalized. In response, Blaine Ray developed the method now known as Teaching Proficiency through Reading and Storytelling (TPRS). According to Lichtmann, the main principles that underlie TPRS are:

- Students need huge amounts of input to acquire language – this means as much class time as possible should be spent providing students with comprehensible input through teacher speech and through reading.
- Language should always be comprehensible – teachers should use the target language throughout, making comprehensibility clear through the use of visuals, gestures, cognates and glosses, and using vocabulary which students already know or by giving meanings in the first language if necessary.
- Students should learn a small number of high-frequency words and phrases to mastery.
- Words should be introduced in forms which are in common use so that students develop a full mental representation of the meanings through usage rather than through explicit teaching.
- TPRS is centred around the students and their interests – students are often the main 'characters' in the stories – this engages students' participation and develops their comprehension of new vocabulary because it is something that matters to them.
- The teacher structures the lesson so that vocabulary is met repeatedly and in different ways to maintain student interest.
- Students work on comprehension (through listening and reading) before working on production (through speaking and writing). Comprehension does not have to be shown through speaking – nods and shakes of the heads, expressions and other gestures all show comprehension. Indeed, minimal lesson time should be spent on output activities – the focus on the lesson is on input and comprehension. If the teacher detects a lack of compression, they should include further examples of input.

After Lichtmann 2018: 9–11

In a TPRS lesson, the following stages are usually followed:

Stage 1: Introduction of new language words and structures. Rather than introducing a vocabulary list, chart or table or grammar rule, the TPRS teacher incorporates the new vocabulary and grammar in common words and phrases that are based around what is already familiar to the student, but which takes them a little further. Input is provided mostly by speaking, and by actions which are copied by the students, for example. Comprehensibility is maintained at all times, as noted above.

Stage 2: Story-asking. Traditional methods which use stories usually include extra vocabulary to help the students comprehend the meaning of the text; often, therefore, the text is set as a test of the student's knowledge of vocabulary which has been previously given and the objective is for the students to read, comprehend and then translate the story in writing. Story-asking, however, turns this approach on its head. The story is the starting point, not the end point, and exposes the students to a flood of language in a comprehensible and enjoyable way so that vocabulary and syntactical features are acquired without anxiety. The story-listening may be supplemented with pictures, paraphrase and extra-linguistic materials such as gesture, tone of voice, facial expressions and props – what Krashen, Mason and Smith (2018) call 'Comprehension-Aiding Supplementation'. Following Krashen's input hypothesis, Mason uses the telling of a story in the target language as the focus for developing a student's competence in the foreign language (Krashen and Mason 2020). According to Mason, there should be no attempt to highlight particular words or phrases that have been chosen to suit a particular vocabulary learning objective (such as a vocabulary list). Instead, she recommends 'optimal input', using comprehension-supplementation. The story should be naturalistic and unforced (Krashen and Mason 2020.). Frequent storytelling, recycling similar vocabulary and even versions of the same stories, is recommended for language acquisition. A number of Latin teachers have experimented with this approach, with apparent success. In a Facebook blog, Patrick (2021) suggests some adaptations:

- While the teacher tells the story first, they draw the scenes on the board. Then, straight after, they retell the story using the drawings already completed.
- While the teacher tells the story, the students draw the scenes as well.
- While the teacher tells the story, they add Latin (and possibly English) words to the drawing, saving it for future readings. While the annotations could be considered to be supplementations for language compressibility, their writing and saving by the students seem not entirely in the spirit of story-listening, per se; however, Patrick (2020), is interested in the creation of the annotated picture as a means of supporting students absent from class who miss the experience and as a resource for other teachers.

Lance Piantaggini's *Latin Stories Video Series* (2017) YouTube channel provides simple, comprehensible Latin based around familiar mythological stories. Telling stories aloud, of course, is far quicker than reading words on a page and therefore more repetitions and more tailored examples can be offered to students. By observing the students' reactions as they listen (expressions of puzzlement or understanding, such as nods and shakes of the head) the teacher is able to gauge how much more support the students need to achieve the learning objective.

Stage 3: Reading. From processing aural input, the student now turns to process written input. The reading material is related to the new vocabulary and structures which have been met in the lesson: it will contain a very high proportion of familiar vocabulary so that the students will be able to read it without the need for a dictionary or vocabulary lists. Sometimes students may use (Lichtmann 2018) novellas or participate in free voluntary reading (see Chapter 3). Students might discuss the story as a class, before their friends, draw versions of the story (or parts of it), add further details to show their comprehension.

MovieTalk

The MovieTalk concept was originally designed by Hastings (1995) for college-level TESL classes and has been adapted for use in the school classroom. Essentially, the teacher shows a movie to the class, sound off, and narrates the story extempore or from a prepared script in the target language. Hastings intended whole movies to be used, but for practical reasons teachers prefer to use shorter clips in the classroom. Hastings also intended that, in the spirit of comprehensible input, students should not be asked questions on the subject matter of the clip, nor should the narrative supplied by the teacher focus on particular vocabulary or grammatical forms. Teachers may choose to replicate the main storyline itself, or may use it for other purposes. Herman (2014) provides a useful guide:

1. The teacher narrates the scenes, paraphrasing where appropriate.
2. The teacher's voice simplifies the soundtrack, making the meaning comprehensible to the students.
3. The teacher selects the movie for the students' age and interest.
4. The vocabulary is contextualized in the story – the visual images are powerful aids to vocabulary comprehension.
5. The vocabulary is concentrated, through the repetition of words within the movie and repetitions of the movie clip itself.
6. Short 4-minute clips seem to hold the interest best.
7. The teacher can employ an embedded listening approach – like embedded or tiered reading (see Clarcq 2012; and also in this volume) – with several versions of the same movie, but with increasing levels of language.
8. The teacher can screen-shot the movie scenes and turn them into individual scenes for projection in sequence on the whiteboard. These can act as a preview for the whole movie segment – a 'picture walk', which can increase the comprehensibility of the movie talk itself.

After Herman 2014

Further suggestions which personalize the experience and aid engagement and motivation include the use of personal information, where appropriate, in the narration (such as student's names), and allowing the students to choose the videos which they would like to watch.

Latin teachers' experiences of using movie talks have been generally positive (see Ramahlo 2019; Ash 2017; and Patrick 2014). The following blogs, by Latin teachers, also offer helpful guides:

- John Piazza: Movie Talk Resources for Teachers of Latin (and Other Languages) (Piazza n.d.).
- Keith Toda: Movie Talks (Toda 2016).
- Lance Piantaggini: Movie Talk (Piantaggini 2019).

Listen-and-do activities

These are good for vocabulary recycling:

1 The teacher provides students with a black-and-white drawing of a room, or the forum, or some other kind of busy scene. As the teacher describes the scene in Latin, the students colour in the various parts of the picture.

2 The teacher reads or retells a simple Latin story. As they do so, they mime the story, with the students copying the actions. The story might be shown on the whiteboard. The teacher retells the story, without miming, but the students continue to mime, using the actions they used before or using others of their own. The teacher retells the story for the last time, but with the students' eyes closed, so that they are listening only to the words as they hear them: meanwhile, they mime the actions.

3 The teacher describes a scene – a room, a place, or an event. The students draw the scene as the teacher describes it. This is good for semantically related vocabulary. The teacher and students check their drawings for accuracy. An extra might be to add in adjectives (especially superlatives).

Podcasts

Many teachers have turned to the podcast as a way of providing students with readily accessible and easily comprehensible Latin input. Some neurodiverse students find recordings of the notes from exercise books or from an English translation beneficial to enable them to follow along at reading speed and access, navigate and absorb information more easily. Advanced students might find the news delivered in Latin a useful means of developing their comprehension skills: the news channels *nuntii Latini* (2021) and *Radio Finnica Generalis* (2021) (sadly no longer transmitting, but archived) provide considerable, somewhat challenging, but rewarding aural comprehensible input.

Films

There are numerous films or television series set in the Roman historical period, many of which are very suitable for supporting students' background knowledge. The very small number which are in Latin may provide samples of spoken Latin sufficient for further interest and stimulation (although the pronunciation of the Latin may not be entirely satisfactory). For school students, such films as *Sebastiane* (Jarman and Humfress 1976) with its frequent homo-erotic content, *The Passion of the Christ* (Gibson 2004) with occasional suffering and violence, and the television series *Barbarians* (Heckmann, Nolting and Scharf 2020/2021) with its occasional violence may not be suitable for watching. All is not lost, however, and there are a small number of shorts created by film students which are much less risky: teachers have recommended *Barnabus and Bella* (Corn 2010), 'an original Latin-language musical comedy about high school life and love' and *Pacifica* (SLAM 2009), 'a Latin-language teen drama set in current times in a California beach community' in four episodes, created by students at Santa Monica High School. There is, of course, nothing to stop students preparing their own films in Latin. Snippets of Latin may be found on YouTube segments, some of which can provide unusual sources of learning about how Latin might be used in 'real-life' situations.[5]

Music and singing

Singing along to recorded or live music can be helpful for students to improve their pronunciation and to recycle vocabulary. Students are more likely to recall vocabulary heard in songs than in speech (Smith-Salcedo 2002). Carlsson (2015) suggests a significant impact on helping students learn vocabulary; Conti and Smith (2019) are less convinced, considering that specific grammar or vocabulary needs to be drawn out once engagement through singing has occurred. Some songs are more useful for supporting vocabulary learning than others: simple structures work best, with predictable verses and chorus (Kellaris 2003); and with simple rhyme schemes (Rubin and Wallace 1990). Many medieval Latin songs, for example, feature repetitions of words or phrases, and choruses, too. There has been little research specific to Latin on this subject, but a number of Latin teachers have attested to the usefulness of listening to Latin songs for their students to assimilate vocabulary and detect Latin phraseology (see, for example, Letchford 2021 and Domagala, Loch and Ochman 2021). A small collection of songs in Latin can be found online in *carmina convivalia* (Kuhner 2018) and in the ARLT Songbook (ARLT 2021). Conti (2019) has published *Carmina Latina Per Se Illustrata*, a set of songs based on the vocabulary of Ørberg's *Lingua Latina Per Se Illustrata*. The *Disney Songs – Classical Latin* YouTube channel must surely have its attractions (0livette 2017). A good number of activities in which songs are used as initial stimulus material for language development, including grammar knowledge, can be found in Conti and Smith (2019).

Notes

1. Pettersson and Rosengren (2021) suggest that a student who listens to the text as they read it begins to appreciate it more as a real language than as a code. The *Cambridge Latin Course, Minimus* and *Suburani* Latin coursebooks all have digital audio recordings of all the stories, although I have rarely heard them in use in the classroom.
2. There are many contrasting views as to how to pronounce Latin. For a brief and approachable introduction, see Swift (2021). For more detail, see *vox Latina* (Allen 2008). If the teacher is using a commercial course which has its own audio supplementary materials, it would be wise to stick with the pronunciation which they use, to save confusion. Both the *Cambridge Latin Course* and *Suburani* have good, consistent Latin pronunciation in their digital audio resources. There is a great deal of anecdotal evidence that teachers make use of chanting and mnemonic songs from social media (see, e.g., HI_PAWS 2019, among many others). If the teacher uses resources from social media, they should be aware that there may be considerable variation.
3. I am reminded of the similarity of experience to that described in the often quoted anecdote of Winston Churchill's first schoolday at Harrow School, when the future statesman was required to memorize the paradigm for *mensa*, in vain (Churchill 2002). There the similarity ends. But the practice goes on: I, along with the invited teachers, was treated to a similar display of paradigm-chanting by the arch-traditionalist online teacher Neville Gwynne at a Prince's Trust Classics Summer School in 2016. Charts for chanting also appear in the traditionally inspired Latin books *Gwynne's Latin* (Gwynne 2014) and *Amo Amas Amat and All That* (Mount 2006). They are noticeably absent in other coursebooks.
4. See, e.g., p. 30 of *Suburani*, p. 37 of *Cambridge Latin Course*, p. 18 of *Latin to GCSE* and p. 26 of *De Romanis*.
5. These include the famous 'Romans Go Home' scene from *Monty Python's Life of Brian* (Jones 1979) and, more recently, a scene from Marvel Studios' *Loki* (Waldron 2021), in which actor Tom Hiddleston (himself a Cambridge Classics undergraduate) warns the inhabitants of Pompeii about the imminent destruction of their town in (relatively) fluent Latin.

References

01ivette (2017, 23 Sept.). Disney Songs – Classical Latin. Retrieved from YouTube. Available at: https://www.youtube.com/playlist?list=PL70AC3BA7B0E4442C.

Allen, S. (2008). vox Latina: *A Guide to the Pronunciation of Classical Latin.* Cambridge: Cambridge University Press.

ARLT (2021). *ARLT Songbook.* Retrieved from Association for Latin Teaching. Available at: http://www.arlt.co.uk/songbook.html.

Ash, R. (2017). The Movie Talk: A Practical Application of Comprehensible Input Theory. *Teaching Classical Languages*, 8 (2): 70–83.

Asher, J. (2012). *Learning Another Language Through Actions*. Los Gatos, CA: Sky Oak Productions.

Bailey, J. (2016). The 'Ars' of Latin Questioning: Circling, Personalization, and Beyond. *The Classical Outlook*, 91 (1): 1–5.

Bell, B. (2003). Minimus. In J. Morwood, *The Teaching of Classics* (pp. 61–6). Cambridge: Cambridge University Press.

Bracey, J. (2019). TPRS, PQA & Circling. *Journal of Classics Teaching*, 39: 60–4.

Carlsson, L. (2015). Singing as a Tool for English Pronunciation Improvement: An Experimental Study. Unpublished Research Paper, Lund University.

Churchill, W. (2002). *My Early Life: A Roving Commission*. London: Eland Publishing.

Clarcq, L. (2012). Embedded Reading: A Scaffolded Approach to Teaching Reading. *International Journal of Foreign Language Teaching*, 21–4.

Conti, A. (2019). *Carmina Latina Per Se Illustrata*. Madrid: Cultura Clasica.

Conti, G. and S. Smith (2019). *Breaking the Sound Barrier: Teaching Language Learners How to Listen*. Self-published. Imprint/G. Conti and S. Smith.

Corn, E. (Director). (2010). *Barnabus and Bella*. Motion Picture.

Cullen, H. and J. Taylor (2016). *Latin to GCSE, 1*. London: Bloomsbury Academic.

Domagala, S., M. Loch, M. and K. Ochman (2021). Latin Teaching in Poland – A New Renaissance with Communicative Approaches? In M. Lloyd and S. Hunt, *Communicative Approaches for Ancient Languages* (pp. 161–78). London: Bloomsbury Academic.

Forrin, N. and C. MacLeod (2018). This Time It's Personal: The Memory Benefit of Hearing Oneself. *Memory*, 26 (4): 574–9.

Gibson, H. and J. England (2008). The Inclusion of Pseudowords within the Year One Phonics 'Screening Check' in English Primary Schools. *Cambridge Journal of Education*, 46 (4): 491–507.

Gibson, M. (Director) (2004). *The Passion of the Christ*. Motion Picture.

Gwynne, N. (2014). *Gwynne's Latin*. London: Ebury Press.

Hastings, A. (1995). The FOCAL SKILLS Approach: An Assessment. In F. Eckman, D. Highland, P. Lee, J. Mileham and R. Weber, *Second Language Acquisition: Theory and Pedagogy* (pp. 29–44). Malwah: Lawrence Eribaum Associates.

Heckmann, A., A. Nolting and J. Scharf (Directors) (2020/2021). *Barbarians*. Motion Picture.

Herman, E. (2014). How to Use MovieTalk to Teach with Comprehensible Input. *International Journal of Foreign Language Teaching*, 18–24.

HI_PAWS (2019, June 21). *HI PAWS*. Retrieved from YouTube. Available at: https://www.youtube.com/watch?v=__Ba1Q4j_AA.

Hipfner-Boucher, K., K. Lam and X. Chen (2014). The Contribution of Narrative Morphosyntactic Quality to Reading Comprehension in French Immersion Students. *Applied Psycholinguistics*, 36: 1375–91.

Hunt, S. (2016). *Starting to Teach Latin*. London: Bloomsbury Academic.

Jarman, D. and P. Humfress (Directors) (1976). *Sebastiane*. Motion Picture.

Jones, T. (Director) (1979). *Monty Python's Life of Brian*. Motion Picture.

Kellaris, J. (2003). Dissecting Earworms: Further Evidence on the 'Song-Stuck-in-Your-Head' Phenomenon. In C. Page and S. Prosavac, *Proceedings of the Society for Consumer Psychology Winter Conference* (pp. 220–2). Potsdam: Society for Consumer Psychology.

Krashen, S. and B. Mason (2020). The Optimal Input Hypothesis: Not All Comprehensible Input is of Equal Value. *CATESOL Newsletter*, May.

Krashen, S., B. Mason and K. Smith (2018). Some New Terminology: Comprehension-Aiding Supplementation and Form-Focusing Supplementation. *Language Learning and Teaching*, 60 (6): 12–13.

Kuhner, J. (2018, 19 Jan.). *Carmina Convivalia*. Retrieved from in medias res. Available at: https://medium.com/in-medias-res/carmina/home.

Letchford, C. (2021). Communicative Latin for All in a UK University. In M. Lloyd and S. Hunt, *Communicative Approaches for Ancient Languages* (pp. 81–90). London: Bloomsbury Academic.

Lichtmann, K. (2018). *Teaching Proficiency through Reading and Storytelling (TPRS)*. New York: Routledge.

Lightbown, P. and N. Spada (2017). *How Languages are Learned*. Oxford: Oxford University Press.

Mason, B. (2020). Story-Listening: A Brief Introduction. *CATESOL Newsletter*, June.

Milton, J., J. Wade and N. Hopkins (2010). Aural Word Recognition and Oral Competence in English as a Foreign Language. In R. Chacon-Beltrain, C. Abello-Contesse and M. Torreblanca-Lopez, *Insights into Non-Native Vocabulary Teaching and Learning* (pp. 83–98). Bristol: Multilingual Matters.

Mount, H. (2006). Amo Amas Amat *and All That*. London: Short Books.

nuntii Latini. (2021). *nuntii Latini. occidentalis studiorum universitatis vasintoniensis*. Retrieved from nuntii Latini. occidentalis studiorum universitatis vasintoniensis. Available at: https://nuntiilatini.com/.

Patrick, R. (2011). TPRS & Latin in the Classroom: Experiences of a US Latin Teacher. *Journal of Classics Teaching*, 22: 8–10.

Patrick, R. (2015). Making Sense of Comprehensible Input in the Latin Classroom. *Teaching Classical Langauges*, Spring: 108–36.

Patrick, R. (2021, 11 Feb.). *Latin Best Practices: The Next Generation in Comprehensible Input*. Retrieved from Facebook. Available at: https://www.facebook.com/groups/122958344965415/?multi_permalinks=804075066853736.

Patrick, M. (2014, 29 May). *Movie Talk/Movie Shorts*. Retrieved from Pomegranate Beginnings, web blog. Available at: http://pomegranatebeginnings.blogspot.com/2014/05/movie-talkmovie-shorts.html.

Pettersson, D. and A. Rosengren (2021). The Latinitium Project. In M. Lloyd and S. Hunt, *Communicative Approaches for Ancient Languages* (pp. 195–210). London: Bloomsbury Academic.

Piantaggini, L. (2017, 9 Aug.). *Latin Stories Video Series*. Retrieved from YouTube. Available at: https://www.youtube.com/playlist?list=PLx10fugjczknvXe5E2VqmgepCc_EZhhOx.

Piantaggini, L. (2019, 31 July). *MovieTalk.* Retrieved from Magister P, web blog. Available at: https://magisterp.com/2017/09/07/movietalk/.

Piazza, J. (n.d.). *Movie Talk Resources for Teachers of Latin (and Other Languages).* Retrieved from John Piazza, web blog. Available at: http://johnpiazza.net/movie-talk/.

Radio Finnica Generalis (2021). *Radio Finnica Generalis.* Retrieved from Areena Audio. Available at: https://areena.yle.fi/audio/1-1931339.

Ramahlo, M. (2019). On Starting to Teach Using CI. *Journal of Classics Teaching,* 39: 45–50.

Rivers, W. (1981). *Teaching Foeign Language Skills.* Chicago, IL: University of Chicago Press.

Rubin, D. and W. Wallace (1990). Rhyme and Reason: Analyses of Dual Retrieval Cues. *Journal of Experimental Psychology: Learning, Memory and Cognition,* 15 (4): 698–709.

Schmidt, R. (1990). The Role of Consciousness in Second Language Learning. *Applied Linguistics,* 11 (2): 129–58.

Seo, S. (2014). Does Reading Aloud Improve Foreign Language Learners' Speaking Ability? *GSTF International Journal on Education (JEd),* 2 (1): 46–50.

Service, E. (2011). Phonology, Working Memory, and Foreign-Language Learning. *Quarterly Journal of Experimental Pschology Section A,* 45 (1): 21–50.

Shonozuka, K., S. Shibata and Y. Mizusawa (2017). Effectiveness of Read-Aloud Instruction on Motivation and Learning Strategy among Japanese College EFL Students. *English Language Teaching,* 10 (4): 1–14.

SLAM (Director) (2009). *Pacifica.* Motion Picture.

Smith, S. (2019, 15 Jan.). *Delayed Dictation.* Retrieved from Language Teacher Toolkit: Steve Smith's Blog. Available at: https://frenchteachernet.blogspot.com/search?q=delayed+dictation.

Smith-Salcedo, C. (2002). The Effects of Songs in the Foreign Language Classroom on Text Recall and Involuntary Mental Rehearsal. Unpublished PhD thesis, Louisiana State University.

Swift, N. (2021, 14 July). *What did Ancient Languages Sound Like?* Retrieved from *Antigone Journal.* Available at: https://antigonejournal.com/2021/07/what-did-ancient-languages-sound-like/?fbclid=IwAR032H4NBazroyFriqv_f00YdFGsoLN1sGBqczNxh01F1bDPs48DmLYG3es.

Toda, K. (2016, 30 June). *Movie Talks.* Retrieved from Toda-lly Comprehensible Latin, web blog. Available at: http://todallycomprehensiblelatin.blogspot.com/2016/06/movie-talks.html.

Waldron, M. (Director) (2021). *Loki,* Motion Picture.

Wong, W. and B. Van Patten (2003). The Evidence is IN: Drills are OUT. *Foreign Language Annals,* 36 (3): 403–23.

Woo, M. and R. Price (2015). The Pronunciation-Reading Connection. In T. Jones, *Integrating Pronunciation with Other Skills Areas* (pp. 129–42). Alexandra, VA: TESOL Press.

3

Reading

Reading and not reading Latin

Reading is complex. Logically, reading must precede translation; despite this, translation of a Latin text into written or spoken English is often described by Latin teachers as 'reading', perhaps because written translation is the dominant mode of assessment for examinations and so many conflate translation and reading as being the same thing. Commonly-used Latin coursebooks also fail to make this distinction, many of them providing passages of Latin text for the teacher to decide how to use.[1] Aside from that, teachers often utilize a number of different strategies in the classroom which purport to be 'reading' but actually are neither that nor translating. Instead, as US Latin teacher Lance Piantaggini (2021b) says in his blog, the following may be more realistic descriptions of 'reading' a text in the classroom:

- Discussing . . .
- Puzzling through . . .
- Parsing out . . .

- Understanding parts of . . .
- Analysing the language of . . .
- Reading English in support of . . .
- Applying memorized translations to the text . . .

Piantaggini 2021b

So, for Latin teachers, 'reading' has often become a synonym for a variety of activities which are supposed to help students develop skills for reading Latin texts, but which are perhaps not as efficient and effective as they might be.

How does the student, then, really read? The two models of reading a whole text most often mentioned are a top-down approach (in which the reader infers the meaning by activating semantic, pragmatic, syntactic and discourse knowledge) and a bottom-up approach (a decoding approach, word by word). Macaro (2003) suggests that students should use both in an interactive model – a process which draws on different sources of knowledge, in which:

> there is a constant interaction between the surface structure of the text and the reader's own knowledge of the topic which the text is trying to communicate. This model involves the reader in elaborating on the meaning of the text, inferring learning but also at times stopping to pause and ponder over individual words and syntactic patterns and their relationships with other words and phrases in order to confirm hypotheses, strengthen connections and build up layers of interpretation.

Macaro 2003: 120–1

Confident learners do not, therefore, 'just read'. Here we explore how Latin teachers can help students develop language understanding using continuous Latin narratives.

One of the persistent problems of coursebook materials is that the subject matter of the passages and some of the vocabulary is often uninteresting or insufficiently familiar (or both) so as to engage the student to make the effort to read. Coursebooks do try to minimize this by providing supplementary vocabulary (glossing) and by locating the narrative in a familiar setting. Nonetheless, they expect students to *work at* the story, rather than *read* it fluently. The nature of the coursebook methodology – to insert new material every time, while consolidating prior knowledge – may make language learning through analytical or reading-comprehension methods feel rather like a treadmill, with no end in sight. Although both methods are meant to provide students with the skills to be able to read, it is a long-term process and, if numerous anecdotes over the years are true, a not especially effective one.

For this reason, some teachers have chosen to stop using the coursebook (see, for example, Ash 2019). Instead, they have adopted other approaches to reading materials which they have chosen for themselves, including tiered readers and novellas. The preference for coursebooks to prepare students to read the canon of Latin literature from the classical period has also been questioned: would late antique or neo-Latin be a more reasonable aim for students learning on short courses? If, however, the teacher does decide to stay using coursebooks, I recommend that students could read stories that they have read some weeks or months before, to consolidate grammar and vocabulary and enhance motivation when they realize how far they have come in so short a time.

Grabe (2004) makes ten recommendations for reading instruction in the classroom:

1 Ensure word recognition fluency.
2 Emphasize vocabulary learning and create a vocabulary rich environment.
3 Activate background knowledge.
4 Ensure effective language knowledge and general comprehension skills.
5 Teach text structures and discourse organization.
6 Promote the strategic reader rather than individual strategies.
7 Build fluency reading rate.
8 Promote extensive reading.
9 Develop intrinsic motivation for reading.
10 Plan a coherent curriculum for student learning.

Grabe 2004: 46

Strategies for reading

Nuttall (2005) identifies three main cognitive reading strategies for dealing with a text. These include:

Predicting

- Using all available information including own world and linguistic knowledge to predict likely contents of text/gaps.

Inferring

- Using context to infer the meaning of missing words or chunks of text or the next chunk of text in as sequence/deducing.
- Using knowledge of rules to decide on the form of missing words or the next word in a sequence.

Reasoning

- Seeking clarification and or additional information and explanation including grammar hints and vocabulary from other students, teacher, grammar refences book or dictionary.
- Creating own resource by note taking.

For the text as a whole, Nuttall (2005) suggests that the reader (and, by inference, the teacher) should make some early decisions about how to 'attack the text'. What are the students reading the narrative for?

1 Efferent reading: The reader is using the text to find out some information that they did not know before.
2 Aesthetic reading: The reader is assessing the text for its artistic qualities.
3 Analytical reading: The reader is focusing on the encoding of meaning through vocabulary and grammar.

The teaching of original Latin texts means that all three approaches will be necessary. Teachers and students who prefer an analytical approach will start there. Those who prefer a reading-comprehension approach will start with a reading for meaning, and move on to a more analytical approach of the parts which need it when the encoding of the meaning is not immediately obvious. It is likely that teachers and students will complete several readings of the same piece, ending with an aesthetic reading. Older and high-attaining students may be able to handle all three approaches at the same time; younger students will probably need to take a more stage-by-stage approach, in order to reduce cognitive overload. It is worth mentioning that VanPatten's Input Processing Theory suggests that people tend to listen for meaning first, and grammar afterwards (and often not even that) (VanPatten 1993). Evidence from transcripts of novice Latin students show this to be frequently the case with reading too (Jacobs 2022 forthcoming; Wright 2017; Hunt 2016). If we work with this, then we can see how a meaning-first/grammar-afterwards approach fits with most students' normal experiences of reading a text, and how the teacher needs to modify their expectations of what the student is likely to do – and then teach them to adjust their practice accordingly. Take this very simple example, drawn from a recent classroom observation, where the student focuses first on the meaning conveyed by the vocabulary, and then comes to refine the meaning through their knowledge of grammar forms, prompted by the teacher:

Latin: ex una navium ... puella pulcherrima exiit [From one of the ships ... came a very beautiful girl].[2]

Student   [*Orally translating*] From one of the ships came a girl.

Teacher   What sort of girl?

Student   A beautiful one.

Teacher   Are you sure?

Student   Oh. It's superlative. The most beautiful?

Teacher   The whole sentence?

Student   From one of the ships came the most beautiful girl.

Teacher   Sure? Have we met her before?

Student   Hmm. *A* most beautiful . . . a . . . *very* beautiful girl. From one of the ships came *a very beautiful* girl.

In this episode, the student understands the main message of the passage, but misses some of the details. The teacher prompts the student first to recall the missed adjective, and then to recall the superlative form. The student gradually refines their original understanding of the meaning of the sentence, calling on their grammatical knowledge. It is not that the student does not know, it is just that the student needs reminding about the details. With practice, the student will no longer need reminding.

Thinking about the text

Rather than just reading along and finding out as we go, the teacher can guide students to look for particular structural features of a story. This is not just to help students understand what the story is, or how the narrative flows, but it (a) sends out an expectation about *how* to read the story – which helps language learning if we know the features are going to happen- and (b) we can predict how the story is going to move along. There are simple ways in which most narratives follow. Latin is no different. The teacher should use a variety of strategies to get students to pre-read the passage.

Schemata are categories of information stored in long-term memory. A schema contains groups of linked memories, concepts or words, which acts as a cognitive shortcut and makes storing new information in the long-term memory and their retrieval quicker and more efficient. Students who have well-developed schemata are more likely to be able to read and comprehend a text than others. Teachers therefore need to provide opportunities for their students to develop rich schemata about the socio-historical location of the text, and also the way the text 'works'. There are three types of schemata which are useful to learners when they are faced with a narrative text:

1   External schemata: using existing knowledge.
2   Content schemata: using an understanding of the text genre.
3   Narrative and expectations/predictions schemata: using an understanding of the way a narrative unfolds.

External schemata

The teacher can elicit information about the subject matter of the text prior to reading it. This can be challenging if the text is new and concerns something about which the students have no prior knowledge. In some coursebooks, there is little to go on except a title and the possibility that the passage concerned is part of a sequence from which references might be picked up by the teacher.[3] In other cases, the coursebook provides some additional reading material which might provide the necessary support.[4] In coursebooks which are richly illustrated, external schemata are much easier to provide.[5] Examples will be given below.

Content schemata

Students might be asked to skim the passage for a general gist of what it is about. Students are given a short period of time to read through and then submit their ideas to the rest of the class, which the teacher collates on the board, to give a picture of the whole story.

Students might scan the passage for particular events in the narrative or what happens to characters within it. They submit their ideas back to the class as above.

With either of these, the teacher may prompt for further features. The contributions which have been put on the board can be colour coded, arranged in particular ways or left as they are. These notes act as a silent scaffold for the students to use in the lesson, or for drawing their attention to as the teacher monitors progress. They may be added to as the lesson progresses. If an Interactive White Board (IWB) is used, the notes may be manipulated, and/or saved and provided for students to continue with at another time.

Narrative and expectations/predictions schemata

The teacher might quiz the students on the likely structural forms that are evident in the passage. The following forms are common in Latin coursebooks and reading materials:

1 A description of a scene, a place, or an occasion.
2 A speech.
3 A will.
4 An argument between two people.
5 A court case.
6 A fight or battle scene.
7 A myth involving a metamorphosis.
8 A dream or portent.
9 A reversal in circumstances.

10 A declaration of love or admiration.

11 A mystery with a resolution.

12 A comedic scene.

13 A punchline or revelation.

The teacher can also recall common narrative tropes, such as zooming in, zooming out, the rules of dialogue, changes of focus/character/location, flashback and flashforward, foreshadowing, repetition and cyclical structure. We cannot assume that a student can just pick these up and they all help a student make meaning from a passage which otherwise looks to them like nothing more than a set of words on a page.

Building reading schemata: Examples

Example 1

The extract below is from *Latine Legamus [Let's Read Latin]* (Harrison and Wilson 1968), which is the sort of 'reader' from the 1960s which was published for preparing students for the old O level examination in Latin. This is from Part 1, by the end of which students were expected to have learnt 'most of the accidence and some elementary syntax' (Harrison and Wilson 1968: vi). Part 2 was designed to take students to a point where they would be able to 'tackle undiluted Caesar'. The authors typically conflate the separate skills of reading and translation, conceiving of the book as an intermediate reader but anticipating that the texts will be used as translation practice. Any teacher using this sort of material – and there is still plenty of it in more recent publications – needs to decide how to use the resource. Is it for testing the student's skill at translating? The book itself is unclear, but there are scattered here and there useful admonitions to translate certain words. If the teacher does want to set the passage as a translation exercise, then they need to make some choices. In this publication, no glossed words are given. There are two vocabulary lists given at the end of the book: one of these is a general vocabulary of all the words in the book, the other a specific vocabulary list which pertains to individual stories. For this passage, the book instructs the student to use the general vocabulary. One can imagine that a great deal of use will have to be made of it. Within the first two lines we come across four proper nouns: *Romanis, Poenos, Syracusas, Siciliae [the Romans, the Carthaginians, Syracuse, Sicily]*; the adjective *Romanus [Roman]* and *Graecus [Greek]* appear (probably not too many problems with them) and two more proper nouns: *Syracusanos [the Syracusans]* and *Archimedes [Archimedes]*, who is the hero of the piece, as evidenced by his name given as the title of the piece (but nothing more).

Archimedes

eodem bello, quod a Romanis contra Poenos gestum est, consul Romanus Syracusas, urbem Siciliae maximam, terra marrique obsidebat murosque omni genere machinarum oppugnabat. sed erat tum in urbe homo quidam, qui mira sua arte Syracusanos adiuvabat. Archimedes is erat, vir Graecus, artis mathematicae peritus, qui non solum caelum stellasque observabat, sed etiam novas belli machinas invenerat.

Romani in navibus suis machinas multas posuerant, quae in eam partem muri, quae prope mare erat, multitudinem telorum iactabant. contra eas Archimedes non solum tormenta, e quibus saxa ingentia mittebantur, sed etiam machinas cum manibus ferreis in muris collocaverat; his machinis primo naves Romanae ex aqua trahebantur, deinde, ubi manus relaxatae erant, naves repente cum magno nautarum timore cadebant.

omnes tamen Archimedis machinae Syracusanos non servaverunt. consul tandem cum copiis suis urbem iniit militesque urbem vastaverunt. Archimedes, victoriae Romanorum ignarus, tum formas mathematicas spectabat, quas in terras scripserat. invenit enim miles Romanus; qui Archimedem, quod ei non erat notus, statim gladio occidit. Marcellus consul aegre mortem eius tulit.

exinde ob sapientiam magnam semper in memoria hominum nomen Archimedis habitum est.

Archimedes

In the same war, which was being conducted by the Romans against the Carthaginians, the Roman consul was besieging Syracuse, a very large city in Sicily, by land and sea and he was attacking the walls with every kind of military engine. But there was in that city a certain man, who helped the Syracusans with his amazing skill. That man was Archimedes, a Greek man, experienced in the art of mathematics, who not only used to observe the sky and the stars, but also invented new military engines.

The Romans had placed on their ships their military engines, which hurled a great number of projectiles at that part of the wall, which was near the sea. Against them Archimedes had placed on the walls not only catapults, from which huge rocks were thrown, but also military engines with iron claws; with these military engines first of all he dragged the Roman ships out of the water, and then, when the claws were relaxed, the ships suddenly fell to the great fear of the sailors.

However, all the military engines of Archimedes did not save the Syracusans. Eventually, the consul with his forces entered the city and his soldiers destroyed the city. Archimedes, not knowing about the Romans' victory, was looking at some geometrical figures, which he had drawn on the ground. A Roman soldier found him; immediately this man, because he was not known to him, killed Archimedes with his sword. Marcellus the consul took his death badly.

And so, because of his great wisdom, the name of Archimedes was always kept in the memory of mankind.

Author's own translation

The title is opaque. Is there a picture or a map which might help students understand the physical and geographical features mentioned in the passage? Even a picture of Archimedes 'at work' might be helpful to provide the entry point to the passage.

We could number the lines. It's helpful, when discussing the passage, to be able to navigate it easily. We might split the passage into sections with subtitles for each paragraph. The first subtitle might be: 'The Romans and the Syracusans are at war. The Romans attack the city. But the Syracusans have their own secret weapon – an inventor called Archimedes.'

We might provide some grammar alerts – we might note, for example, the fact that all the tenses are imperfect, perfect or pluperfect, or that there are quite a few relative clauses. We might ask students to find these in advance on their own or in pairs, although this is quite a traditional way and takes up time when students could be reading the passage. Alerting students to particular grammar does not necessarily mean explaining those grammar items all over again: the students will have plenty of opportunities to explore them while reading the passage all that needs at this stage is some priming of the grammar.

A better method might be to do a number of these collaboratively with the whole class, perhaps with students annotating their own texts or with the teacher annotating a projected version on the whiteboard or IWB. It is probably not necessary to do every single one: enough to make the point and to model what to look for should be all that is necessary. So much doing time can be wasted in time spent searching for individual words when students could be reading whole sentences. The teacher is the most precious resource – they know *how* to do something as well as *what* to do – and needs to spend time modelling how for the students to follow for themselves.

We might need to clarify some of the unfamiliar features. What *happened* in a siege? What *is* a 'military machine'? Are they familiar with the meaning of Roman-specific words like 'consul'?

Vocabulary may need clarification. Personal names might need spelling out on the board. Vocabulary that is perhaps not quite familiar might need setting out. If this is the case, the teacher needs to think where to put it: it is best at the right-hand side of the text, because that is where the eye naturally leads when reading – across not down. Underline the words that have been given in the list. What forms will the vocabulary list provide? Will they be dictionary-standard, or suit the present level? Do the students know how to recognize the forms given in a standard Latin dictionary, or will they be using a form that is modified at this stage in their learning (for example, the exact form that is given in this passage)?

Rereading is so important: did the students understand what they had read? Rereading in the original Latin provides consolidation.

The teacher should tick off answers to comprehension questions, made as guides during the reading or on a checklist afterwards:

1 Where did the Romans put their military engines? What did they do with them?
2 What military engines did the Syracusans have? Where did they put theirs? How did they work? What was the effect on the Romans?
3 How can we think of the whole story? What words/moments express turning points in the narrative?
4 How are the individual people named do/act/behave? The consul Marcellus? The Roman soldier? Archimedes? What Latin words describe them? Can you think of other Latin words that might describe them with hindsight?

Example 2

The example below is drawn from the *Cambridge Latin Course*, UK 4th Edition, Stage 17. The story contains rich visual details, and also a coherent narrative in which the new grammar (in this example, the genitive case) naturally arises from the content.

The title image is a coin from Alexandria. The coin is reproduced in superscale (it is nearly 14 cm across in the printed book) and the details are easy to make out, either through elicitation or explicit teaching. In the following transcript, the features are discussed – a lighthouse to the left and a vessel to the right:

Teacher   Which direction is the boat going?

Students   To the right – away from the lighthouse.

Teacher   Where might it be going?

Students   Across the sea.

[Students may have heard of the city of Alexandria and know that it is in Egypt. If not, tell them.]

Teacher   The boat is sailing from Egypt, from Alexandria, in the direction of?

Students   Rome perhaps?

Teacher   And what might it be carrying?

Students   Goods of some sort?

Teacher   Grain. This is a grain ship, perhaps, showing the importance of Alexandria as a Roman port in an overseas country. Who might be growing the corn? The Romans. Or . . .?

Students   The Egyptians?

Teacher   Indeed – and how do you think they might feel about putting the corn they grew onto ships bound for Rome?

[The answer can be left ambiguous. Future stories will provide possible answers.]

The students turn to the next page. In the model sentences 1–5, they meet the some richly detailed illustrations and accompanying texts. The pictures are included for two reasons: to provide rich contextual schemata for the student to grasp the meaning of the unfolding narrative, and to provide clear linguistic schemata for the new grammar feature (the genitive case, here represented as a descriptive or possessive) and new vocabulary with which the following stories are going to be written.

It is worth examining each of the pictures in detail. Some teachers like to do this sequentially as they read the Latin text; others prefer to examine all the pictures first, before going back to look at the text. There is an argument that looking at all the pictures together establishes a narrative in the students' minds which the text then elaborates. Also, it could be said that looking at the pictures first reduces the cognitive load of having to bounce back and forth between image and text. This extract looks at the first two passages.

Passage 1. A large image of the Pharos (lighthouse) of Alexandria, with Egyptian statues at the door and Egyptian obelisks visible in the distance in a Roman or Greek-styled city; two Roman merchant vessels are leaving the harbour.

- Content schemata – Alexandria has a harbour and a lighthouse. Alexandria is an Egyptian city, styled by the Romans and/or Greeks. It is an important harbour for Roman trade.
- Narrative schemata, built up with semantically connected words: harbour, island, ships, huge lighthouse. Notice the way that the new word *ingens [huge]* is foreshadowed by the word *magnus [big]* and the way that the meaning of the *hac* in *in hac insula [on this island]* comes naturally enough because of the repetition of the word *insula [island]* immediately before.

Passage 2. A street in Alexandria. At the steps of a Greek or Roman temple a group of people is gathering: there seems to be a group of men arguing or brawling. A brigade of soldiers in Roman armour approaches.

- Content schemata – Alexandria is a dangerous city in which the population is policed by Roman soldiers. The picture and the English derivative *turbulent* both support the meaning of the new word *turbulenta [rowdy]* and it is easy to understand that it describes *Alexandria* – the city of Alexandria. The word *turba [crowd]* has been met before but is probably unremembered. It is supported by the word *turbulenta* (with which it is connected) and what one can see in the picture itself – the number of people in the streets comprise a rowdy, crowded city. *Complet [fills]* is also suggested by the visual clues and the lexical context. *Ingens [huge]* is met again (from the previous paragraph). Various forms of *multus [many]* are met across the first two paragraphs: *multae naves … multi mercatores … multi servi [Many ships … Many merchants … Many enslaved people …]*. None of the words (*naves, mercatores, servi*) are unfamiliar. However, *milites [soldiers]* has been infrequently met up to this point. The picture, the English derivative word 'military' and the repetition of *multi* all separately and altogether give clues to the new word.

- Narrative schemata: Look at the patterns of the three parallel phrases:

  o *multi mercatores per vias ambulant [Many merchants are walking through the streets].*
  o *multi servi per urbem currunt [Many slaves are running through the city].*
  o *multi milites per vias urbis procedunt [Many soldiers are proceeding through the streets of the city].*

As a result of the patterning of sentences, the support given by derivatives and semantically related, familiar vocabulary, the repetition of vocabulary units and the strong visual hints, students' cognitive dissonance is low: the patterns are all regular, the vocabulary is familiar and the meaning of the genitive is natural 'streets *of* the city'.

Tiered readings

The sorts of texts selected for study by Latin students are well known to be considerably beyond the comprehensibility of most school students of only a few years' study (Dutmer 2020; Sears and Ballestrini 2019). The works of Cicero, Livy, Virgil and even Catullus would be considered by the American Council of Teachers of Foreign Languages (ACTFL) to be *Distinguished* texts, 'characterised by one or more of the following: a high level of abstraction, precision or uniqueness of vocabulary; density of information; cultural reference; or complexity of structure' (ACTFL 2012). As few as 15 per cent of US students, after the standard four years' study at school, are able to read these texts fluently (Dutmer 2020). This experience is echoed in the UK, where students often study Latin for only an hour or two a week for between three and five years: from my own observations in classrooms, students are not ready to study the original authors set for examination. Instead, many teachers have to find ways make the original Latin text sufficiently comprehensible for the students to understand. Numbering the words to follow standard English word order, the provision of interlinear translations of individual words, or the provision of extensive glossing all seem to be variations on standard practice to get them through the translation part.[6] The problem then becomes, as I see it, that students taught to approach the original texts this way come to see Latin as some form of encoded English, to be mechanically transferred word by word from the Latin. The efficacy of this approach is almost guaranteed and, sadly, a memorized translation will get students a good way through a GCSE examination; but it could be argued that the engagement with the original Latin is rather superficial. In other cases, the teacher subdivides the complete text into shorter sections, or even line by line, in the belief that shorter passages are easier for the students to comprehend than larger; however, this sort of subdivision of the text into isolated chunks hides the way in which the narrative unfolds and impedes how one element of the passage informs or reflects another. And this is not just a question of the student enjoying the story as a whole – although enjoyment can be a sufficient motivation to go on. It is more about how the student develops reading fluency by taking cues from earlier parts of the text, and by reading, checking and rereading the whole passage for narrative coherence, for making predictions about the narrative direction of travel, and for understanding the meaning of the piece as a whole. A fragmented approach is not sufficient. Some teachers believe tiered reading approaches provide a possible answer.

Tiered (or embedded) readings are a form of scaffolding, by which the original text is manipulated to make it more comprehensible for the learner (Clarcq 2012; Clarcq and Whaley 2012). Standard approaches to scaffolding texts provide support, such as extra vocabulary, images and heavy contextualization, which is gradually taken away. The scaffolding in a tiered reading passage, however, is designed to support a student so that they can get to the point where they are able to understand the meaning of the passage without these extrinsic measures: the text itself suffices. The benefits of tiered readings, according to Clarcq (2021), are:

1 Students are given the time and opportunity to develop a clear picture of the information provided in the reading, one step at a time.
2 Scaffolding provides opportunities for review and repetition.
3 Scaffolding provides opportunities for summary and prediction.
4 Scaffolding provides opportunities for the reader to interact intellectually and emotionally with the reading material.

Clarcq 2012: 21–2

Top-down tiering is characterized by the rewriting of an original text which lacks comprehensibility for the student as it stands. The rewriting involves 'thinning out' complex syntax or vocabulary so that there is a baseline text which is now easy for the student to comprehend. A middle tier is composed, which reintroduces some of the vocabulary and more of the syntax structures of the original. The final tier is the original. Clarcq (2012) recommends three tiers, but there is no reason not to do more with particularly complex texts. Indeed, there is something to be said for introducing a fourth tier with the most complex Latin texts. The student works on each tier, starting with the baseline text, to comprehend the essential meaning of the passage, before passing on to the middle and finally the original. What makes this different from scaffolding? Scaffolding is extra support, provided by the teacher, which is gradually taken away. This might comprise dictionaries and/or vocabulary glosses, visuals of the vocabulary, diagrammatic representations of the syntax, the provision of reading strategies and so on. However, with tiered reading, the student deals with the original text as it stands.

Students read simplified and comprehensible versions of the original text. The principle is that the cognitive load of trying to understand vocabulary, syntax and context all at once is reduced leaving the students to focus on a smaller number of features at a time as they return in stages to the original text. The student is presented with something that they can reasonably understand: it is within their grasp, the meaning is relatively clear from the start, and so the purpose of the reading is not one of guesswork but of understanding and comprehension throughout. The gradually increased cognitive demand made by the addition of original words and structures is piece by piece and therefore manageable and not off-putting. Moreover, the process provides opportunities to develop their understanding of the aesthetic aspect of the text as they see how each word, phrase or clause enhances the original simple meaning until they finally arrive at the complete, complex, layered text.

A simple three-tier approach might consist of three stages, in which the more complex subordination and unfamiliar vocabulary is omitted or simplified, to be gradually reinserted in the second tier and fully restored in the third:

Tier 1: Basic tier, where the bare bones of the original passage are present.

Tier 2: Middle tier, where more of the original detail is restored.

Tier 3: Final tier, the original Latin passage in its entirety.

Variations of basic tiering might comprise:

1 Changing the word order (to match that which appears in students' normal coursebooks, or to follow English word patterns *in extremis*).
2 Replacing rare and unfamiliar vocabulary is replaced with more familiar, high-frequency vocabulary.
3 Simplifying syntax by replacing, for example, one type of subordinate clause for another.

Whichever system is used, it helps students gain confidence in reading Latin not just for its meaning, but also for developing an understanding of something of the

Roman author's artistry. This is something that students often miss – the lengthy, often mechanical and sometimes rather tedious process of translation from Latin into English means the student loses the chance to appreciate the writing itself; getting students to look at how the additional words and syntactical structures enhance the basic meaning can be eye-opening. Most important of all, contrary to the approaches discussed above, where the text is numbered or interlinear translations are provided, the tiered reading, carefully constructed, keeps students in the Latin language for longer: at least three reads for each passage and the exposure to synonyms and alternative syntax ensures it (Ramahlo 2019).

The process of making tiered readings has been well documented, albeit mainly of shorter extracts rather than longer works. Most have concerned tiered reading materials based on original texts at ACTFL's *Distinguished* level. The degree of tiering is dependent on two things: the learning objective and the complexity of the original text. In Dutmer's (2020) account, tiered versions of Lucretius and Seneca rendered the essence of Roman stoic philosophy more accessible to his students than he considered would be possible by traditional means: the tiering was a means to a rapid comprehension of the subject matter. By contrast, Gall (2020), in her small-scale study of tiering Tacitus' *Annals*, approached the task from the position of language teacher: the improvement of students' reading fluency was the aim and so the tiering kept the structure of the original author more or less intact, with judicious omission of vocabulary and a restructuring of word order in the initial tier. Likewise, Sears and Ballestrini (2019) wanted to develop students' reading fluency: however, their account of tiering Ovid's *Metamorphoses* shows a greater willingness to adapt the original in forms that they felt were more familiar to their students at their stage of learning.

Gall's (2020) study revealed generally positive student perceptions. The Roman historical author Tacitus is notorious for the lexically demanding and complex syntax of his Latin, in which most of the norms of the sort of Latin which one reads in coursebooks are thrust aside. But Gall noted that the students began to realize that 'underneath all the "foliage" the basis of each chapter had actually been quite simple' (Gall 2020: 17). This suggested that in making the essential meaning clear right from the start, the initial tier provided a secure foundation for appreciating the artistry of Tacitus more readily than other methods had usually provided. The tiers helped students as visual points of reference: they approved of the way in which the rearrangement of words into 'normal' Latin word order helped them not just to comprehend the meaning but also to appreciate Tacitus' own choices of word order because they could see the effect for themselves rather than be blinded by the original text being marked up traditionally with arrows and underlining. Students felt they understood the passage better, the benefit of having read it three times. This made it easier to remember, at least for the purpose of examination technique.

A small number of modern authors have compiled tiered texts of original Roman authors. For example, Olimpi's *Daedalus et Icarus* is a worked-out version of the text into three tiers, ending with selections from the Ovid and Hyginus originals (Olimpi 2019a). Further details of similar books can be found on his website (Olimpi 2021).

The preparation of a tiered text is lengthy, as Gall (2020) notes. In the UK, GCSE and A level texts change regularly (as frequently as every two–three years) and a teacher may be responsible for teaching texts at both levels at the same time. The responsibility of tiering texts could be shared between groups of teachers, by social media, for example, provided that the group regulated for consistency. In the US, by comparison, the situation is more manageable: the texts set for the AP examinations are lengthy, but are drawn from the same Caesar and Virgil texts each year. The Pericles Group (2021) has tiered readings of the whole of the AP syllabus available on its website. Perusal of this site reveals an internally consistent approach. The tiered readings for Virgil's Aeneid, for example, only restores the hexameter verse at the final tier: earlier tiers are rewritten in prose form. The earlier tiers use finite verbs and simplify the vocabulary; the middle restores the original vocabulary and the sentence structure; the final tier brings back the hexameters. This arrangement – convenient as it is – might not suit every teacher or learner.

And I wonder if asking students to read through the text three or more times, each of which is of increasing complexity, might become rather boring, or that the student becomes over-dependent. Might there come a point when the student is primed enough actually to read the original for themselves in the way intended? The teacher needs to know the class well enough to predict what problems there will be. Might they consider weaning the students off tiered readings after a number of lessons, or bringing the tiers back in when there are moments of greatest lexical or syntactical challenge?

Making an original text more comprehensible

The extract below comes from Pliny's Letter 7, 27. It is part of a longer piece, but for reasons of space I have chosen to focus just on the first section. It's a ghost story, written in epistolary style. I want to look at how many ways we can make this lexically dense and aesthetically complex piece of literature comprehensible to the student in the school classroom.

Pliny the Younger, Letter 7, 27

erat Athenis spatiosa et capax domus sed infamis et pestilens. per silentium noctis sonus ferri, et si attenderes acrius, strepitus vinculorum longius primo, deinde e proximo reddebatur; mox adparabat idolon, senex macie et squalore confectus, promissa barba horrenti capillo; cruribus compedes, manibus catenas gerebat quatiebatque.

There was in Athens a large and roomy house, but it was notorious and dangerous. During the silence of the night echoed the sounds of iron, and if you were to listen closely, the clanking of chains far away at first, and then close by; soon – right there – was the spectre, an old man consumed by wasting and filth, with a long beard with hair bristling; he wore fetters on his legs, chains on his hands, and he rattled [them].

Author's own translation

Priming the students' knowledge of the context

We will start with some observations about the piece the students are going to read. These knowledge schemata are important for them to 'tune in'. What sort of background knowledge is going to be useful for this passage?

That Pliny was a writer of the 1st century CE and was present at the eruption of Mount Vesuvius, a governor of Bithynia and Pontus and a prolific letter writer is of little use for the particular task – although it is of some passing interest.

(Incidentally, by printing out the text in larger format, with wider spacing between the lines and with each sentence on a separate line makes it much easier for students to follow the process of how to learn the strategies we want to teach them. An inclusive approach to teaching would recommend this.)

We should point out that the passage falls into a number of parts which follow traditional literary tropes: for the students to know the gene, context and author's arrangement of the passage is to equip them with tools to start to understand the meaning of the passage.

This is a ghost story.

Explore what happens in ghost stories – making sure that the topic stays on or reaches the conventions of haunted house stories (avoid sidetracks). Rivers (1981) calls this the 'script' – the pieces of the story fit together in a way that the author and the audience together understand, even if not everything is spelled out. Pedagogically, the teacher has invited the students to contribute their own ideas which will be tested in the reading of the story itself. Personal engagement and interest is a motivation to find out more.

The teacher might then ask students to skim read the first few lines and then ask questions to elicit information as follows:

Teacher   Looking briefly at the story, can anyone spot where the action takes place?

Student A   Athens

Teacher   And the name of the man who is involved?

Student A   Athenodorus.

Teacher   And what is this man Athenodorus' job?

Student B   A philosopher.

Teacher   Yes – funny kind of job. What does a philosopher do – or rather – what sort of person do you think becomes a philosopher?

Student A   He thinks a lot?

Student B   He's wise? He wants to work out the truth?

Teacher   Yes – he wants to work out what is true. So, this is a ghost story, set in Athens, involving a philosopher called Athenodorus. Do you think a philosopher would believe in ghosts?

Student C   No.

Teacher   Well, he might do. Let's see.

After some further reading, the teacher might introduce some ideas about whether the ghost described here is similar to or different from what they would expect a ghost to be like. Allow one anecdote from a student. Many students love to tell a ghost story at this moment and, indeed, an anecdote can often serve to pick out salient features which resonate with the story under discussion; too many anecdotes run the lesson off-schedule and occasionally into unchartered and diffiuclt waters.

Of course, you might say: you are giving them so many clues! But *learning* to comprehend Latin is not meant to be a *test*. Setting everything as a test is simply not learning, because, for the most part, the teacher cannot guarantee that the students possess the contextual clues which they need. If that means that many of the narrative passages are heavily scaffolded in this way, then so be it. As the students become more proficient, they will be able to apply the same ways of looking at a text for themselves without having to be told.

Pliny aloud

In *Starting to Teach Latin* (Hunt 2016), I talked about how important it is for students to hear Latin spoken aloud both as a kind of 'live' experience and also as a way of beginning to develop a sense of the interconnectedness of words and phrases. Earlier in this book, I discussed the part played by listening and speaking for vocabulary retention and recall. Now we want to hear the way in which the phraseology of the writing enhances the narrative's aesthetics. An oral/aural approach will add salience to the narrative and help prime the students' understanding of the meaning. (We should make recordings of all the set texts, all the passages we ever read and ask students to listen to them regularly, to follow them, and to read along with them.)

The teacher should use an appropriate tone of voice, gesture and even use props if they are available. For an example of this very passage, watch Justin Slocum Bailey's YouTube-telling of the story (Bailey 2015). In the suggested sample below, the markings indicate that:

- Underlined words run together into phrase units.
- Short pauses are indicated by . . .
- Longer pauses are indicated by [. . .].
- Particular *emphasis* of a word is shown by the word in *italics*.

These are suggestions only: personal taste will dictate what really happens. After each section I have indicated gestures, but you can, of course, think of your own.

erat Athenis . . . spatiosa et capax domus [. . .] *sed* [. . .] infamis et pestilens.	There was in Athens . . . a large and roomy house [. . .] *but* [. . .] notorious and dangerous.
Gesture to show: • size of the house – hands outstretched palms up. • notoriety of house – hands to lower part of face – scared expression.	
per silentium noctis . . . sonus ferri, [. . .] et [. . .] si attenderes acrius, . . . strepitus vinculorum . . . longius primo, [. . .] deinde . . . *e proximo* reddebatur;	During the silence of the night . . . the sounds of iron, [. . .] and [. . .] if you were to listen closely, . . . the clanking of chains . . . far away at first , [. . .] and then . . . *close by* echoed;
Gesture to show: • listening to distant sound – hand cupped around ear. • more intent listening – move head 'closer' to source of sound. • noises getting closer – head jerks and eyes widen.	
mox . . . adparabat *idolon*, [. . .] *senex* . . . macie et squalore confectus . . ., promissa barba . . . horrenti capillo;	soon . . . right there was the *spectre*, [. . .] *an old man* . . . consumed by wasting and filth . . ., with a long beard . . . with hair bristling;
Gesture to show: • expression of sudden shock – jerk of body – eyes widening. • recognition of spectre – eyes wide in horror. • filth of spectre – hands brushing length of body – dirt on hands. • length of beard – hands brush out imaginary beard from chin. • hair standing on end – hand brushes hair up on head.	
cruribus compedes, . . . manibus catenas gerebat [. . .] *quatiebatque*.	on his legs fetters, . . . on his hands chains he wore [. . .] and *he rattled* [them].
Gesture towards legs and hands so as to represent shaking of chains.	

Does this mean that you have to use gestures and props with every reading? Of course not! But the tone of voice and gesture are, I suggest important clues to the meaning of the whole passage, to individual phrases and words and serve to prime students' knowledge.

A follow-up after a reading of the whole passage might be for the students themselves to perform a dramatic reading, which could take place in front of the class. Discussion afterwards could profile the best demonstrations and improvements – all the while developing students' awareness of vocabulary and style.

Think-alouds

Think-alouds are usually used when a teacher models their own thought process on the board for the whole class. But they can also be used in a telling of a story, as a way of modelling the impact of words, phrases and events to help develop students' understanding. Whether this is effective on a first telling or on a subsequent one is a moot point and probably depends on the complexity of the passage and the students' knowledge of the vocabulary. My feeling is that it is something that could best be done once the initial meaning of the Latin has been understood. Nevertheless, one can imagine a teacher reading the text in the box.

> erat Athenis spatiosa et capax domus *[Well, that sounds nice!]* sed infamis et pestilens *[Oh-oh! Doesn't sound too good!]*. per silentium noctis sonus ferri *[Creepy!]*, et si attenderes acrius, strepitus vinculorum longius primo *[My!]*, deinde e proximo reddebatur *[Gosh! How scary!]*; mox adparabat idolon *[Whistles]*, senex macie et squalore confectus, promissa barba horrenti capillos *[Ugh!]*; cruribus compedes, manibus catenas gerebat quatiebatque. *[Whew!]*

Text manipulation

Word-processing makes text manipulation very easy.

Example 1

Try rearranging the text in more 'standard' Latin word order, rather than Pliny's finely wrought form.[7]

> Athenis domus spatiosa et capax erat, sed infamis et pestilens. per silentium noctis sonus ferri, et si attenderes acrius, strepitus vinculorum reddebatur, longius primo, deinde e proximo; mox idolon adparabat, senex confectus macie et squalore, barba promissa horrenti capillos; compedes cruribus [gerebat], catenas manibus gerebat quatiebatque.

Example 2

Here is an arrangement of the text into sense units, which is designed to support students' understanding of the 'shape' of the text in visual form:

Athenis domus spatiosa et capax erat
    sed infamis et pestilens.
per silentium noctis sonus ferri,
    et si attenderes acrius,
    strepitus vinculorum reddebatur,
      longius primo,
      deinde e proximo;
mox idolon adparabat,
    senex confectus macie et squalore,
      barba promissa horrenti capillos;
compedes cruribus [gerebat],
catenas manibus gerebat
quatiebatque.

Example 3

Here I have made a series of tiered readings of the passage: first, simplification of the sentences by missing words out; second, restoration of some of the missing words; finally, the original passage.

1 erat Athenis domus. per silentium sonus et strepitus vinculorum reddebatur; mox adparabat idolon, senex promissa barba; compedes [et] catenas gerebat quatiebatque.
There was in Athens a house. During the silence echoed the clanking of chains; soon – right there – was the spectre, an old man, with a long beard; he wore fetters on his legs, chains on his hands, and he rattled [them].

2 erat Athenis spatiosa domus, sed infamis. per silentium noctis sonus ferri, et strepitus vinculorum reddebatur; mox adparabat idolon, senex, promissa barba horrenti capillos; compedes [et] catenas gerebat quatiebatque.
There was in Athens a roomy house, but it was notorious. During the silence of the night echoed the sounds of iron, and the clanking of chains; soon – right there – was the spectre, an old man, with a long beard with hair bristling; he wore fetters on his legs, chains on his hands, and he rattled [them].

3 Back to the original Pliny.

Example 4

The teacher could simplify the vocabulary itself. However, while the students may be able to understand what happens in the story, it seems that this would take them further away from reading Pliny, and not be helpful in teaching the students how to read original Latin. You might find, however, that reading a 'version' of the original earlier in a Latin programme would help to prime students for the original when it did come along. However, we want the students to understand the language that *Pliny* is using and I think you would have a revolt on your hands if you read a version of the story that was not actually Pliny, only to go over it again in the 'real' version.

Example 5

An alternative to rewriting Pliny with familiar vocabulary might be to provide the student with a list of synonyms for the original words which Pliny uses. This is the method Ørberg's *Lingua Latina Per Se Illustrata* (2011) uses and could help them to elaborate and extend their vocabulary knowledge more generally. A possible list might be as shown in the box.

---

spatiosa – magna
capax – erant multi loci/multae
   casae
infamis – prava
pestilens – terribilis
sonus ferri – id quod ferrum facit/
   pulsum
attenderes – audires
acrius – diligenter
streptius – sonus/fragor
vinculorum   –   vincula/catenae/ea
   quae captivus in manibus gerebat

reddebatur – (iterum) audiebatur
adparabat – aderat
idolon – umbra
macie et squalore – macies et
   squalor/sordidsissimus
confectus – male factus
promissa – missa / (pro)fundens
horrenti – horribilis
capillos – ea quae sunt in capite
compedes – vincula circa pedes
quatiebat – in manibus tenebat

Example 6

In this final version of the passage, I have simplified the syntax, replacing the participle forms with indicatives, and have taken out all the subordination. It does not feel like Pliny, but it is closer to Pliny's original and, with vocabulary support, is eminently readable. Once the meaning has been grasped, you can move back to the original and see how much better it is!

> erat in urbe Athenis spatiosa et capax domus. sed erat infamis et pestilens. per silentium noctis sonus ferri audiebatur. Athenodorus attendebat acrius. strepitus vinculorum audiebatur. longius primo audiebatur, deinde proximo audiebatur. mox adparabat idolon. senex macie et squalore confectus erat. promissa erat barba horrens capillos. cruribus compedes gereabat. manibus catenas gerebat. quatiebat.
>
> There was in Athens a large and roomy house. But it was notorious and dangerous. During the silence of the night echoed the sounds of iron. Athenodorus listened closely. The clanking of chains was heard. It was heard far away at first, and then close by. Soon – right there – was the spectre. It was an old man consumed by wasting and filth. His long beard bristled with hair. He wore fetters on his legs. He wore chains on his hands. He rattled [them].

Narrow reading

Narrow reading is an activity devised by Steve Smith and Gianfranco Conti (2016), two MFL teachers. The student reads the same passage again and again, in different ways, which cumulatively build up vocabulary knowledge and develop reading skill. Narrow reading employs skimming and scanning as pre-reading strategies, with students looking for key vocabulary and simple factual elements at the start, and introducing more inferential comprehension questions once the basic skeleton of the passage has been grasped. The scaffolding is reduced, too, so that towards the end of the process, the student is encouraged to write down their own understanding of the passage. The student could finally write a translation of the passage. Narrow reading followed by a translation is might be appropriate for students who find 'straight-to-translation' tasks too cognitively overwhelming. The sample Latin is from an old O level practice paper.

> Tarquinius rex a Romanis expulsus, cum a Porsinna auxilium petivisset, multis cum militibus in agros Romanorum mox rediit, urbem Romam obsessurus. milites eius, cum collem vicinum, nomine Ianiculum, subito impetu cepissent, inde ad flumen Tiberim celeriter decurrebant. tum cives perterriti, armis relictis, ad urbem confugiebant, muris se defensuri. Pons tamen Sublicius iter

paene hostibus dedit. unus vir, Horatius Cocles, in statione pontis illo die forte positus, urbem servavit.

Expelled by the Romans, Tarquinius the king, after he had sought help from Porsinna, soon returned with soldiers to the fields of the Romans, ready to besiege the City of Rome. His soldiers, when they had captured a neighbouring hill, called the Janiculum, with a sudden attack, quickly ran down from there to the River Tiber. Then the terrified citizens, leaving their arms behind, fled all together to the city, ready to defend themselves with the walls. However, the Sublicius Bridge almost provided a way for the enemy. One man, Horatius Cocles, by chance stationed that day on the bridge, saved the city.

Author's own translation

Stage 1: Find the Latin for the following:

    a) King.
    b) Help.
    c) In the Romans' fields.
    d) A nearby hill.
    e) Quickly ran down.
    f) Terrified citizens.
    g) Walls.
    h) A way.
    i) On that day.
    j) By chance.

Stage 2: Answer the questions:

    a) Who was Tarquinius?
    b) What did he ask for from Porsinna?
    c) What did he take to the Romans' fields?
    d) What was the name of the hill?
    e) What was the name of the river?
    f) Where did the citizens go?
    g) What was the name of the bridge?
    h) Who stood on the bridge?

Stage 3: Answer the questions:

    a) What had happened to Tarquinius?
    b) Why did he go to Porsinna?
    c) What did he take with him back to Rome?
    d) What was his intention to do there?
    e) What did his soldiers do first?
    f) What did they do second?

g) What did the citizens do to their weapons?
h) Why did they go inside their city?
i) Why was the bridge a danger to the citizens?
j) What stopped the soldiers crossing the bridge?

Stage 4: Fill in the table below in your own words.

Name	Actions
Tarquinius	
Porsinna	
The soldiers	
The citizens	
Horaatius Cocles	

Stage 5: Translate the story into English.

Linear reading: Read like a Roman

Traditional approaches to reading (or, rather, translating) a Latin text have involved a student treating the sentence as a kind of disarrangement of English. Nearly every coursebook advocates that students should find the verb or analyse the formation of every word, before slotting the words together into English.[8] With simple passages, as found in those same coursebooks, this seems to work, if the student is prepared to put in the effort to memorize the vocabulary and the grammar notes: it all seems to hang together. But as the Latin texts become more sophisticated and the student starts to read original authors, this process slows up, becomes significantly cognitively challenging and, as Kitchell (2000) has pointed out, is less than successful for students of even several years' practice: Romans did not write like the authors of coursebooks.

Instead of atomizing a carefully constructed sentence, a linear reading approach has much to recommend it. For a full description of the theory and some of the practice, I direct to Dexter Hoyos' article *Translating: Facts, Illusions, Alternatives* (Hoyos 2006) and his excellent handbook, *Latin: How to Read It Fluently* (Hoyos 1997) and to Deborah Pennell Ross' *Latin Pedagogy at the University of Michigan, USA: Linear Reading Using a Linguistic Perspective* (Ross 2008). Linear reading requires students to see the sentence not as a string of random words which must be reassembled, but as a series of sentence units or partial sentences which, read from left to right, contribute to the overall meaning. The student uses their morpho-syntactic knowledge to make connections both within the smaller sentence units and between them. Ross recommends that students, while reading along the sentence unit ask themselves a 3-step set of questions: (1) What can I see? (a check of lexical and morphological information); (2) What do I have? (a check of syntactic function); (3) What do I expect? (using the information). She advocates using a card to cover up part of the sentence as a prompt for students to make predictions from what they can see. She notes that students sometimes like to annotate their texts to provide support. Two examples of small-scale practitioner research with beginner/intermediate students also suggest annotations are helpful to students (Russell 2018; McFadden 2008). Hoyos (1997) recommends that students should make use of knowledge of typical word groups, signposting words for subordinate clauses and how different types of clause 'embrace' each other. Each clause has to be complete in itself before the sentence moves on:

> Once context, arrangement and signposts are recognised, the logic of how an author structures any type of sentence turns out to be natural and recognisable. Recognizing sentence-structures is again a task that improves with practice. The more the principles of correct reading are practised, the more accustomed and comfortable they become, and the easier to apply to new texts.
>
> Hoyos 1997: 58

McCaffrey (2006, 2009) provides abundant examples of how linear reading resolves morphological ambiguities. Harrison (2010) provides further practice sentence examples with which to train students.

Free Voluntary Reading (FVR)

In the US, extensive reading in Latin for students to develop vocabulary growth and attain reading fluency is an emerging trend. To meet the demand for resources, a small but growing number of teachers have started to make available self-published short Latin stories or 'novellas', designed to provide students with extensive reading material in Latin at an age-appropriate level for novice and intermediate-level students. Piantaggini (2021c), a self-publisher of Latin novellas, captures the moment in his blog:

> Our modern language colleagues have long since recognized the benefits of reading compelling novellas with sheltered vocabulary—boasting selections of hundreds of titles for teachers and students to choose from. For Latin, this is only the beginning . . .
>
> Piantaggini 2021c

Teachers have been exploiting digital media to support the growth. Self-publication and sales through organizations such as Amazon Publishing and self-promotion through social-media feeds, websites and blogs make the production and advertisement of novellas easy. This challenge to the traditional control over the curriculum by commercial publishers, and to typically traditional, grammar-led publications to suit it, have contributed to a lively debate about the purpose and uses of novellas in the classroom.

Extensive reading is a method used in the classroom in which learners read lots of easy material in the target language (Day and Bamford 1998). Learners choose their own stories, read them for pleasure and information, sometimes in and sometimes out of class. They change them when they get bored or have finished them, and they seek out stories for themselves or with encouragement from their peers and their teachers, sometimes easier, sometimes a little harder than they are used to reading. Through extensive reading practices, researchers suggest that learners of languages 'become better and more confident readers, better writers, better listeners and speakers; their vocabulary improves; they enjoy learning languages' (Bamford and Day 2004: 1).

Readers have long been available to students of modern languages, but in very short supply for students of Latin. There has long been a tradition of individual Latin teachers writing stories for their own students, often incorporating storylines and characters which are of personal interest to them. Publishers, too, have issued graded readers which run alongside the established coursebooks. They are not designed for pleasure reading, however, but as collections of supplementary passages for practice in comprehension or translation.[9] Traditional approaches to reading a Latin text often only involve intensive reading, that is, paying close attention to vocabulary, grammar and the commentary.[10] Olimpi suggests such approaches 'treat Latin as an object of study not a vehicle for communication' (Olimpi 2019b: 84). Breaking point was reached when he realized:

> Only the most intellectually gifted students continued in my 'puzzle-solving' course; consequently, my enrolment dropped off steeply after the second year. Looking for more help, I even implemented various 'rules for reading' and 'reading strategies' advocated by others, yet rather than improve student reading ability, I felt my curriculum begin to feel increasingly cluttered with activities and processes that stole away from my students the valuable time needed to interact with the language itself.
>
> Olimpi 2019b: 83

The treatment of a text as a language artefact which must be dissected slows the development of reading fluency. By contrast, it has long been realized that readers learn to read better by *reading* rather than by being *given instructions on how to read* (William 1986). Novellas are designed to provide extensive reading material in the target language which is not dominated by grammatical forms presented in the traditional sequence: authors restrict (or 'shelter') vocabulary so that the meaning of the text remains comprehensible and therefore interesting enough for the student to read extensively. Krashen describes traditional grammar-first approaches to teaching modern languages as a 'serious error in language education ... Only after hard and tedious work do we earn the right to actually enjoy the use of language'

(Krashen 2004b: 3). While the aim of students of modern languages is to use all four skills – listening, reading, speaking and writing in the language – and (arguably) students of Latin only aim to be able to read and comprehend original Latin authors, Krashen's criticism of delayed gratification still remains pertinent. Taking their cue from Krashen, therefore, a number of US Latin teachers have begun to self-publish their own Latin novellas for use in their own and other teachers' classrooms. Some use them as supplements to standard available commercial resources, but there is also a trend towards using them as instructional materials in their own right.

The effectiveness of direct instruction of vocabulary has long been debated, and while it is considered to have its place in the classroom, researchers have suggested that extensive reading can help with vocabulary acquisition (Grabe and Stoller 2013). McQuillan (2019) compared the relative efficiency of free voluntary reading and direct instruction of English academic vocabulary, concluding that students were more likely to meet academic vocabulary through reading works of fiction than would be the case through direct instruction by the teacher. In his view, reading was between two and six times more efficient than explicit teaching and therefore should be considered an important component of language teaching.

There is still a lack of agreement whether extensive reading does, indeed, deliver the sorts of gains in vocabulary knowledge that some of its advocates claim. Bruton (2002) shows early anxiety about the arguments of Day and Bamford (1998). This was echoed by Laufer's (2003) observation that, in the case of second language teaching in schools, only small gains in the number of words learnt through extensive reading occurred, when compared with direct instruction. By contrast, Krashen (2013), drawing on multiple case studies, maintains that vocabulary gains are at least as good as if not better through extensive reading than through direct instruction. He goes on to make the argument that long-term and regular extensive reading routines deliver better language outcomes generally. According to Krashen, vocabulary instruction focuses on a restricted list of words, whereas stories 'contain a rich supply of vocabulary as well as grammar and cultural information' (2013: 37). This is an argument with which Laufer (2003) might find common ground: while extensive reading might not deliver many more new words, it does consolidate the learning of partially-learnt words and deepen students' understanding of their usage in context. Grabe (2009) reports that extensive reading practice automatizes second language leaners' lower-level reading processes, thereby aiding reading fluency. The benefit of reading fluency is that it improves the comprehension of a text (Nation 2007). In Aka's (2018) comparative study of students receiving extensive reading practice or direct instruction, pre- and post-tests of grammar, vocabulary and reading indicated that the scores of the low-to-middle-proficiency students improved dramatically in the extensive reading group compared to those in the direct instruction group. McLean and Roualt's (2017) study of Japanese university students found that the group receiving extensive reading instruction improved their reading rate more than those who received grammar instruction. If extensive reading can develop vocabulary and reading fluency and comprehension in English and other languages, it ought to be able to do the same in Latin.

Bamford and Day (2004) describe ten principles of extensive reading practices as part of a school programme:

1 The reading material is easy.
2 There is a wide variety of reading material available for students to choose from.
3 The students choose for themselves.
4 The students read a lot – maybe a book a week.
5 The students' reading speed should be faster rather than slower; they should not need to use the dictionary, but should be able to guess unfamiliar words.
6 The students should read for pleasure, to learn something new for themselves.
7 The students should read silently, in class or out of it, at their own pace.
8 Reading is its own reward – there may be some follow up, but there is nothing that a teacher does to dissuade students from reading more.
9 The teacher orientates the students to reading, and keeps track. Sometimes they make suggestions.
10 The teacher models reading.

After Bamford and Day 2004

For greater clarity and to help teachers decide what it might look like pedagogically, Krashen (2004) subdivided extensive reading into three groups: extensive reading itself, which is accountable; sustained silent reading, which is not; and free voluntary reading, which is self-selected reading for the entire class period with minimal or no accountability. Many Latin teachers, however, seem to use the terms interchangeably, although there seems to be a preference for the term free voluntary reading.

Cloelia, puella Romana (Arnold 2016), one of the earliest of the new Latin novellas, stands as an example of a novella written only with the intention of providing material for free voluntary reading: a complete story without attendant accountability materials. Other authors, however, have published novellas with an array of supplementary materials for teachers and students. For example, the novella *Piso Ille Poetulus [Piso the Little Poet]* (Piantaggini 2016) is partnered by a Student Workbook (Piantaggini 2017a) and a Teacher's Guide (Piantaggini 2017b) with grammar notes and culture guide, amongst other things. Similarly, *Templum Romanum [The Roman Temple]* (Craft 2018a) can be used on its own as a reader; but it also has a teacher's manual (Craft 2018b) with questions and activities.

I am not suggesting that there is anything inherently wrong with having extra materials checking comprehension – in the end, it is an author's choice and a teacher's professional judgement what to write and how to use them. However, an inexperienced teacher might be confused as to what free voluntary reading really is, looking at these products. The original point of the novella was that the story should be fully comprehensible for its intended audience at the point of language proficiency they had reached. They are not intended as instruction manuals for grammar – although some teachers use them for this purpose. Institutional accountability, as always, makes its presence strongly felt. Should the student be made accountable for reading the novella? How should students be reading if there are series of worksheets and other accountability measures on offer? Recent concerns expressed on social media suggest that these issues are not fully resolved in teachers' minds. But if the teacher's purpose in using voluntary reading is as a supplementary pedagogical tool to developing skills that may be tested elsewhere, then holding students to account for self-selected reading does not seem appropriate.

Part of the interest in providing accountability measures may derive from the need to legitimize free voluntary reading in the eyes of senior management (Macalister 2014): there needs to be visible evidence of learning outcomes; grades need to be supplied. Bamford and Day (2004) noted that giving students time *just to read* felt like an abrogation of duty: teachers like to teach. Researchers note that teachers often folow up supposedly free voluntary reading with assessments (Rodrigo et al. 2007; Green 2005; Helgesen 2005; Lida and Smith 2001). However, assessment undemines the students' wilingness to read (Prowse 2002; Hsui 2000; Lida and Smith 2001; Fox 1990). One has to ask if institutional accountabilty should outweigh pedagocial appropriateness. But, as Fenton-Smith (2010) argues, without some form of accountability, the practice itself can become marginaslied, lessened in the eyes of the teacher and the students themselves. Miriam Patrick (2019), in her reflections over three years when introducing free voluntary reading in Latin lessons at her school, after trialling various measures, decided to have no accountablity: 'I have seen much more success this year, across levels, with this new process of indiviual reading, complete free choice, and full immersion in the experience, than I ever saw with my accountability measures' (Patrick, M 2019: 82). On the other hand, Piazza (2017) recommends a personal reading log – a form of accountablity that keeps everyone informed of what the student is reading, but which does not necessarily hold them to account for it. This log later forms the basis of a self-reflective document at the end of the school term or year.

There's another anxiety that I have myself drawn attention to – students might only *pretend* to read (Hunt 2018). However, research by Von Sprecken and Krashen (1998) showed that in a class where sustained silent reading was taking place, 90 per cent of the students were engaged in reading; and they noted from other observations that the students' reading concentration was better in those classes where teachers modelled reading, read themselves in class, recommended books for reading to the students, and provided them with a large choice of reading materials (Krashen 2004). Reading should be a joyful experience: the students need to be receptive to the language exposure, not just exposed to it (van Lier 1996).

Dealing an institution's attitude towards accountability, particularly in today's results-driven mode, however, may be problematic. Davis (1995) notes that the results take some time to reveal themselves, and not always obviously in examination grades; Krashen (1993) cautions against short-term projects as not making much impact. How, then, to bring together the requirements of showing evidence to the senior management, while maintaining the integrity of the free voluntary reading approach? Some have suggested that the book report might be an answer. However, Fenton-Smith (2010) notes objections even to these: book reports can be demoralizing (Lida and Smith 2001; Krieger 1992), make students think of reading as some sort of study (Cliffe 1990), take time from reading (Mason 2020; Fox 1990). Moreover, book reports are not done well by lower proficiency students (Krieger 1992) – such students could better spend their time reading. Fenton-Smith (2010) argues that the focus should be on getting students to read and to see how language is used, not get them to analyse it: the story should provide meaningful and compelling input of itself, and that it should provoke a need for meaningful communication afterwards. It is not just a question of vocabulary. As Waring (2009) points out there should be an overarching structure, rich language and a reason for interaction. These are what encourage higher order thinking skills (Helgesen 2005).

Fenton-Smith (2010) makes a number of suggestions for post-reading activities:

1   Write a summary to describe some of the characters in the story.
2   Draw a scene or scenes from the story and label them.
3   Find an example where the character made a choice. What did they do? What if they chose differently?
4   Quote 1–3 senteces which made a strong impression on you – why?
5   'Dear diary.' 4 diary extracts from a character in the story.
6   Make a movie poster – characters, plot, information.
7   Choose a gift for one of the characters and write a gift card explaining why.
8   Change the genre. What would you do?
9   Write a comparision between two books.
10 School visit. Someone from the book is coming to visit.
11 2 characters from the story have a conversation a year later.
12 Debate the good and bad parts of the story with a friend.
13 3 objects in the book. What is the significance of any of them?

After Fenton-Smith 2010

All of these activities promote student–student and teacher–student interactions, with minimal preparation and applicability to different circumstances. They encourage student self-regulation, can involve the teacher in a non-threatening way and provide instituonal accountabiity.

Brown (2008) suggests that there is an opportunity for authors to provide reading materials as an integral part of their more traditional published textbooks – not to replace, but to act as a significant supplement. He notes that textbooks often *become* the curriculum (this is especially the case in the UK, where textbooks for Latin are often 'badged' as leading to the public examinations[11]). There are very few examples of these integrated reading resources at present for Latin at the novice–intermediate level. Stan Farrow's *fabulae ancillantes* for the North Amercian edition of the *Cambridge Latin Course* (NA-CSCP 2007) might be considered as an example of the type: further stories based around the familiar characters and themes of the *Cambridge Latin Course*. However, perosnal observation suggests that teachers do not use them as free voluntray reading material. Indeed, they are hard to do so: the stories are brief passages and contain much the same level of lexical and syntactical complexity as the instructional texts of the main course.

By contrast, more closely aligned to the principles of materials set at a level for easy reading are Barbara Bell's *Minibooks*, which supplement the primary level beginners' Latin course *Minimus*. These booklets, a scarce dozen pages long, are, hwoever, on a very small scale, as is suited to the absolutae beginners for which they are intended. Another example might be the coursebook *Suburani*, which has a thriving online community resources site where contributors share materials, including a number of extra stories based around the coursebook themes. While these stories are presently few in number, the publication of a spin-off story *Celer* (the deerhound which has an important role in the main coursebook) by *Hands Up Education* itself might form a useful trend in the develiopment of suitable 'spin-off' readers. Perhaps the future lies in these sorts of digital self-publications, moderated and curated by the publishers and made accessible online to all.

Indeed, publishers' own versions of free voluntary reading materials might act as a pedagogical Trojan Horse against more traditionalist school leadership. Hutchinson and Torres (1994) note that it is easier to effect changes in practices through experimental resources which have been created as additions to established coursebooks resources than through 'outsider' publications. Perhaps one could see publishers thinking more creatively by providing a core textbook made up of intensive readings, supplemented by multiple extensive reading materials based on the characters and situations in the core. The publishers' desires to develop and improve textbook materials in the light of research can sometimes meet resistance from teachers to changes in practices that might be required (Carter, Hughes and McCarthy 1998). It is not that teachers dislike change, but that pedagogical habits become engrained, refined and finessed over time. Habits *can* be good. Change is hard, especially if it is not felt necessary. On the other hand, successful textbooks are usually those that break new ground while at the same time having something familiar about them (Bell and Gower 1998). Can Latin teachers, then, break new ground, with the support of the established publishers? Perhaps, despite the notoriety of Latin teachers to be old-fashioned stick-in-the-muds, it might be easier in a subject discipline where commercial interests are smaller and less pushy. Latin teachers have always been good at creating their own resources. In the UK, where there are no restrictions on which textbooks a teacher uses, except financial ones, there is much freedom for experimentation with self-published novellas. In the US, however, where textbook adoption across a state or school district is more common, the purchase and use of a wide variety of self-published novellas might be more difficult to achieve in publicly funded schools. If this is so, and the opportunity to improve students' reading fluency through free voluntary reading is an option for private schools only, there opens up an awkward conversation about equitable practices.

Conway, a Latin teacher and specialist researcher in Latin novellas, in a YouTube interview (Conway 2021), comments on his perceptions of the challenges which Latin teachers face in adopting new and unendorsed pedagogical practices:

1 There is no agreed measurement of comprehensibility for a Latin story. The number of words may or may not be a guide. Other features, such as extensive use of images, aid understanding, as does the use of cognates and glosses.

2 There is no consensus about what constitutes appropriate reading for standardized progression markers.

3 Novellas can shelter (i.e. restrict) vocabulary, but they do not have to do the same with syntax: often the meaning is perfectly clear from a lexical point of view and from comprehension of the narrative flow of the story.

4 Students need not worry about analysing the syntax (that's not the point of extensive reading): the meaning should be obvious from the context.[12] Lexical simplicity and syntactical simplicity work together; but lexical simplicity trumps syntactical simplicity.

5 Teachers need to 'let go' of syntax analysis during extensive reading. This is hard for them, and for their students brought up on a traditional analytical approach to Latin.

6 The purpose is not to learn new vocabulary, but to consolidate existing vocabulary knowledge through frequent repetition and seeing it in comprehensible context: vocabulary is best learnt through connections.

7 There's nothing wrong with reading below 'your level'. It should be easy and pleasurable.

Subject matter/Latinity

Birketveit, Rimmerreide, Bader and Fisher (2018) carried out extensive research of foreign languages reading practices in primary schools. Noting that the choice of reading material varied according to gender, they recommended a wide variety of books should be provided for everyone to dip into. They also cautioned against there being accountability measures for reading, since this had a negative impact on students' willingness to read, especially amongst those who did not have a home reading culture. This last point correlates with earlier research which suggested that sustained silent reading was more effective for students who had a higher value of reading, fostered by joint reading activities with their parents at home (Siah and Kwok 2010). Birketveit et al. (2018) recommended that a reading culture needed to be introduced into the curriculum at an early stage.

We should aim to achieve variety in Latin, too. It is important for students to 'hear' other voices, ones which interest them for their own sake. The predominantly male-dominated narratives of most Latin coursebooks have rightly met with sustained criticism (Amos 2020; Upchurch 2014; Churchill 2006). To counteract this, there has been a growth in the number of novellas which feature female protagonists and promote female agency. Among the earliest of these were *Cloelia, puella Romana [Cloelia, a Roman girl]* (Arnold 2016), set at the time of the fall of the Roman monarchy, and *Pluto, fabula amoris [Pluto, a tale of love]* (Ash and Patrick 2015), a version of the myth of Proserpina. The story *provincia Iudaea [The province of Judaea]* (LiCalsi 2020) tells the story of the Roman occupation through the ideas of its young Jewish heroine, in Latin and in Hebrew. The recently published *carmen Megilli [Song of Megillus]* (Belzer-Carroll 2021), based on a text from Lucian, is perhaps the first novella with a trans man as protagonist. Another, *Virgo Ardens [Girl Aflame]* (Cunning 2021b), portrays LGBTQ+ characters. For the author, who started his teaching career at the time of the notorious Clause 28 legislation,[13] it is a remarkable moment in educational history that such stories can be welcomed for use in the Latin classroom.

Conway (2021) notes that there should be a good plot: twists and turns maintain interest for the reader. It is not just the vocabulary that make the story comprehensible, the way the narrative works makes it comprehensible – the anticipation of the sort of story that it is. He concludes that predictability is a good thing for beginning- and novice-level language learners: the ending should be a reward – strong and worth waiting for (Conway 2021). To these points, I would add:

1   The story should be a recognizable genre type.
2   The characters should be reasonably recognizable types, but not stereotypes.
3   The student should be able to see themselves in the characters and the events described.
4   The plot should generally be episodic for beginners; more complex timelines may be appropriate for novice-intermediate/high readers.
5   There should be many images, carefully detailed and closely supportive of the meaning of the Latin, especially new or unfamiliar vocabulary that cannot be intuited.
6   There should be a gloss for new or unfamiliar words on the same page as the text.
7   At least 95 per cent of the words should have been encountered beforehand.

8 The story should be readable in one sitting, or clearly divided into manageable chapters.

9 There should be links for other stories in the sequence or range.

10 There should be links for further reading, such as historical background.

11 The stories should be cheaply made or available free online, for access anywhere at any time to anyone.

12 Recordings of the stories should be available and their use encouraged while reading. The readings should be fluent and clear.

Debate continues whether the subject matter in Latin novellas needs to be strictly historical. It is clear that in modern foreign languages novellas set in the contemporary world provide a realistic timeframe for the communicative interactions that take place within the narrative and help develop the students' language competency. Some authors of Latin coursebooks have been – and continue to be in some cases – resistant to the idea that the cultural setting is important for language learning: the 'background material' is felt to be an added extra that is strictly unnecessary.[14] However, teaching language *is* teaching culture (Kramsch 1996), and in Latin coursebooks, generally, there has been a gradual move since the 1960s towards integrating language and culture in ways that are more than just using culture as an attractive feature.[15] Most teachers would agree that the historically authentic location of the most commonly used reading-comprehension coursebooks provide a natural setting *in* which students learn about the language, and *for* which comprehension of the language provides further insight.

Does then a Latin story set in more modern times run counter to the generally agreed idea that learning the language is an aid for developing intercultural understanding? Perhaps an answer can be found if one considers that all reading – any reading – of Latin is beneficial and that there is a time and a place even (perhaps especially) for light reading. Perhaps we should stop worrying and just learn to love the fact that students might enjoy reading without particular intentions in mind other than pleasure. As for Latinity, while we would not want students to be exposed to incorrect Latin which misled them, we might be perfectly satisfied with stories which engaged them with relatively simple, unadorned Latin, such as might actually have been used in the street rather than the elaborate, lexically dense and aesthetically complex literature of the classical canon. Whether the text has been written by a Roman of, say, the first century CE or not should not detain us: in our search for a supposedly 'authentic' text from that period suitable for the beginning or even novice level student in the classroom, we would be disappointed. The texts in coursebooks and modern novellas are as 'authentic' for learners as any other natively produced works that are written are for non-learners – a point made by Simmonsen (2019) about the experiences of students of modern foreign languages.

A number of Latin novellas depict the modern world. *Legonium* (Gibbins 2019), for example, a spin-off novella from the website of the same name, capitalizes on widespread interest both by young learners and adults in the plastic construction toy Lego. Its lengthy single story is set in the present day, although its subject matter is concerned with a visit to the archaeological site of Pompeii (in Lego, of course). The story draws much of its appeal from its many illustrations of Lego scenes populated by its Lego protagonists and some contemporary 'famous faces' in Lego.[16] The website *Dinosaurs Speak Latin* (Berg n.d.) provides a range of purely informational Latin texts about places and events in the world, not all of which are focused on Roman history. *Erucula: fabula metamorphosis* (*Erucula: a story of changing*) (Cunning 2021a) tells the life-story of a caterpillar, illustrated by the images Maria Sibylla Merian used to describe the lifecycle of insects in her book *Metamorphosis Insectorum Surinamensium*, which she published in 1705. The key thing must be that the stories are worthwhile reading. As far back as the 1960s, at a time when the present ability to self-publish online was unimaginable, Dora Pym (1962), Lecturer in Classics Method at the University of Bristol, noted teachers' preference for story-based practices:

> Many teachers do recognize in practice the principle of teaching language in a significant context by composing serial stories as a vehicle for new grammar and syntax. The heroes [*sic*] of these stories are always the same, and the new work is encountered in a familiar setting; there is a motive for following their adventures and finding out what happens. So the story, whatever it may be, becomes part of a child's life; expressed in a Latin language-pattern it must convey some personal understanding. If this living experience can be provided, it is the germ from which understanding of Latin literature will later grow.
>
> Pym 1962: 37

I think she would have approved of novellas set even in the contemporary world.

Waring (n.d.) is in favour of light reading over academic, recommending even comics and online texts as sure-fire ways of engaging students with relatively simple texts that are fun and align with their own interests. Some recently published novellas are stand-alone, one-of-a-kind comedies. From the mildly scatological *Brando Brown canem vult [Brando Brown wants a dog]* (Bailey n.d.) or *Walter, canis inflatus [Walter, the farting dog]* (Colman and Kostwinkle 2004) to the more erudite *pugio Bruti [The Dagger of Brutus]* (Pettersson and Rosengren 2018), there is a growing repertoire to explore.

Latin versions of familiar stories are worth consideration: one thinks of short stories like the *Asterix* comics, beloved of old, which might fit into this category (although their humour might be dented by age; Asterix n.d.); or the Latin versions of *Cattus Petasatus [The Cat in the Hat]* (Tunberg and Tunberg 2000), *The Gruffalo* (Harris and Donaldson 2012) or *ubi fera sunt [Where the Wild Things Are]* (LaFleur 2016). A small number of graphic novels depicting the Greek and Roman myths, in Latin, is available through the Booxalive website (n.d.).

Repeated reading of the same text series should develop reading fluency even if some of the vocabulary is uncommon or perhaps not even Latinate. Novella collections or series are recommended: we have all seen how young people eagerly read on from one story to the next in a sequence, unspooling the narrative thread almost as fast as they can go, as they engage with the familiar scenes and characters, week after week. One is reminded of how, when the first editions of the *Cambridge Latin Course* were being written and trialled in schools, the authors had to speed up writing to keep pace with the demand for the next instalment (Pat Story, personal communication). Publication, even self-publication, of hard copies of whole sequences of novellas might be daunting, however. One of the ways to provide sufficient readers might be for community groups to come together to make their own contributions to a shared website. Consistency across the group might be difficult to achieve, but is not impossible if the novellas are peer reviewed within the group. For example, Schwamm's *Let's Build a Thing* online projects have successfully crowd-sourced several community co-authored novella series, drawing inspiration from Roman tombstone inscriptions for the characters which populate a Saturnalia story (Schwamm n.d.).

Another way is for teachers and students to co-create novellas for use in their own classroom and to share them with younger and older students, building up a stock over time. Such collections might not be so attractive to outsiders: the in-jokes and personal interest might not travel well. Buczek (2021) co-creates stories which incorporate the students' own interests and characters, revisiting the passages for additional storylines and improvements. The publication of these stories seems to encourage student participation and commitment. Schwamm and Vander Veer (2021) describing their own experience of co-authoring stories with students, note how much they value the inclusion of their own characters (perhaps, avatars?) and interests (including pets) which weave in and out of the co-telling and co-reading of their story, that lasts a term in its creation. Student motivation and interest in reading Latin remains high while they engage in writing alternative histories, Romans in the future, and LGBTQ+ issues.

The role of educational technology in FVR

Educational technology has a large part to play in supporting the reading process. Reading extensive texts and listening at the same time helps students perceive semantic phrasing better than silent reading: it prevents them from splitting up the words into incorrect chunks and thereby helps develop comprehension skills (Brown, Waring and Donkaewbua 2008). Students who were allocated recordings of the text assigned for reading reported greater enjoyment and motivation for the reading compared to when there was no audio (Isozaki 2018). A number of websites dedicated to Latin novellas contain audio recordings. These include the website *latinitium*, a compendium of text and audio resources linked to *pugio Bruti [The dagger of Brutus]* (latinitium n.d.), Piantaggini's *Magister P* website and blog, linked to the *Piso* stories (Piantaggini 2021a) and Piazza's edited *Seneca's Letters to Lucilius* contains simplified versions of the original Latin text and audio to facilitate reading comprehension (Piazza 2019). While these resources are admirable, the collections remain somewhat diffuse. It would be desirable for future publications to have embedded audio and available to enjoy on all tech platforms, anywhere at any time.

Podcasts, interactive stories, choose-your-own adventures, authentic materials created for or by students, realia – all of these can provide materials suitable for free voluntary reading (Reinagel 2018). Is it beyond the realms of possibility to think of video gaming as a means of supporting language development (Horowitz 2018)?

Interactive books, supported on such platforms as inklewriter and Twine have huge potential, as yet almost completely unexplored.[17] In Classics, there has been some interest in using Twine as a medium for developing students' understanding of historical events (see, e.g., the *Path of Honors* project, McCall 2018; and the *Melian Dilemna*, Morley 2019). The simple interactive story *tu in via ambulas [You are walking in the street]* (Hahn n.d.) demonstrates an online media model for serious consideration for teaching languages, which is easy for teachers to create and share online.

With the proliferation of online social networking, the potential use of Latin as a *lingua franca* to communicate with Latinists from across the world has never been greater. Reinhard (2009) described the importance of building online social networks for students and teachers of Latin as well as for instructions on how to set up a network. Today, we barely need to understand the tools to do the job ourselves – educational technology is so intuitive, and our students are often ahead of the game.

While they may not provide much in the way of extensive reading on their own, taken together, might we see Latin Twitter, Instagram and TikTok as ways to engage students in Latin every day?

Notes

1. Of the commonly used reading-comprehension courses, the *Cambridge Latin Course* and *Ecce Romani* are the only ones to draw a distinction between passages meant for reading and those meant for translation (this is no idle matter: texts written for reading are longer, more complex syntactically, and contain much more vocabulary than those written for translation, which are shorter, tightly focused on the new linguistic features of the stage and use a small list of familiar vocabulary); the *Oxford Latin Course* and *Suburani* make no distinction between reading or translation passages, allowing the teacher to decide for themselves what is appropriate. In the

commonly used grammar-translation courses, such as *De Romanis* and *Latin to GCSE*, the continuous passages are not intended as reading material but as translation passages which test previously learnt vocabulary and grammar.

2. Extract from *Cambridge Latin Course*, Book 4, UK 4th Edition, p. 43.

3. E.g. *Latin to GCSE* has virtually no content schemata beyond that which has been deduced from the previous passages.

4. E.g. *De Romanis* has translation passages which broadly align with the historical/ cultural reading material provided at the start of each section. Images are occasionally provided.

5. E.g. *Ecce Romani,* the *Oxford Latin Course,* the *Cambridge Latin Course* and *Suburani* all provide richly detailed images drawn from a variety of ancient and contemporary sources which pertain closely to the reading material.

6. Examples of this approach to facilitating the reading and comprehension of original Latin literature for GCSE and A level examinations can be found in resources published by Zig Zag Education (2020) and on the website of Carter (2014). For an explanation of Carter's rationale in using interlinear translations, see Carter (2019). The GCSE examination boards themselves endorse similar, digital resources, which are available online through the Cambridge School Classics Project's website: for Eduqas, see CSCP (2021a); for OCR, see CSCP (2021b).

7. I prefer this to practices where individual Latin words are numbered in 'English' word order (see, e.g., Zig-Zag Education 2020) and where interlinear translations are provided (see, e.g., Carter 2019) as I feel they focus the students too much on mechanically extracting the English meaning and not enough on the way in which the Latin encodes it.

8. A recent Twitter thread (February 2021) declared that, 'as Latin is not a linear language', the student needed to analyse every word in a sentence before translating, thereby simultaneously forgetting the fact that Latin (along with every other language) must be linear for the purpose of making sense to the listener/reader, and complicating the reading process for the student. No Latin coursebook I am aware of teaches students how to read a sentence or paragraph in the order in which the information is written. Some advocate the 'find the verb' approach; others require analysis of every word. The *Cambridge Latin Course* and *Suburani* are the only coursebooks which show by their use of subordinate clauses how information is presented in a text, but leave much of the explanation to the teacher.

9. See, e.g., CSCP's *fabulae ancillantes* (NA-CSCP 2007), a collection of supplementary stories which match the style, content and reading-comprehension methodology of the Cambridge Latin Course books. Cullen, Dormandy and Taylor's (2011) *Latin Stories* similarly provides a collection of short stories for preparing students to take the UK GCSE examination. Neither of these would be considered to be extensive reading materials.

10. Even when coursebooks include passages of Latin, traditional grammar-first approaches are nearly always espoused. See, e.g., the following UK Latin coursebooks: *So You Really Want to Learn Latin* (Oulton, 1999), *Variatio* (Clarke 2015), *Oxford Latin Course, Latin to GCSE, De Romanis*. Even the story-based

reading-comprehension coursebooks, such as the *Cambridge Latin Course* and *Suburani* follow almost the same grammar-based sequence and include explicit grammar instruction.

11. *De Romanis* and *Latin to GCSE* are both explicitly oriented towards the GCSE examinations. These textbooks and also the *Cambridge Latin Course* are often treated by teachers as if they are the Latin curriculum.

12. In Goddard's (2020) review of *pugio Bruti [Brutus' Dagger]* (Pettersson and Rosengren 2018), she notes the difficulties students brought up on a more traditional grammar-based, analytical course (A level) had with simply 'reading' the story, due to the prevalence of apparently quite complex syntax. In a study of Japanese students of English, Tabata-Sandom (2017) observed that their students who had been exposed to intensive reading as part of the everyday curriculum were similarly thrown. Perhaps students brought up with extensive reading materials on a regular basis might not experience the same feelings.

13. Clause 28 was a 1988 addition to the Local Government Act 1986, which affected England, Wales and Scotland, that stated that a local authority 'shall not intentionally promote homosexuality or publish material with the intention of promoting homosexuality' or 'promote the teaching in any maintained school of the acceptability of homosexuality as a pretended family relationship'. For details, see Pink News (2019).

14. See, e.g., Clarke (2018), who considers the use of images in a coursebook a distraction from the language.

15. In 1963, Bolgar, in the first issue of the classics journal *Didaskalos*, wrote, 'If Latin studies have any value, that value must lie either in the language, or in the literature, or in the knowledge we gain generally about Roman culture, or, of course, in any two or three of these fields' (Bolgar 1963: 15). The ideas contributors brought to *Didaskalos* profoundly influenced the development of the British reading courses of the 1970s.

16. *Professor Maria Beard, homo peritissima [Professor Mary Beard, a very clever person]* arrives on a bicycle in Pompeii, e.g., on p. 67.

17. One of my teacher-trainees presented some unfinished and experimental narrative based on characters in the *Cambridge Latin Course* using the Twine app, thereby demonstrating the potential for students and alerting me to the ease of the app for writing simple interactive stories.

References

ACTFL (2012). *ACTFL Proficiency Guidelines 2021*. Retrieved from ACTFL. Available at: https://www.actfl.org/sites/default/files/guidelines/ ACTFLProficiencyGuidelines2012.pdf.

Aka, N. (2018). Reading Performance of Japanese High School Learners Following a One-Year Extensive Reading Program. *Reading in a Foreign Language*, 31 (1): 1–18.

Amos, E. (2020). A Case Study Investigation of Student Perceptions of Women as Seen in the Cambridge Latin Course in a Selective Girls' Grammar School. *Jounral of Classics Teaching*, 42: 5–13.

Arnold, E. (2016). *Cloelia, puella Romana.* Self-published. Amazon.

Ash, R. (2019). Untextbooking for the CI Latin Class: Why and How to Begin. *Journal of Classics Teaching*, 39: 65–70.

Ash, R. and M. Patrick (2015). *Pluto, fabula amoris.* Self-published. Pomegranate Beginnings Publications.

Asterix (n.d.). *Asterix.* Retrieved from Asterix. Available at: https://www.asterix.com/en/.

Bailey, J. (n.d.). *Brando Brown canem vult.* Self-published. Justin Slocum Bailey.

Bailey, J. (2015, 30 Oct.). *Pliny's Haunted House/Domus Infamis (Epist. 7.27) – Latin Narration.* Retrieved from YouTube. Available at: https://www.youtube.com/watch?v=vPPUZBV4pSs.

Balme, M. and J. Morwood (2003). The Oxford Latin Course. In J. Morwood, *The Teaching of Classics* (pp. 92–4). Cambridge: Cambridge University Press.

Bamford, J. and R. Day (2004). *Extensive Reading Activities for Teaching Language.* Cambridge: Cambridge University Press.

Bell, J. and R. Gower (1998). Writing Course Materials for the World: A Great Compromise. In B. Tomlinson, *Materials Development in Language Teaching* (pp. 135–50). Cambridge: Cambridge University Press.

Belzer-Carroll, A. (2021). *carmen Megilli.* Self-published.

Berg, L. (n.d.). *Dinosaurs Speak Latin.* Retrieved from Dinosaurs Speak Latin. Available at: https://dinosaursspeaklatin.blog/stories-informational-texts.

Birketveit, A., H. Rimmerreide, H. Bader and L. Fisher (2018). Extensive Reading in Primary School EFL. *Acta Didactica Norge*, 12 (2): 1–23.

Bolgar, R. (1963). A Theory of Classical Education. *Didaskalos*, 1 (1): 5–26.

Booxalive (n.d.). *Booxalive.* Retrieved from Booxalive. Available at: https://booxalive.nl/klassieke-strips/.

Brown, D. (2008). Why and How Textbooks Should Encourage Extensive Reading. *ELT Journal*, 63 (3): 238–45.

Brown, R., R. Waring and S. Donkaewbua (2008). Incidental Vocabulary Acquisition from Reading, Reading-While-Listening, and Lisetning to Stories. *Reading in a Foreign Language*, 20 (2): 136–63.

Bruton, A. (2002). Extensive Reading is Reading Extensively, Surely? *The Language Teacher*, 26 (11): 23–5.

Buczek, C. (2021). Novella Corner. *Prima*, 25 (1): 139.

Carter, D. (2014). *Classical Workbooks.* Retrieved from Classical Workbooks. Available at: http://www.classicalbooks.co.uk/workbooks.

Carter, D. (2019). Using Translation-Based CI to Read Latin Literature. *Journal of Classics Teaching*, 39: 90–4.

Carter, R., R. Hughes and M. McCarthy (1998). Telling Tails: Grammar, the Spoken Language and Materials Development. In B. Tomlinson, *Materials Development in Language Teaching* (pp. 78–100). Cambridge: Cambridge University Press.

Churchill, L. (2006). Is There a Woman in this Textbook? Feminist Pedagogy and Elementary Latin. In J. Gruber-Miller, *When Dead Tongues Speak: Teaching Beginning Greek and Latin* (pp. 86–112). Oxford: Oxford University Press.

Clarcq, L. (2012). Embedded Reading: A Scaffolded Approach to Teaching Reading. *International Journal of Foreign Language Teaching,* 21–4.

Clarcq, L. and M. Whaley (2012, 25 July). *About Embedded Reading,* web blog post. Retrieved from Embedded Reading. Available at: https://embeddedreading.com/about/.

Clarke, E. (2015). *Variatio, Part 1.* Unknown.

Clarke, E. (2018). In Their Own Words: Some Recently-Published Latin and Greek Course Books. *Journal of Classics Teaching,* 38: 75–88.

Cliffe, S. (1990). How to Set Up a Class Reading Library. *The Language Teacher,* 14 (12): 29–30.

Colman, A. and W. Kostwinkle (2004). *canis inflatus.* Frog Ltd.

Conway, D. (2021). *Interview with Dan Conway, 2,* video file. Retrieved from YouTube. Available at: https://www.youtube.com/watch?fbclid=IwAR0wqCcbImn3I4ZytEZcOiRY3Qwa_UqMrZnoWZ8VoeVdrBNAsUOqigrsmWQ&v=8exTlMM4cl4&d=n&app=desktop&ab_channel=BeneNarras%21.

Craft, J. (2018a). *Templum Romanum.* Self-published. Magister Craft/Amazon.

Craft, J. (2018b). *Templum Romanum. Teacher's Manual.* Self-published. Magister Craft / Amazon.

CSCP (2021a). *Cambridge School Classics Project. Exams. Eduqas GCSE Latin (9-1).* Retrieved from Cambridge School Classics Project: https://www.exams.cambridgescp.com/Array/eduqas-gcse-latin-9-1

CSCP (2021b). *Cambridge School Classics Project. OCR GCSE Latin (9-1).* Retrieved from Cambridge School Classics Project: https://www.exams.cambridgescp.com/Array/ocr-gcse-latin-9-1

Cullen, H., M. Dormandy and J. Taylor (2011). *Latin Stories: A GCSE Reader.* London: Bristol Classical Press.

Cunning, R. (2021a). *Erucula: fabula metamorphosis.* Self-published.

Cunning, R. (2021b). *Virgo Ardens.* Self-published. Bombax Press.

Davis, C. (1995). Extensive Reading: an Expensive Extravagance? *ELT Journal, 49,* 4, 329–336.

Day, R. and J. Bamford (1998). *Extensive Reading in the Second Language Classroom.* Cambridge: Cambridge University Press.

Dutmer, E. (2020). Teletherapeia: Ancient Consolation in the Distance Latin Classroom. *Journal of Classics Teaching, 42,* 75-79.

Fenton-Smith, B. (2010). A Debate on the Desired Effects of Output Activities for Extensive Reading. In B. Tomlinson and H. Masuhara (eds), *Research for Materials Development in Language Learning: Evidence for Best Practice* (pp. 50–61). London: Contiuum Publishing Group.

Fox, M. (1990). Increasing Intrinsic Motivation in Second Language Readers. *The Language Teacher,* 14 (3): 13–15.

Gall, A. (2020). A Study in the Use of Embedded Readings to Improve the Accessibility and Understanding of Latin Literature at A Level. *Journal of Classics Teaching,* 41: 12–18.

Gibbins, A. (2019). *Legonium*. Self-Published. Legonium Latin Press/Lulu Press.

Goddard, C. (2020). Review: *pugio Bruti*. *Jounral of Classics Teaching*, 41: 107.

Grabe, W. (2004). Research on Teaching Reading. *Annual Review of Applied Linguistics*, 24: 44–69.

Grabe, W. (2009). *Reading in a Second Language: Moving from Theory into Practice*. New York: Cambridge University Press.

Grabe, W. and F. Stoller (2013). *Teaching and Researching Reading*. London: Routledge.

Green, C. (2005). Integrating Extensive Reading in the Task-Based Curriculum. *ELT Journal*, 59: 306–11.

Hahn, M. (n.d.). *tu in via ambulas*. Retrieved from inklewriter. Available at: https://www.inklewriter.com/stories/29369?fbclid=IwAR1YJLwLG1ONFpDM1mW_RJa2Z1U0AfI1UBSuj5ywWtjkfbhX5dPIdDcBPpA.

Harris, B. and J. Donaldson (2012). *The Gruffalo (Latin Editon)*. London: Macmillan Children's Books.

Harrison, J. and S. Wilson (1968). *Latine Legamus*. London: G. Bell and Sons.

Harrison, R. (2010). Exercises for Developing Prediction Skills in Reading Latin Sentences. *Teaching Classical Languages*, 2 (1): 1–30.

Helgesen, M. (2005). Extensive Reading Reports – Different Intelligences, Different Levels of Processing. *Asian EFL Journal*, 7 (3): 25–33.

Horowitz, K. (2018, 31 July). *The New Free Voluntary Reading?* Retrieved from Language Magazine. Available at: https://www.languagemagazine.com/2018/07/31/the-new-free-voluntary-reading/.

Hoyos, D. (1997). *Latin: How to Read It Fluently*. CANE Press.

Hoyos, D. (2006). *Translating: Facts, Illusions, Alternatives*. Retrieved from CPL Online, 3 (1). Available at: https://camws.org/cpl/cplonline/files/Hoyoscplonline.pdf

Hsui, V. (2000). Guided Independent Reading (GIR): A programme to nurture lifelong readers. *Teaching & Learning*, 20 (2): 31–8.

Hucthinson, T. and E. Torres (1994). The Textbook as Agent of Change. *ELT Jounral*, 48 (4): 315–28.

Hunt, S. (2016). *Starting to Teach Latin*. London: Bloomsbury Academic.

Hunt, S. (2018). Latin is Not Dead: The Rise of Communicative Approaches to the Teaching of Latin in the United States. In A. Holmes-Henderson, S. Hunt and M. Musié, *Forward with Classics: Classical Languages in Schools and Communities* (pp. 89–108). London: Bloomsbury Academic.

Isozaki, A. (2018). Reading-Listening and Reading Circles: Bimodal Approaches Building Fluency. *The Reading Matrix*, 18 (1): 82–103.

Jacob, T. (2022, forthcoming). How do Students Translate? A Study of the Translation Process from Student Perspectives at Key Stage 3. *Journal of Classics Teaching*, 45.

Kitchell, K. (2000). Latin III's Dirty Little Secret: Why Johnny Can't Read Latin. *New England Classical Journal*, 27 (4): 206–26.

Kramsch, C. (1996). *Context and Culture in Language Teaching*. Oxford: Oxford University Press.

Krashen, S. (1993). The Case for Free Voluntary Reading. *Canadian Modern Language Review*, 51 (1): 72–82.

Krashen, S. (2004a). *Free Voluntary Reading: New Research, Applications, and Controversies.* Retrieved from sdkrashen.com. Available at: http://www.sdkrashen.com/content/articles/singapore.pdf.

Krashen, S. (2004b). Why Support a Delayed-Gratification Approach to Language Education? *The Language Teacher*, 28 (7): 3–7.

Krashen, S. (2013). Reading and Vocabulary Acquisition: Supporting Evidence and Some Objections. *Iranian Journal of Language Teaching Research*, 1 (1): 27–43.

Krieger, E. (1992). The Book Report Battle. *Journal of Reading*, 35: 340–1.

LaFleur, R. (2016). *ubi fera sunt.* Mundelein: Bolchazy-Carducci Publishers.

latinitium. (n.d.). *latinitium.* Retrieved from latinitium. Available at: https://www.latinitium.com/.

Laufer, B. (2003). Vocabulary Acquistion in a Second Language: Do Learners Really Acquire Most Vocabulary by Reading? Some Empirical Evidence. *Canadian Modern Language Review*, 59 (4): 565–85.

LiCalsi, L. (2020). *provincia Iudaea.* Self-published.

Lida, K. and A. Smith (2001). Alternative Assessment for Graded Readers. *The Language Teacher*, 25 (8): 26–8.

Macalister, J. (2014). Teaching Reading: Research into Practice. *Language Teaching*, 47: 387–97.

Macaro, E. (2003). *Teaching and Learning a Second Language: A Guide to Recent Research and Its Applications.* London: Continuum.

Mason, B. (2020, 15 Dec.). *Extensive Reading: Why Do It, How to Do It, How Not to Do It.* Retrieved from: http://beniko-mason.net/publications/: http://beniko-mason.net/content/articles/extensive_reading_why_to_do_it_how_to_do_it_how_not_to_do_it.pdf.

McCaffrey, D. (2006). Reading Latin Efficiently and the Need for Cognitive Strategies. In J. Gruber-Miller, *When Dead Tongues Speak: Teaching Beginning Greek and Latin* (pp. 113–33). Oxford: Oxford University Press.

McCaffrey, D. (2009). When Reading Latin, Read as the Romans Did. *The Classical Outlook*, 86 (2): 62–71.

McCall, J. (2018, 21 Jan.). *Path of Honors: Towards a Model for Interactive History Texts with Twine.* Retrieved from epoiesen. Available at: https://epoiesen.library.carleton.ca/2018/01/21/path-of-honors/.

McFadden, P. (2008). *Advanced Level Latin without Translation? Interactive Text-Marking as an Alternative Daily Preparation.* Retrieved from CPL Online, 4 (1). Available at: https://camws.org/cpl/cplonline/files/McFaddencplonline.pdf.

McLean, S. and G. Rouault (2017). The Effectivenss and Efficiency of Extensive Reading at Developing Reading Rates. *System*, 70: 92–106.

McQuillan, J. (2019, April). *Where Do We Get Our Academic Vocabulary? Comparing the Efficiency of Direct Instruction and Free Voluntary Reading.* Retrieved from *The Reading Matrix: An International Online Journal*, 19 (1). Available at: http://www.readingmatrix.com/files/20-d7ceydef.pdf

Morley, N. (2019, 4 Feb.). *The Melian Dilemna: Remaking Thucydides.* Retrieved from epoiesen. Available at: https://epoiesen.library.carleton.ca/2019/02/06/the-melian-dilemma-remaking-thucydides/.

NA-CSCP (2007). *fabulae ancillantes.* Cambridge: Cambridge University Press.

Nation, I. (2007). The Four Strands. *Innovation in Language Learning and Teaching*, 1: 2–13.

Nuttall, C. (2005). *Teaching Reading Skills in a Foreign Language.* London: Macmillan Education.

Olimpi, A. (2019a). *Daedalus and Icarus: A Tiered Latin Reader: Selections from Ovid's Metamorphoses and Hyginus' Fabulae.* Darcula: Comprehensible Classics Press.

Olimpi, A. (2019b). *legere discitur legendo*: Extensive Reading in the Latin Classroom. *Journal of Classics Teaching*, 39: 83–9.

Olimpi, A. (2021). *Comprehensible Classics: Publications.* Retrieved from Comprehensible Classics, web blog post. Available at: https://comprehensibleclassics. wordpress.com/publications/.

Oulton, N. (1999). *So You Really Want to Learn Latin, Book 1.* Tenterden: Galore Park Publishing.

Patrick, M. (2019). Free Voluntary Reading and Comprehensible Input. *Journal of Classics Teaching*, 39: 78–82.

Pettersson, D. and A. Rosengren (2018). *pugio Bruti.* Self-published. Latinitium.

Piantaggini, L. (2016). *Piso Ille Poetulus.* Self-published. Poetulus Publishing/Amazon.

Piantaggini, L. (2017a). *Piso Ille Poetulus: Student Workbook.* Self-published. Poetulus Publishing/Amazon.

Piantaggini, L. (2017b). *Piso Ille Poetulus: Teacher's Guide.* Self-published. Poetulus Publishing/Amazon.

Piantaggini, L. (2021a). *Magister P: Latin audio.* web blog. Retrieved from Magister P. Available at: https://magisterp.com/latin-audio/.

Piantaggini, L. (2021b, 20 Jan.). *'Not-Reading' Synonyms.* Retrieved from Magister P, blog. Available at: https://magisterp.com/2021/01/20/not-reading-synonyms/.

Piantaggini, L. (2021c). *Why Novellas?* Blog post. Retrieved from Magister P. Available at: https://docs.google.com/ document/d/1bF8hZuxTDtgNMSSdonEX112JJaVYqoPH7w27Oju9ETs/edit.

Piazza, J. (2017). Beginner Latin Novels: A General Overview. *Teaching Classical Languages*, 8 (2): 154–66.

Piazza, J. (2019). *Seneca's Letters to Lucilius: Selections, with Simplified Versions, and a Glossary.* Self-published. Piazza/Amazon. Retrieved from: http://johnpiazza.net/ seneca-book/.

Pink News (2019, 18 Nov.). *The Terrible History of Margaret Thatcher's Homophobic Section 28, 16 Years Since it was Repealed in England and Wales.* Retrieved from *Pink News.* Available at: https://www.pinknews.co.uk/2019/11/18/section-28-homophobic-repealed-england-wales-history-margaret-thatcher/.

Prowse, P. (2002). Top Ten Principles for Teaching Extensive Reading: A Response. *Reading in a Foreign Language*, 14 (2): 142–5.

Pym, D. (1962). The Fig-Tree. In The Classical Association, *Re-Appraisal: Some New Thoughts on the Teaching of Classics* (pp. 35–41). Oxford: Clarendon Press.

Ramahlo, M. (2019). On Starting to Teach Using CI. *Journal of Classics Teaching*, 39: 45–50.

Reinagel, R. (2018). *Developing Online Extensive Reading and Listening Materials.* Retrieved from University of Hawai'i at Mānoa. Available at: http://www.hawaii.edu/sls/wp-content/uploads/2018/07/Reinagel.pdf.

Reinhard, A. (2009). Social Networking in Latin Class: A How-to Guide. *Teaching Classical Languages*, 1 (1): 4–29.

Rivers, W. (1981). *Teaching Foeign Language Skills.* Chicago, IL: University of Chicago Press.

Rodrigo, V., D. Greenberg, V. Burke, R. Hall, A. Berry, T. Brinck, H. Joseph and M. Oby (2007). Implementing an Extensive Reading Program and Library for Adult Literacy Learners. *Reading in a Foreign Language*, 19 (2): 106–19.

Ross, D. (2008). Latin Pedagogy at the University of Michigan, USA: Linear Reading Using a Linguistic Perspective. In B. Lister, *Meeting the Challenge: International Perspectives on the Teaching of Latin* (pp. 44–53). Cambridge: Cambridge University Press.

Russell, K. (2018). Read Like a Roman: Teaching Students to Read in Latin Word Order. *Journal of Classics Teaching*, 37: 17–29.

Schwamm, J. (n.d.). *The Tres Columnae Project:* Retrieved from The Tres Columnae Project. Available at: http://trescolumnae.com.

Schwamm, J. and N. Vander Veer (2021). From Reading to World-Building: Collaborative Content Creation and Classical Language Learning. In M. Lloyd and S. Hunt, *Communicative Approaches for Ancient Languages* (pp. 47–54). London: Bloomsbury Academic.

Sears, L. and K. Ballestrini (2019). Adapting Antiquity: Using Tiered Texts to Increase Latin Reading Proficiency. *Journal of Classics Teaching*, 39: 71–7.

Siah, P. and W. Kwok (2010). The Value of Reading and the Effectiveness of Sustained Silent Reading. *The Clearing House: A Journal of Educational Strategies, Issues and Ideas*, 83 (5): 168–74.

Simmonsen, R. (2019). An Analysis of the Problematic Discourse Surrounding 'Authentic Texts'. *Hispania*, 102 (2): 245–58.

Smith, S. and G. Conti (2016). *The Language Teacher Toolkit.* Self-published. CreateSpace Independent Publishing Platform.

Tabata-Sandom, M. (2017). L2 Japanese Learners' Responses to Translation, Speed Reading, and 'Pleasure Reading' as a Form of Extensive Reading. *Reading in a Foreign Language*, 29 (1): 113–32.

The Pericles Group (2021). *Tiered Reading List for Operation Caesar.* Retrieved from Project Arkhaia. Available at: http://lapis.practomime.com/index.php/operation-caesar-reading-list.

Tunberg, J. and Tunberg, T. (2000). *Cattus Petasatus.* Mundelein: Bolchazy-Carducci Publishers.

Upchurch, O. (2014). How do Students Perceive Women in Roman Society as a Result of Studying the Cambridge Latin Course? A Case Study of a Year 9 Class at an Urban Comprehensive School. *Journal of Classics Teaching*, 29: 30–6.

van Lier, L. (1996). *Interaction in the Language Curriculum: Awareness, Autonomy and Authenticity.* London: Routledge.

VanPatten, B. (1993). Grammar Teaching for the Acquisition-Rich Classroom. *Foreign Languages Annals,* 26 (4): 435–50.

Von Sprecken, D. and S. Krashen (1998). Do Students Read during Sustained Silent Reading? *California Reader,* 32 (1): 11–13.

Waring, R. (n.d.). *Rob Waring's Extensive Reading Pages* (blog). Retrieved from Rob Waring's Extensive Reading Pages. Available at: http://robwaring.org/er/.

Waring, R. (2009). The inescapable case for extensive reading. In A. Cirocki (ed.), *Extensive Reading in English-Language Teaching* (pp. 93–111). Munich: Lincom.

William, R. (1986). 'Top Ten' Principles for Teaching Reading. *ELT Journal,* 40: 42–5.

Wright, R. (2017). What are They Talking About? Pupils Talk while Translating Latin Stories: A Case Study of a Year 7 Class Using the Cambridge Latin Course. *Journal of Classics Teaching,* 35: 13–25.

Zig Zag Education (2020). *2020 GCSE Latin Exams.* Retrieved from Zig Zag Education. Available at: https://zigzageducation.co.uk/keywords/2020-gcse-latin-exams.

4

Speaking

Why speaking?

I happen to be writing this chapter at the moment of publication of the volume I co-edited with Mair Lloyd, *Communicative Approaches for Ancient Languages* (2021), which covers many points far more eloquently than I can here and from many different points of view (university/school, formal/informal learning). Because that book has only just been published, I inevitably point readers to it for a more fulsome set of expositions of communicative practices than are possible in this short chapter. Spoken Latin has been of serious interest in continental Europe for many years (Leonhardt 2013), and has started to take root in the modern US (and some very few UK) classrooms (Hunt 2018). At the present time, teaching approaches in which spoken Latin is used are perhaps more widely described and discussed than any other. However, it is worth remembering that 'Living Latin' in the modern era classroom is not all that recent. We can look back a bare hundred years for practical examples of speaking Latin in the classroom, to W. H. D. Rouse (1863–1950), the Cambridge Classics teacher and headmaster, whose employment of the Natural or Direct Method for Latin teaching aroused significant interest in the UK in the early part of the twentieth century. At this time, there was a general spirit of reform throughout Europe concerning the education of the different classes (Bayley 1998). Rouse himself, disillusioned by the traditional grammar-translation approach to teaching Latin, was interested in the innovations in modern foreign language teaching on the Continent, where oral methods seemed to be producing positive results (Stray 1992). Rather than spending most of the lesson in explanation of grammar rules, teachers who used the Direct Method remained in the foreign language throughout and encouraged activities for students to use it spontaneously (Richards and Rogers 2009). At the time, even for the teachers of modern foreign languages, the Direct Method was felt to put too much pressure on teachers' skills, something especially keenly felt by Latin teachers, for whose students speaking fluency was clearly not the aim (Stray 1992). In answer, Rouse's version of the Direct Method blended oral approaches at the start and explicit grammar instruction after. He explained his method as follows:

> The Direct Method means that the sounds of the foreign tongue are associated directly with a thing, or an act, or a thought, without the intervention of an English word; and that these associations are grouped by a method, so as to make the learning of the language as easy and as speedy as possible … It follows that speaking precedes writing, and that the sentence (not the word) is the unit. The method is largely oral, but not wholly so: on the contrary, all the practices of indirect methods are used, but not at the same time or in the same proportion. Language is an art, and we proceed from art to science, from idiom to accuracy; the idiom and the feeling for a language is easily taught thus, and accuracy can wait.
>
> Rouse and Appleton 1925: 2–3

A more recent account of Rouse's Direct Method for teaching Latin can be found in Peckett (1992), from which language teachers today would be able to identify several features of the contemporary modern foreign languages classroom: the importance of forms of input first (listening followed by reading) and forms of output afterwards (speaking followed by writing); a carefully planned sequence of activities whereby the use of an oral activity is targeted to achieve the specific language objective; the greater speed and efficiency with which language understanding can be achieved through listening and speaking rather than through reading and writing; the employment of other 'indirect' methods in proportion; the understanding that learning a language – even Latin – does not have to mean that the student has to get it perfectly right at the start, as long as they get it right in the end (Lightbown and Spada 2017).

This last point can be the cause of much consternation: traditionally Latin teaching has emphasized perfection and measured it through written translation from Latin to English and from English to Latin (Richards and Rogers 2009). In Rouse's time, criticism came from the universities, who considered the Direct Method an inadequate preparation for their students in any language, not just Latin (Bayley 1998). Such beliefs have continued to echo over the years: in the 1910s, the Classical Association and the Association for the Reform of Latin, which Rouse had founded, had a 'difficult relationship' (Stray 2003:18); in 1923, the Prime Minister's Commission on Classical Studies came out against the Direct Method; in 1954, the authors of *The*

Teaching of Classics were more ambivalent, calling it 'a high adventure', although 'worthy of experiment' (perhaps damning it with faint praise) (Incorporated Association of Assistant Masters in Secondary Schools 1954: 79). But, in general, the status of Latin as a difficult subject reserved for only the best was to be maintained – its very difficulty and the difficulty with which it was taught was felt to be the point (McLelland 2018): not so much a language as an intellectual discipline. Latin had become little more than 'the sum of its grammatical rules' (Leonhardt 2013: 288).

After the crises of the 1960s, with concerns about enrolments, the terrible attrition rate of students and the suitability of the O level Latin examination for all (Baty 1962; Brink 1962), attention tuned to developing courses based on the reading-comprehension method and more realistic forms of assessment than the English-to-Latin translations ('prose composition') which formed the bulk of the exercise. Yet, Sharwood Smith (1977), one of the most influential of the specialist Classics educationalists of the late twentieth century, remained doubtful of the Direct Method's efficacy, especially for preparation for the study of Latin literature – a bookish activity which dealt with demanding texts. He did, however, consider it might 'provide ample opportunity for performance as well as for experience of the language' (Sharwood Smith 1977: 36).

I suspect that by 'performance' Sharwood Smith (1977) was not envisioning the sorts of conversational badinage which Ball and Ellsworth (1996) criticize as leading nowhere. He preferred, as many have done since, to recommend reading-comprehension methods. But performance is now exactly what is needed to enthuse take-up by our students, if by it we mean some kind of productive language activity. Some deny it. They argue that that is fine for modern foreign languages: Latin is different, they say; we should be teaching students how to read Latin and nothing more. Clearly, we are not aiming to speak Latin to others because of need. But I would draw attention to Tunberg's (2011b) maxim that 'speaking to learn' Latin rather than 'learning to speak' emphasizes speech as a tool, not as a product. And it can be a very simple and efficient and enjoyable one. Coffee (2012) noted that successful modern languages teaching engaged students in speaking, listening and writing as well as reading. The four skills are interdependent. Why should Latin – a language like any other – be different? Mair Lloyd, in the introduction to *Communicative Approaches for Ancient Languages*, says:

> We want to help students to experience reading ancient languages without having to painstakingly transpose texts into their own language in order to achieve comprehension. We want to escape the image of ancient languages as codes to be deciphered and to move towards students experiencing them as a normal means of communication in spoken as well as written form. In short, we hope to make ancient languages recognizable as languages and to make them lively and attractive to as wide a range of modern learners as possible.
>
> Lloyd and Hunt 2021: 13

Latin teachers teach students who are often also in modern languages classes, where they enjoy the opportunity to express themselves in the target language. It seems curious to deny students the same opportunities in Latin, especially if it served to motivate and engage them through activities which promoted self-expression and personal satisfaction. And although Latin teachers choose to assess Latin through written responses to reading texts, it does not mean that they must always teach it in those ways: we are, after all, teachers of Latin not just teachers of Latin tests.

Rasmussen (2015), in an overview of why oral Latin should be part of classroom practices, drawing on Mackey and Abbuhl (2005), notes that, for students, spoken Latin promotes automatization, pushes them to notice gaps in their own learning, encourages them to process syntactically rather than just semantically, and provides opportunities to test hypotheses they have constructed about the target language. Drawing on Wills (1998), she suggests that interactional communication (such as discussions, conversations and debates) promote opportunities for self-correction, where the speakers listen to each other and modify their own speech for comprehensibility. Vocabulary is better remembered when the student has to recall and use it with appropriate intonation and attention to phraseology. It appeals to students in a class who have diverse learning styles (Deagon 2006); it has historical precedent; it is enjoyable. From an institutional point of view, spoken Latin aligns with ACTFL (2012) guidelines for interpersonal, interpretative and presentational communication.

Patrick's (2011, 2015, 2019) written contributions and conference presentations on teaching Latin, as informed by SLA research, have significantly impacted on the practices of a generation of US Latin teachers (although less known across the Atlantic). For a full description of how to teach using comprehensible input, including spoken Latin (and also listening and reading), see Patrick (2015). Patrick notes the main considerations: that the teacher should deliver messages in Latin that are understandable to the students; the material should be interesting to the students; and the classroom should be stress-free. Students do not have to speak themselves if they are not ready – they can show appreciation and understanding non-verbally. A communicative approach which puts these ideas into practice is more likely to meet these conditions than one in which the focus is primarily on grammar exposition and memorization, testing and translation.

Activities for speaking Latin

Stories

Teaching Proficiency through Reading and Storytelling (TPRS) has become a staple practice (Bailey 2016; Patrick 2011, 2015). The teacher tells a simple story to the students, in Latin that is appropriate to their level. Props can be used. Stopping at various points, the teacher invites the students to respond to questions in Latin to check their comprehension of the story. The teacher is able to repeat (or modify) elements of the story – sentences, phrases, vocabulary – to ensure comprehension, and they can personalize it and the questions according to the students' own knowledge and interests. The teacher needs to explain to the students how to respond, as part of the activity (yes/no/don't understand answers). Students may initially only respond by nodding or shaking their heads; as they become more proficient, they may start to utter simple answers such as *minime [no]* or *ita [yes]*, individual words, phrases and so on. If there is total confusion, the teacher can use English to get back on track. Grammar can also be addressed as it arises in the same way.

Extemporizing a story through TPRS is quite a challenging first step. Using a printed copy of an interesting and easy text (or displaying it on the IWB) might provide a first step in the process. Although the opportunity to personalize the text itself is lost, there remains the opportunity to personalize the questions.

Stories have a powerful hold over on our imaginations and our memories. Language teachers and language learning textbooks have given examples of stories to amuse, interest, provide input and provoke interaction. What is the aim of learning Latin if not to read ancient stories? Stories enable the teacher to deploy a range of productive activities which provide large amounts of meaningful input and opportunities to practise with it. Stories provide many examples of action and event words, and sequences of events. This makes it easy to ask questions, elicit responses, and let students read aloud and manipulate the text – by changing the point of view, for example. Grammar is seen in context, not in isolation. Vocabulary is seen in meaningful chunks. Some classroom suggestions:

1 Read the text aloud, while students follow with their fingers. The teacher reads a chunk aloud, which the students repeat back, chorally or individually. A translation of the text might be also provided, if necessary.
2 Practice individual words which have difficult phonology as they arise in the story.
3 One student at a time reads a sentence aloud. To speed things up, the teacher might read alternate sentences. Or the students read aloud in pairs to each other.
4 The teacher asks students to find an individual Latin word or phrase in the text, giving the word in English.
5 The teacher makes false statements which resemble the content of the text. The students have to correct the teacher.
6 The teacher asks a series of questions, of increasing complexity. The aim here is to provide more comprehensible listening input and elicit output at various levels of complexity. Question types would look like this:

- Yes/No   (Yes/No question).
- Is X a – or a – ?   (Either/Or question).
- Is X a –, a – or a – ?   (Multi-choice question).
- Is he searching for X? (No, he's searching for ...) (Yes/No question).
- Is he looking for X or Y?   (Either/Or).
- Whom is he looking for?   (Question word question).

7 Pupils can answer with hands up, no hands up or on mini-whiteboards. The teacher may wait until the students have had sufficient time to rehearse their answers mentally.

8 The teacher repeats some of the questions that have been used earlier, but this time pupils write down their answers. The teacher elicits responses.

Dictation

The teacher dictates four or five sentences. See also the other sort of dictation, where the students hear, but they do not write; instead, they rewrite the sentences that they have heard, and then share afterwards in recreating the whole passage. It is not a sentence-by-sentence rewrite, rather it is a rewrite of a short continuous passage which the students compose together through speaking to each other.

Pictures

Example 1

The teacher points to pictures on the whiteboard and reads a number of sentences aloud, three times for each. The students are called out to answer questions in Latin about the pictures, with the expectation that they will use some of the sentences completely, or partially, or some of the vocabulary used within them. More simply, the teacher asks questions expecting yes or no answers about the pictures. Teacher and the other students support the responses.

Example 2

The class is studying a passage from a Roman author. The students draw an image of the scene, and, through talking in Latin with the teacher and other students, using the Latin from the original passage, annotate the picture. It is a good way to get students to interrogate the text closely, improve vocabulary recognition, and clarify understanding of the meaning of the text by representing it on the board and talking about it. The student is not panicking about getting the answer 'right', because this seems on the surface to be more about sharing information and having fun. The teacher's judicious questioning seems more to be a conversation about the picture than a test of the language.

Example 3

The teacher provides an image on the IWB which they use as a 'talking' point, much like TPRS (above). The teacher describes the image, eliciting responses to questions as they go. A variant on this is providing the students with a copy of the picture to share between two. The students, as they become more proficient, take it in turns to ask questions about the picture. A supplementary vocabulary list may be provided. A further variation is that the paired students share their observations with the rest of the class.

Key question starters:

- quis est? [Who is?]
- ubi est/sunt? [Where is/are?]
- quid est? [What is?]
- quid facit? [What is s/he doing?]
- quid agit? [What is s/he doing/]
- estne ...? [Is s/he ...?]
- -ne? [Is?]
- an ...? [or ...?]
- quid est in pictura? [What is in the picture?]
- in pictura video ... [In the picture, I see ...]
- cur faciunt? [Why are they doing ...?]
- hic sunt ...[Here there are ...]

Corrective feedback

Sometimes students will not benefit from any feedback on spoken errors. The teacher could simply say that the focus of the activity is on promoting spoken fluency and that errors will be taken care at another time. If, however, corrective feedback is desired, MFL immersion lessons can provide useful approaches for dealing with error correction (see, for example, Lloyd 2017). Even in MFL immersion lessons, students do not attain fluency (Tedick and de Gortari 1998) and teachers are not always able to provide sufficient language teaching to provide fluency on matters that are engaging and interesting enough for students as subject content is often circumscribed by institutional requirements (Lyster and Ranta 1997). In the case of Latin, it could be argued that fluency is never going to be the aim, especially if one takes the maxim that students are speaking to learn Latin rather than learning to speak it. There are increasing opportunities at the university level and in immersion events (see Lloyd and Hunt 2021). Terence Tunberg, on the subject of error correction in a fully immersive Latin *conventiculum*, notes:

> We very rarely correct people. It is more important for people to gain confidence in communication and learn not to fear errors. Of course, correctness in expression is always our goal, especially in a classical language where the norms of usage (I believe) are more fixed in canonical texts than is the case in the still-evolving national languages. But we all strive for this goal of correctness, and there is no need for 'language police' to make overt corrections to help us reach this goal. The more experienced speakers will constantly model the desired patterns. Most of the people trying their hand at this will want (of their own accord) to advance in this direction.
>
> Tunberg, quoted in Lloyd 2016: 46

For MFL (and by extension, Latin) teaching in the classroom, however, different considerations may apply. To my knowledge, no research has been carried out on error correction in the language, and so I shall have to turn to the extensive research for MFL. Hendrickson (1978) identified five considerations: (1) Should learners' errors be corrected? (2) When should learners' errors be corrected? (3) Which errors should be corrected? (4) How should errors be corrected? (5) Who should do the correcting? Assuming that the teacher would be the one who provided corrective feedback, Lyster and Ranta (1997, 2013) researched which sort of corrective feedback was the most likely to encourage learners' uptake and self-repair. The researchers considered student generated self-repairs were important in language learning because they showed that the student was actively engaged in the learning process. Self-repair, they claim, requires negotiation between teacher and student and happens when the student has to reformulate language with the help of the teacher's cues.

The effect of different types of corrective feedback is given below (Lyster and Ranta 1997):

> Types of corrective feedback (percentage relates to the number of occasions when students self-repaired):
>
> 1 Explicit correction: 0 per cent self-repair. The teacher indicates that the response was incorrect and provides the correct form.
> 2 Recast: 0 per cent self-repair. The teacher does not indicate that the student's utterance was incorrect, but implicitly reformulates the students' error or provides the correction.
> 3 Clarification request: 20 per cent self-repair. The teacher indicates that the message has not been understood (sometimes just a raised eyebrow or expression of puzzlement; more often a question, 'Sorry, can you say that again?') and implies that a repetition or reformulation is required.
> 4 Metalinguistic clues: 26 per cent self-repair. Without providing the grammatical form, the teacher poses questions or provides comments or information related to the formation of the students' utterance ('Was that feminine?').

5   Elicitation: 43 per cent self-repair. The teacher directly elicits the correct form from the student by asking questions, but pausing for the student to complete the teacher's utterance or asking the student to reformulate the utterance.

6   Repetition: 11 per cent self-repair. The teacher repeats the student's error and adjusts intonation to draw the student's attention to it.

Lyster and Ranta 1997

The research suggests that prompts, such as eliciting, metalinguistic clues and clarification requests produce more examples of self-repairs than the other forms of corrective feedback. Other researchers have made greater claims for the effectiveness of recasts, drawing attention to the wide range of options available and the specificity of their purpose in language learning (Goo and Mackey 2013). Recasts work well with form-focused teaching (Nicholas, Lightbown and Spada 2001); with higher-ability students (Bigelow, delMas, Hansen and Tarone 2006); and with students with good working memories (Mackey, Philp, Egi, Fujii and Tatsumi 2002) and good phonological memories (Trofimovich, Ammar and Gatbonton 2007). However, their value in the average school classroom is disputed (Lyster and Ranta 2013). What is being corrected by the recast might be ambiguous: younger students tend to focus on meaning rather than grammatical form. The recast might not be recognized at all: younger students do not tend to notice as much as older ones. The recast can work if there is salience and intonation that indicates the recast is taking place. Not all recasts are repeated by the students: is the expectation that just the one or that all students should notice? Does there have to be a sign that uptake has occurred? Sometimes there are forms of words that are insufficiently different to make recasting effective. This is a major problem for Latin, where the change of one or two letters makes a big difference in meaning – hence the importance of developing phonological awareness early. If the question is binary (masculine or feminine, singular or plural, active or passive) there is a risk that recasting is insufficient and actually reinforces the error.

If recasting is insufficient, it is better to prompt by eliciting or asking the student to clarify their response? The teacher can hold back information to encourage the student to recall – but they need to know the information to recall first. Some help may be needed to fully recall information and the process may help to secure it. Prompts do not have to be questions; they can be pointing to the board, posters on a wall, or giving instructions to find the information in a book. The teacher can repeat the word with an incredulous (or suspicious) intonation.

One can see that in the communicative Latin classroom, the research on corrective feedback has direct applicability. But much everyday Latin instruction involves comprehension and translation and of Latin texts carried out orally in English. If we assume that students are responding directly to questions asked by the teacher about a Latin text, corrective feedback which encourages self-repair could still be useful. It is clear that oral corrective feedback of this kind would have little value if students were to be correcting written translations of Latin.

Where to learn

Patrick (2011, 2015) notes that teachers feel they lack proficiency in using Latin communicatively and, understandably, are reluctant to try. For those teachers who wish to develop experience, there are now many places which offer a chance. Gratius Avitus (2018) gives perhaps the best overview of places (both physical and virtual) where Latin speaking may be learnt. More specifically, the *Lexington conventiculum*, an annual immersion event, which Terence Tunberg organizes, has been the subject of several articles (Minkova and Tunberg 2021; Lloyd 2016; Tunberg 2011a). Student-led Latin-speaking circles at Oxford and Cambridge are reported by Ivan Parga Ornelas and Josey Parker (2021) and typify opportunities for informal learning in some universities. The *Accademia Vivarium Novum* in Rome has excellent reports (Letchford 2021). Digital resources are ever-increasing in number. Perhaps the original *Association for Latin Teaching* can have a future role?

Reading resources

For further examples of articles which discuss and demonstrate practical experiences of using communicative approaches in the Latin classroom, see the following:

Journal of Classics Teaching, 22 (2011):

- Editorial: *omnis lingua usu potius discitur quam praeceptis [Every language can be learnt through use rather than through instructions]* (Rogers 2011).
- Krashen and Second Language Acquisition Theory – A Re-evaluation of How to Teach Classical Languages (Macdonald 2011).
- Success and Failure: W. H. D. Rouse and Direct-Method Classics Teaching in Edwardian England (Stray 2011).
- The Use of Latin as a Spoken Language in the Humanist Age (Tunberg 2011b).
- TPRS and Latin in the Classroom: Experiences of a US Latin Teacher (Patrick 2011).
- Educating the Educators (Carlon 2011).
- *de instituto studiis Latinis provehendis, quod annum iam decimum in Acadmeia Kentukiana floret* (Tunberg 2011a).

Journal of Classics Teaching, 39 (2019):

- Comprehensible Input FAQs (Rogers 2019).
- Comprehensible Input and Krashen's Theory (Patrick 2019).
- On Starting to Teach Using CI (Ramahlo 2019).
- TPRS, PQA and Circling (Bracey 2019).

The Classical Outlook, (94) 2 (2019):

- 'Aut Latine aut nihil'? A middle way? (Keeline 2019).
- A Day in the Life of an Active Latin Teacher (Shirley 2019).
- Comprehensible Output, Form-Focused Recasts, and the New Standards (Anderson 2019).
- What Can Active Latin Accomplish? Well Let Me Just Show You Some Facts and Figures Illustrating the Benefits of Active Latin Instruction (Stringer 2019).
- Toward a Collegial, Post-Method Latin Pedagogy: A Response to the SCS Panel 'What Can "Active" Latin Accomplish?' (Bailey 2019).

Communicative Approaches for Ancient Languages (Lloyd and Hunt 2021), contains chapters by several teachers of Latin in school and university classrooms, and immersive and informal Latin language learning events.

Making Sense of Comprehensible Input in the Latin Classroom (Patrick 2015).

The Biduum Experience: Speaking Latin to Learn. Contains a number of illustrated examples of communicative activities (Lindzey 2015).

The *Ars* of Latin Questioning: Circling, Personalization, and Beyond (Bailey 2016).

The Virtue of Variety: Opening the Doors to Wider Pedagogical Practices in UK Schools and Universities (Hunt, Letchford, Lloyd, Manning and Plummer 2018).

Latin is Not Dead: The Rise of Communicative Approaches to the Teaching of Latin in the United States (Hunt 2018).

References

ACTFL (2012). *ACTFL Proficiency Guidelines 2021.* Retrieved from ACTFL. Available at: https://www.actfl.org/sites/default/files/guidelines/ACTFLProficiencyGuidelines2012.pdf.

Anderson, P. (2019). Comprehensible Output, Form-focused Recasts, and the New Standards. *The Classical Outlook,* 94 (2): 72–80.

Bailey, J. (2016). The *Ars* of Latin Questioning: Circling, Personalization, and Beyond. *The Classical Outlook,* 91 (1): 1–5.

Bailey, J. (2019). Towards a Collegial, Post-Method Latin Pedagogy: A Response to the SCS Panel 'What Can "Active" Latin Accomplish?' *The Classical Outlook,* 94 (2): 94–101.

Ball, R. and J. Ellsworth (1996). The Emperor's New Clothes: Hyperreality and the Study of Latin. *The Modern Language Journal,* 80 (1): 77–84.

Baty, C. (1962). Classics in the Schools: A Survey of the Position and Prospects. In The Classical Association, *Re-Appraisal* (pp. 10–14). Oxford: Clarendon Press.

Bayley, S. (1998). The Direct Method and Modern Language Teaching in England 1880–1918. *History of Education,* 27 (1): 39–57.

Bigelow, M., R. delMas, K. Hansen and E. Tarone (2006). Literacy and the Processing of Oral Recasts in SLA. *TESOL Quarterly*, 40: 665–89.

Bracey, J. (2019). TPRS, PQA and Circling. *Journal of Classics Teaching*, 39: 60–4.

Brink, C. (1962). Small Latin and the Classics. In The Classical Association, *Re-Appraisal* (pp. 6–9). Oxford: Clarendon Press.

Carlon, J. (2011). Educating the Educators. *Journal of Classics Teaching*, 22: 13–14.

Coffee, N. (2012). Active Latin: Quo Tendimus? *Classical World*, 105 (2): 255–69.

Deagon, A. (2006). Cognitive Style and Learning Strategies in Latin Instruction. In J. Gruber-Miller, *When Dead Tongues Speak: Teaching Beginning Greek and Latin* (pp. 27–49). Oxford: Oxford University Press.

Goo, J. and A. Mackey. (2013). The Case Against the Case Against Recasts. *Studies in Second Language Acquisition*, 35 (1): 127–65.

Gratius Avitus, A. (2018). Spoken Latin: Learning, Teaching, Lecturing and Research. *Journal of Classics Teaching*, 37: 46–52.

Hendrickson, J. (1978). Error Correction in Foreign Language Teaching: Recent Theory, Research, and Practice. *Modern Language Journal*, 62: 387–98.

Hunt, S. (2018). Latin is Not Dead: The Rise of Communicative Approaches to the Teaching of Latin in the United States. In A. Holmes-Henderson, S. Hunt and M. Musié, *Forward with Classics: Classical Languages in Schools and Communities* (pp. 89–108). London: Bloomsbury Academic.

Hunt, S., C. Letchford, M. Lloyd, L. Manning and R. Plummer (2018). The Virtue of Variety: Opening the Doors to Wider Pedagogical Practices in UK Schools and Universities. *Journal of Classics Teaching*, 19 (38): 53–60.

Incorporated Association of Assistant Masters in Secondary Schools (1954). *The Teaching of Classics*. Cambridge: Cambridge University Press.

Keeline, T. (2019). 'Aut Latin aut nihil'? A middle way. *The Classical Outlook*, 94 (2): 57–65.

Leonhardt, J. (2013). *Latin: Story of a World Language*. Cambridge, MA: Belknap Press of Harvard University Press.

Letchford, C. (2021). Communicative Latin for All in a UK University. In M. Lloyd and S. Hunt, *Communicative Approaches for Ancient Languages* (pp. 81–90). London: Bloomsbury Academic.

Lightbown, P. and N. Spada (2017). *How Languages are Learned*. Oxford: Oxford University Press.

Lindzey, G. (2015). The Biduum Experience: Speaking Latin to Learn. *Teaching Classical Languages*, 6 (1): 72–107.

Lloyd, M. (2016). Living Latin: An Interview with Professor Terence Tunberg. *Journal of Classics Teaching*, 34: 44–8.

Lloyd, M. (2017). *Living Latin: Exploring a Communicative Approach to Latin Teaching through a Sociocultural Perspective on Language Learning*. Retrieved from PhD thesis, The Open University. Available at: http://oro.open.ac.uk/48886.

Lloyd, M. and S. Hunt (2021). *Communicative Approaches for Ancient Languages*. London: Bloomsbury Academic.

Lyster, R. and L. Ranta (1997). Corrective Feedback and Learner Uptake: Negotiation of Form in Communicative Classrooms. *Studies in Second Language Acquisition*, 19 (1): 37–66.

Lyster, R. and L. Ranta (2013). Counterpoint Piece: The Case for Variety in Corrective Feedback Research. *Studies in Second Language Acquisition*, 35: 167–84.

Macdonald, S. (2011). Krashen and Second Language Acquisition (SLA) Theory – A Re-evaluation of How to Teach Classical Languages. *Journal of Classics Teaching*, 22: 3–5.

Mackey, A. and R. Abbuhl (2005). Input and Interaction. In C. Sanz, *Mind and Content in Adult Second Language Acquisition: Methods, Theory, and Practice* (pp. 207–33). Washington, DC: Georgetown University Press.

Mackey, A., J. Philp, T. Egi, A. Fujii and T. Tatsumi (2002). Individual Differences in Working Memory, Noticing of Interactional Feedback and L2 Development. In P. Robinson, *Individual Differences and Instructed Language Learning* (pp. 181–209). Amsterdam: Benjamins.

McLelland, N. (2018). The History of Language Learning and Teaching in Britain. *Language Learning Journal*, 46 (1): 6–16.

Minkova, M. and T. Tunberg (2021). Global Latin, Active Latin: Kentucky and Beyond. In M. Lloyd and S. Hunt, *Communicative Approaches for Ancient Langauges* (pp. 125–32). London: Bloomsbury Academic.

Nicholas, H., P. Lightbown and N. Spada (2001). Recasts as Feedback to Language Learners. *Language Learning*, 51, 719–58.

Ornelas, I. and J. Parker (2021). Student-Led Initiatives at Oxford and Cambridge. In M. Lloyd and S. Hunt, *Communicative Approaches for Ancient Languages* (pp. 179–88). London: Bloomsbury Academic.

Patrick, R. (2011). TPRS and Latin in the Classroom. Experiences of a US Latin Teacher. *Journal of Classics Teaching*, 22: 8–10.

Patrick, R. (2015). Making Sense of Comprehensible Input in the Latin Classroom. *Teaching Classical Languages*, Spring: 108–36.

Patrick, R. (2019). Comprehensible Input and Krashen's Theory. *Journal of Classics Teaching*, 39: 37–44.

Peckett, C. (1992). The Oral Method. *JACT Review*, 11: 4–8.

Ramahlo, M. (2019). On Starting to Teach Using CI. *Journal of Classics Teaching*, 39: 45–50.

Rasmussen, S. (2015). Why Oral Latin? *Teaching Classical Langauges*, Spring: 37–45.

Richards, J. and T. Rogers (2009). *Approaches and Methods in Language Teaching*. Cambridge: Cambridge University Press.

Rogers, K. (2011). Editorial: *omnis lingua usu potius discitur quam praeceptis*. *Journal of Classics Teaching*, 22: 1–2.

Rogers, K. (2019). Comprehensible Input FAQs. *Journal of Classics Teaching*, 39: 33–6.

Rouse, W. and R. Appleton (1925). *Latin on the Direct Method*. London: University of London Press.

Sharwood Smith, J. (1977). *On Teaching Classics*. London: Routledge and Kegan Paul.

Shirley, S. (2019). A Day in the Life of an Active Latin Teacher. *The Classical Outlook*, 94 (2): 66–71.

Stray, C. (1992). *The Living Word: W. H. D. Rouse and the Crisis of Classics in Edwardian England*. Bristol: Bristol Classical Press.

Stray, C. (2003). The Foundation and Its Contexts. In C. Stray, *The Classical Association: The First Century 1903–2003* (pp. 3–22). Oxford: Oxford University Press.

Stray, C. (2011). Success and Failure: W. H. D. Rouse and Direct-Method Classics Teaching in Edwardian England. *Journal of Classics Teaching*, 22: 5–7.

Stringer, G. (2019). What Can Active Latin Accomplish? Well Let Me Just Show You Some Facts and Figures Illustrating the Benefits of Active Latin Instruction. *The Classical Outlook*, 94 (2): 81–93.

Tedick, D. and B. de Gortari (1998). Research on Error Correction and Implications for Classroom Teaching. *ACIE Newsletter*, 1, 3.

Trofimovich, P., A. Ammar and E. Gatbonton (2007). How Effective are Recasts? The Role of Attention, Memory, and Analytic Ability. In A. Mackey, *Conversational Interaction in Second Language Acquisition: A Collection of Empirical Studies* (pp. 171–95). Oxford: Oxford University Press.

Tunberg, T. (2011a). *de instituto studiis Latinis provehendis, quod annum iam decimum in Academia Kentukiana floret. Journal of Classics Teaching*, 22: 16–18.

Tunberg, T. (2011b). The Use of Latin as a Spoken Language in the Humanist Age. *Journal of Classics Teaching*, 22: 8–9.

Wills, J. (1998). Speaking Latin in Schools and Colleges. *The Classical World*, 92 (1): 27–34.

5

Writing

Writing Latin

The value of writing Latin is contested. How does it develop the ability to read and comprehend original texts such that time should be set aside for it? Nevertheless, there are good pedagogical if not utilitarian reasons for writing Latin. Discussing MFL, Grauberg (1997) dismisses *translation* into the second language, saying that in the real world it is rare even among professional translators. On the other hand, he considers *free composition* valuable as a real-life tool for communication and a useful role in promoting the intellectual development of students through the opportunity for 'individual and sometimes quite personal expression' (Grauberg 1997: 213).

In the UK, there remains a long tradition of what is termed 'prose composition', more rightly described as 'reverse-translation' from English to Latin;[1] conversely, free composition is increasingly common at school and university level in the US. In the first part of this chapter, I will look at the arguments for and against prose composition, with some recommendations for practice. In the second part, I will discuss commonly used free composition activities.

Prose composition in the UK

For UK Latin teachers, however, prose composition, lacking any obvious utilitarian purpose, still seems to retain its allure, and, after a gap of some dozen years, has been reintroduced to GCSE as an option under the education reforms of Michael Gove (Education Minister 2010–14). Whether this was done in the name of pedagogical necessity is doubtful; its reintroduction provided the necessary evidence of the fulfilment of the minister's aim of increasing the rigour of national examinations (Bristow 2021; Hunt 2018). Passions run high on either side, between those who see it as an essential element of a Latin examination (Politeia 2013; Jones 2013) and those who do not (Hunt 2018).

I draw much of the evidence for the value of prose composition from the authors of the textbooks which promote it themselves: these date back from 1913 to the present. For much of that period, until the 1960s, Latin's place in the curriculum was secure and the O level Latin examinations tested prose composition almost as much as translation from Latin to English (Forrest 1996). Both the examinations at that time and the books which prepared students were designed for use in academically selective schools (CSCP 2012). Rarely was literature or civilization formally assessed, it being reserved for students who went on to study Classics at university (Hunt 2013). The introduction in 1988 of the GCSE in Latin saw a decline in interest in prose composition (CSCP 2012); however, changes to the current requirements of national examinations have reintroduced it (Hunt 2018). This has seen the publication of a number of coursebooks which advocate it today, such a *De Romanis* and *Latin to GCSE*. The US experience, as I have said above, is more varied. Having no national Latin examinations of the type seen in the UK gives US teachers a great deal of autonomy to experiment and to adapt their teaching to their own interests and those of the students. US teachers' arguments of the early–mid-twentieth century in favour of prose composition are just as heavily informed by the traditional grammar-translation teaching methods of the time as the UK ones, as we shall see. But as Latin enrolments declined in the 1960s, other methods, such as reading-comprehension and communicative approaches were embraced to try to stem the loss and reverse the trend (Abbott 1998; Drake 1966). Today, there is a growing interest in communicative pedagogies for Latin in schools, which includes both speaking and free composition (Lloyd and Hunt 2021; Ancona 2021). Meanwhile, prose composition and free composition are both popular in the universities, for beginning and more advanced students of Latin, as we shall see in the next chapter. Many of the published articles about contemporary practices for writing Latin in US schools filters down from the universities.

Coursebooks for Latin prose composition: Learning from the past

I have drawn on evidence from coursebooks which include prose composition. The authors' intentions (where known) and the pedagogical concerns that the use of the books draw attention to or which arise from them can be, I think, useful guides for teachers of prose composition today:

1. Arguments that prose composition improves a student's understanding of the Latin language.

Hillard and Botting (1913/2001) provided a lengthy explanation for the importance of teaching prose composition, in comparison with Latin–English translation. Indeed, they claim that prose composition is far superior:

> It is often claimed that this method [Latin–English translation] is more interesting "because, instead of having to learn tenses and declensions, the pupil is introduced at once to a real piece of the language he is learning." This theory bears no relation to actual fact. The subject-matter of the piece of Latin which the boy [sic] at this stage is set to unravel has little or no interest for him. He despises the anecdotes [...], and would far rather, as a matter of fact, be set to learn the forms of the Latin language in a straight and orderly way, than have them filter in in piecemeal and in confusion. The method that has the most interest for the boy is the method that teaches him most quickly.
>
> Hillard and Botting 1913/2001: v–vi

Hillard and Botting's (1913/2001) arguments conflate reading and translation, and assume, according to the *mores* of the time, that the purpose of reading/translating is to learn the grammar of Latin. The purpose of learning the grammar of Latin is, it seems, to enable the student to write Latin sentences – which formed, after all, the major part of assessment at the time. The authors' disparaging reference to 'anecdotes' presumably refers to the sort of short sentences in Latin presented by teachers for translation into English, rather than longer passages. A criticism held against the translation of short sentences is that, composed as they are to illustrate grammatical features rather than to express meaningful communication, they tend to be uninteresting in themselves and lack narrative coherence, both of which are helpful in engaging the student and developing their competence.

Hillard and Botting (1913/2001) follow with an observation which might be surprising for modern readers:

> The authors believe that Latin to English translation is the harder process of the two at this stage of a boy's knowledge. [...] The turning of English into Latin is more conducive than the reverse process to a quick and accurate grasp of the forms of Cases and Tenses. And if the question of interest is raised, it is certain that the constructive,

creative element in composition absorbs a boy much more completely than the analytical element involved in translation.

Hillard and Botting 1913/2001: vi

It should be noted that the authors were school teachers at the academically selective St Paul's School. Quite whether students or teachers in less selective schools would have agreed with these points is difficult to conjecture. Nevertheless, the authors approve of the element of creativity that the process of writing involves – even though the practice consisted of translating English–Latin sentences rather than what we might consider creative writing today. Indeed, it remains a moot point as to whether translating the sentence from Exercise 182, Question 10: 'Since he has been wounded by an arrow, he will die in a few hours' (Hillard and Botting 1913/2001: 148) provides much opportunity to be a creative student at all.

2. Arguments that prose composition provides a means of appreciation of the writing of original Roman authors.

Mountford's 1930s foreword of the early-nineteenth-century *Bradley's Arnold Latin Prose Composition*, still in use today (and, indeed, used to teach me), baldly states: 'When a student has himself [*sic*] employed the language as a tool, he is better able to appreciate the achievements of the great Roman writers' (2006: 1). Such as belief continues to be maintained, as we shall see, with scanty proof.

3. Pedagogical considerations of the challenges of prose composition.

a) Attempts to ameliorate the high cognitive load

Wilding's *Latin Course for Schools: Part 1* (1949) follows a traditional grammar-translation pattern: grammar up front, followed by an assortment of Latin–English practice sentences, a Latin–English narrative passage, more English–Latin sentences, an English–Latin narrative passage and, for those still with time, some additional English–Latin and Latin-English sentences. Perhaps aware that the student might be overwhelmed by so much material, the author tries to reduce the cognitive load (uniquely, I believe, for Latin coursebooks of this period) by fairly closely matching the structure and syntax of the two narrative passages, while using the same vocabulary. Thus, we have by way of example the exercises in the box.

Exercise 34, p. 46

rursus advenae incolas Britanniae oppugnant victoriamque saepe reportant; et Druides et copias reginae Boudiccae superant; Britanniam tamen non omnino superant.

[*The foreigners again attack the natives of Britain and often win a victory; they conquer both the Druids and the troops of queen Boudicca; however, they do not conquer Britain altogether. (Author's translation)*]

Exercise 36, p. 47

The troops of the foreigners again approach and enter Britain. The nature of the land often helps the natives; at length, however, the troops almost conquer the island.

The challenge of too much too soon is echoed only two years later by Jones, in his own book *Facilitas*, where he observes that: '[my book] is written in the belief that we ask our pupils, in writing Latin, to do too much at once, with the result that they are often lost in what has been aptly called the "jungle" sentence' (Jones 1951: 1). Jones' textbook recognizes the problem that too many different types of sentence and narrative passages, back and forth between Latin and English in every combination, make an assessment of a student's strengths and weaknesses difficult for the teacher to perceive. His answer: to provide only English–Latin sentences for the first 158 pages, and, only then, 13 pages of continuous narrative passages to translate into Latin. One can detect an understanding here that the coursebook is not just a set of texts for the student to translate, but it also performs a diagnostic role for the teacher. There is a tendency for coursebooks to offer multiple examples for practice, in the belief that repetition improves learning: *Brevitas* (Hardwick 1960) belied its name, with 149 pages of exercises; while *Latin Prose Composition for the Middle Forms of Schools* (North and Hillard 1960) eclipsed even that with 195 closely-typed sentences and passages for translation into Latin. The modern UK teacher, with often only one or two hours per week to deliver a Latin GCSE over three or four years, would be agog at the enormity of it all. One has to wonder, too, what was realistic for teachers and students at the time.

b) Provision of differentiated activities

The Approach to Latin Writing coursebook (Paterson and MacNaughton 1953) provides a compendious 230 pages of exercises, sentences and extended passages. The authors did not anticipate that all students would attempt every exercise. Rather, they intended that the exercises were differentiated according to whether the students were destined for lower or higher certification. Such an approach would today be frowned upon: schools would expect teachers to provide differentiated support for students of all prior attainment, rather than providing different activities for different groups of students, as a matter of equity and fairness. Besides, few schools today enrol sufficient students for Latin to consider both a higher-attaining and a lower-attaining set.

1960s–70s compromises and the slow death of prose composition

With the removal of O level Latin as a matriculation requirement for entry to Oxford or Cambridge universities in 1960 and the beginnings of the comprehensive school movement of the 1970s onward, Latin's pre-eminent position on the curriculum rapidly began to fade (Gay 2003; Tristram 2003; Forrest 1996). What Latin could be taught to more students, from a wider variety of socioeconomic backgrounds, on a reduced timetable, with a wider range of prior attainment than before, helped to concentrate minds.

In 1962, the Classical Association published *Re-Appraisal*, a special supplement to the journal *Greece and Rome*. A response to concern about the position of Latin and classical studies in schools, at a time when the ramifications of the Oxbridge matriculation decision were beginning to make themselves felt, it aired the views of eight professors and practising teachers of Classics. Charles Brink, Kennedy Professor of Latin at Cambridge, argued for change: the O level Latin examination asked too much of students in the time available; few students who took the examination did so because it formed a foundation for the future classical scholar; it had turned into some kind of general education which had to make sense on its own; prose composition could not find space in such a 'small' Latin course, and it could be saved for later study. He wrote:

> What O level lacks is a clearly defined purpose. The course can either be, *chiefly*, an exercise in elementary prose composition, English into Latin. Or it can be, *chiefly*, an exercise in translation and reading, Latin into English. Personally, I believe the latter to be the natural choice for this course. Far too little Latin is now read, partly because the Latin which is attempted is often too hard, and partly because too much time is spent (to cite a classical headmaster's recent letter to me), "slogging away at English-Latin sentences if the boys are ever to reach O level standard as things as now." But whether it is English into Latin, or Latin into English, I suggest that it should be *chiefly* a one-way road. The sophisticated dual carriage-way of the classical tradition asks too much of the small Latinist, and offers him too little.
>
> Brink 1962: 9

Brink's observations echoed the Board of Education's 'Spens Report' of 1938, which had made similar recommendations that Latin should be taught in a way that students gained something worthwhile even if they did not go on to become classical scholars at university:

In the early stages (which may be taken as roughly covering the first two years of Latin), the *reading of Latin* should occupy the chief place, the reading matter being 'made up' Latin in the very earliest stages which will be replaced as early as possible by suitably simplified passages from Latin authors, chosen primarily as illustrative of Roman life and custom. The pupils should get on to this reading at once, and read as much as possible so as to get the 'feel' of the language. [...] Writing of Latin should not be attempted too soon, it should always be based on the matter read, dealing with the ideas, vocabulary and constructions occurring in that matter, it should be continuous rather than the writing of isolated sentences, and it should always consist of less difficult matter than the Latin which has been read. [...] Probably something like half the time spent at present in translating English into Latin can be saved by this procedure, and the time thus saved will be most profitably filled by increasing the time spent in reading Latin.

Board of Education 1938: 231–2

If Latin in schools needed a change in emphasis in 1938, it was all the more pressing for change after 1960. The debates of the 1960–70s reveal the tensions of this period about what might constitute a Latin course for all students, and what place prose composition had in it.

From the pages of *Didaskalos* came arguments thick and fast. The 1964 volume 2.1 published three arguments back to back. Lee (1964), a Fellow of St John's College, Cambridge, argued for a skills approach to learning language, modified for Latin. No one spoke Latin, he argued; therefore, both reading and writing were essential to compensate. Lee (1964) considered writing to be a more active skill than translation, and therefore a student would become more knowledgeable about the language they were reading if they also wrote in it. Unusually, an advocate for free composition, Lee's suggestions that the writing of hexameter verse and the construction of a period as ways of 'getting inside [Livy and Cicero] in a way [a student] could not before' (Lee 1964: 23) are ideas clearly more suitable for the sort of university community of which he was himself a part than for novice learners in a school.

In direct response, a page later, Bambrough (1964), a Fellow from the same university college, counteracts partially with the wry observation that the students themselves seemed to forget that prose composition was taught to help them improve their reading, rather than the other way around. If, however, prose composition was *not* going to be done, it would lead to more time spent on reading, which, he noted, rather than a passive activity as so often asserted, was actually active: 'There is much more to reading than a capacity to construe' (Bambrough 1964: 26). He dismissed arguments that prose composition had any 'special (and still less any *unique*) power to train the mind' or that it was so necessary that it could not be done without; although he did aver that its practice 'makes school-children and undergraduates read Latin [...] with close attention' (Bambrough 1964: 27), which is a less than forthright denunciation after all.

A page later, from the lofty perch of the university to the ground-level experiences of two school teachers, Leather and Reynell (1964) draw attention to the many other things that could be taught better if prose composition was taken away. The fact that these teachers taught in the academically selective Birkenhead School and Marlborough College gave added grist to the mill of their arguments: if *their* students would benefit from *not* doing prose composition, so, perhaps, would those of other, less academically selective schools. This reminder of the reality of daily life in the classroom was echoed by the Joint Association of Classical Teachers (1964), one of the subject associations for school teachers rather than for university academics. It was a simple equation: schools had less time than before to teach Latin; the removal of prose composition would provide more time for engaging students in reading, comprehending and translating more Latin.

Forward to 1966 and we find Brown, Senior Classics Master at Redruth Grammar School, advocating again for prose composition. But there is a difference to the usual practice of translation sentence by sentence: he adjured the use of even more complex passages than those habitually set for A level, designed to get the students 'under the skin of the language, into the heart of the meaning' (Brown 1966). The most important point: these passages were to be done 'as a combined effort' with students and teacher working together. Brown (1966) also advocated essay writing on a given theme, in Latin, to be completed over a period of a fortnight or more, allowing students ample time to check, refine and polish their work in response to their wider reading about the topic. Still in favour of prose composition as an examination piece, Brown, I think, showed some innovative ideas which foreshadow much of the US experiences in free composition, particularly at the university level, nearly forty years later (see below).

In dismay at the direction that the Joint Association of Classical Teachers was taking, louder voices for the retention of prose composition began to be heard. Loudest was that of Tommy Melluish (1966), one of the joint secretaries of the more traditionally minded, university-focused Classical Association and a Classics master at the Bec School, London, who had edited *Re-Appraisal* a few years before. He now set his heart on pushing back against the reality of the diminished timetable allocation that most headteachers were now providing for Latin. Declaring that 'Latin that can only come in through the portal of the eye is a dead language indeed,' (Melluish 1966: 51), thereby echoing previous arguments that reading was a passive and composition an active skill, he found the answer to bring it to life again through prose composition. Moreover, if prose composition was removed, he warned, it would give headteachers the excuse they needed to reduce the time allocated to Latin yet further. History shows us that the timetable allocation allocated for Latin in the 1960s did not improve despite Melluish's protestations. Something had to give, and that something was prose composition.

By the end of the decade, prose composition was in decline. A report from the Schools Council suggests that teachers themselves were no longer convinced of the arguments for retaining it:

Such methods are still widely used, but they are steadily giving ground to others in which the reading of continuous Latin is central from the earliest stages and grammar and syntax are introduced in a meaningful context. [...] The value of 'composition' – so long the mainstay of a classical training – is increasingly questioned. [...] What was intended to as an ancillary to reading the language came to be looked on as an end in itself and good scholarship at all levels was equated with the ability to compose. [...] In reaction to this situation, many teachers have abandoned the practice of formal composition altogether.

Schools Council 1969: 4–5

A few years later, Dexter (1973), the Assistant Director of the Oxford Local Delegacy Examinations Board, was fighting back. In a speech to the teachers of the Association for the Reform of Latin Teaching (ARLT), a more progressive group than one might have expected such a speech to be given to, Dexter made four arguments for the retention of prose composition: it helped students understand Latin better; he himself enjoyed it; it catered for those who enjoyed it; it was not compulsory. Point one merely reiterated the same unproven arguments as before. As for the reaction to points two and three, history does not relate: the ARLT was perhaps one of the more progressive groups of Latin teachers at the time, broadly supporting the new reading-comprehension courses and founded long ago for the proselytization of the Direct Method of Latin teaching. Just because one liked doing something, surely did not mean that it has to be a compulsory part of an examination: no one was stopping any teacher from teaching prose composition to their students if they wanted, even if, as it might be thought, the delegates of the ARLT might find the activity surprising. The final point, which seemed to open a door to common sense, Dexter swiftly overturned himself: he tried to convince delegates that if prose composition, at examination level, *did* become optional, another matching option would have to be found of equal difficulty, but different in form both to prose composition and to that which had already been assessed. Perhaps he felt he might get support from the delegates of the ARLT, who might have sensed an opportunity to ask for the inclusion of spoken Latin as the other option to prose composition. If so, it was not forthcoming. Perhaps, rather more cynically, he rather expected that finding an alterative would be so difficult that prose composition would have to be compulsory after all.

Pure conjecture, but Dexter's point, however, about the problems caused by optionality in Latin exams, continues to bedevil the current examinations at both GCSE and A level. How can one have an assessment of one skill, which is considered to be a facilitating one for another, when that other skill has already been assessed? You have to provide another subordinate skill of comparable challenge, or merely ask students to repeat what they have already shown they can do in another assessment. Such contortions continue to affect the current UK examinations.

Indeed, the same Schools Council (1969) report noted many of the sorts of things which were becoming common in the classroom and which continue to form many of the practice exercises in commonly used coursebooks today:

> Most of those who have [given up formal prose composition] still agree that some form of active manipulation of the language is valuable to ensure that grammar and syntax encountered in reading are fully understood, but they prefer exercises that are based on the texts read, such as question and answers in Latin, [such as] retranslation, rephrasing of passages, completion exercises or free composition. These keep the lesson closely focused to a meaningful Latin context and often require more flexibility of thought than has the traditional technique but an equal degree of accuracy.
>
> Schools Council 1969: 5

Arguments for prose composition's value were becoming less tenable. Jennings, Headmaster at Ecclesfield School in Sheffield, while not unsympathetic to those for whom time and interest provided the opportunity for it, was under no illusions about its limitations in schools like his own:

> Reading Latin makes you a better Latin reader; understanding English is best done through English; understanding how Latin 'works' is best done through secondary literature specific to the topic; if its strength lies in its difficulty, but not many can do it, then we should find easier ways of achieving that which we found so difficult.
>
> Jennings 1976: 308

Interestingly, Jennings notes that prose composition was almost unknown in girls' schools. Are we to deduce that the peculiar power of prose composition was only worthy of boys' education? Or that girls had no need of it?

John Sharwood Smith, Lecturer in Classics Education at the London Institute of Education, similarly noted the lie to the claim that prose composition (among the other traditional grammar-focused approaches) led to improvements in the students' intellectual development: 'Anyone who looked at the O level papers showed that a very large proportion of students failed to learn precision in the handling of elementary Latin sentences and unseens' (Sharwood Smith 1977: 29).

One cannot but help feel that prose composition had become merely a way of sorting out those who could from those who could not, rather than as a means of developing language proficiency for everyone. But the social mores of the 1970s meant that those who could not meet with success could no longer be so easily discarded as they might have been ten years before: such an approach would likely find no favour in the new all-ability comprehensive schools developed under a more egalitarian education system. Compared to the small minority of pupils interested enough in prose composition to want to pursue it 'there might well be a larger number, not particularly adept at composing, but interested enough in the structure of classical languages to read freely in them, and in due course in the literature' (Department of Education and Science 1977: 3). If Latin was to survive as a subject offered at all, it needed to be presented and taught in ways appealing to all. Prose composition was very much a minority interest.

The answer seemed to lie in the reading-comprehension approach. Courses, designed to maintain and perhaps improve student enrolments, were based on continuous story-based narratives, attractive to students of a wider range of prior attainment than before, and making use of more modern understandings of second language development (Gay 2003; Tristram 2003; Story 2003; Balme and Morwood 2003). Thus, the first edition of the *Cambridge Latin Course* rejected prose composition outright. *Ecce Romani* took a different perspective: while the course consists of a more or less continuous narrative, exercises were included in which students were asked to translate English sentences into Latin, using the vocabulary, forms and structures met in the previous continuous passage. In my view, the idea of rereading a passage and retrieving information from it, and then manipulating it in a new format, has some merit and is not dissimilar to the approach noted above in the case of Wilding's *Latin Course for Schools*, some thirty years earlier. It is an approach the *Cambridge Latin Course* itself took on in its later editions, in response to teacher requests, where exercises which required the manipulation of morphology recycled vocabulary and grammatical structures from the continuous narrative – activities much like the Schools Council (1969) previously reported.

The reading-comprehension courses did not meet with universal favour. Other courses tried to reach a compromise. Harrison's *Latin Reading Course*, by its very name, positions reading in the foreground; but the author is keen to provide support to traditionalists, reflecting doubt on the new-fangled reading courses:

> This course is a compromise; it is hoped a happy compromise. It is intended for those teachers who endorse the importance of acquiring reading skill as soon as possible but who are not entirely convinced of the efficacy of recent experiments in language teaching. It is 'progressive' in that English-Latin is an optional, not an integral part of it.
>
> Harrison 1971: 1

MacNaughton and McDougall's *A New Approach to Latin* held a similar view:

> It is recognised that many teachers still regard a certain amount of English-Latin composition as a useful teaching instrument, and, to meet their needs, we have provided a limited number of such exercises.
>
> MacNaughton and McDougall 1973: 5

These compromise approaches are perhaps indicative of the host of competing attentions: in a declining market, publishers needed to appeal to as many possible purchasers as they could. Without any strong sense of pedagogical principles, or even a consensus about the objectives of teaching Latin, the teachers were wont to take whatever was available, with as much variety of exercise as possible, in order to appeal to their own varying interests and those of their students, who were themselves increasingly drawn from more mixed social groups than had often been the case before. Prose composition, which in the 1970s most teachers of Latin in the UK had grown up with themselves, was something felt to be safe, stable and secure. There were ready answers, no room for manoeuvre, unlike the apparently slippery process of reading, translation and the appreciation of literature. Whether the skill of prose composition transferred itself into reading ability in a way that made it worthwhile doing seems to have been of little concern. SLD research was in its infancy; but, in the teaching of other languages, grammar-translation was being abandoned, and it is difficult to tell whether Latin teachers chose to ignore the fact or did not notice. Only the Cambridge School Classics Project employed a professional linguistic consultant in the development of the *Cambridge Latin Course*. It is significant, surely, that prose composition was not one of his recommendations for the new course. Practice, according to such observers of the time as Story (2003), Sharwood Smith (1977) and Baty (1962), suggested that skill transfer from prose composition to reading had not, in fact, being occurring – at least for most students – and acted instead as a barrier to their engagement, motivation and achievement in Latin more generally. The observations of Sidney Morris, Lecturer in Education at the University of Nottingham, suggest that alternatives to prose composition, such as language manipulation and free composition, were being used in the classroom (Morris 1966). These innovations were overwhelmed by the reality: prose composition continued to be upheld by the examination system.

The new GCSEs of 1988 changed everything. Replacing the O level and CSE examinations,[2] they were designed to enable students to attain the full range of grades through a single qualification route in all subject areas. No longer would the type of examination a student took limit a students' progression to further or higher education. While, for Latin, prose composition of various sorts continued in the classroom, the government itself recommended the practices of language manipulation and free composition: prose composition felt suitable only for the more specialized study at A level (Department of Education and Science 1988). Consequently, at GCSE it withered away, accounting for around 13–25 per cent of the total marks, sometimes compulsory, sometimes optional. By the 1990s, it disappeared from the GCSE altogether (CSCP 2012).

Back to the future: Prose composition *redux*

Of course, teachers still valued prose composition as an activity in the classroom, even if it was not formally assessed in GCSE examinations. A series of coursebooks which maintained the practice continued to find ready purchasers. The *Oxford Latin Course*, ostensibly a reading-comprehension course based on the life of Horace, places the prose composition sentences at the back, as an additional element to the main story, for those who wanted them. Oulton's *So You Really Want to Learn Latin*, designed for preparatory schools teaching Latin predominantly to boys destined for common entrance examinations for major public schools, was less coy:

> Learning Latin is not the easiest thing you could choose to do. In fact, some of you will find it devilishly difficult. But it can be done and you will just have to accept the fact that it involves a good memory and loads of discipline. [...] What's more, your mind will have done so many mental somersaults and press-ups that you will find anything else you turn to laughably easy by comparison.
>
> Oulton 1999:1

The book, with the exception of the inclusion of some line-drawing cartoons, had moved no further pedagogically than the coursebooks of fifty or more years before, with sentences and passages for translation into and out of Latin. Also designed by teachers at preparatory schools, *Latin: A Fresh Approach* (Seigel 1999) and *Variatio* (Clarke 2015) both contain more than enough sentences for translation into Latin to satisfy the entrance requirements for the most selective public schools. *Latin to GCSE* and *Latin Beyond GCSE* offered prose composition in the form of short sentences from the outset, to prepare students for the A level examinations far off in the future.

It was because of political reasons rather than any pedagogical necessity that Latin prose composition returned to the GCSE, under the education reforms of the UK Coalition Government (2010–15). The reasons are complex. The policy of the then Education Minister Michael Gove (2010–14) was to strengthen the academic rigour of all examinations at both the GCSE and A level, which he had felt had become too easy.[3] Latin GCSE, despite a reputation for being among the most difficult of subjects (Middleton 2015), did not escape notice and, in order to make it even more challenging than before, soundings were taken by the Department for Education to find a means to make it so. Some limited consultation took place, and a conference was held by the right-wing think tank Politeia, at which arguments for the reintroduction of Latin prose composition were once again rehearsed.[4] I have referred to the Politeia discussion before (Hunt 2018), but I make no apologies for revisiting it in more detail. The repetition of the same age-old, unproven arguments and cloudiness of thought make it not just an interesting if frustrating read, as if nothing had been learned from the past; but also, the ramifications for the GCSE Latin examination as a whole means it requires detailed study.

First, Sheila Lawlor, the Director of the think tank Politeia, argued that the new Latin GCSEs, to be introduced in 2014, needed to be brought further into line with ministerial thinking. In an explanatory pamphlet *Latin for Language Lovers* (Politeia 2013) she wrote:

> [The] goal: to reduce official prescription to a minimal outline of essential knowledge and liberalise the system for greater professional freedom, so that good teachers can aspire as high as they wish without being held back by the bounds imposed by

bureaucratic rules. The same aims – higher standards, greater rigour, more academic freedom – also apply to the new GCSEs.

Politeia 2013: 2

This initial statement is problematic. Lawlor conflates qualifications with curriculum. There was, of course, nothing to prevent teachers from teaching in the way they preferred at GCSE or any other level. The choices they made – the very autonomy that Lawlor desires – was already available to them: the current GCSE did not *prevent* what happened in the classroom. Assessment itself does not hold back excellent teaching: other constraints, such as time and teacher expertise do. Lawlor also made the same erroneous point as Dexter (1973): that reading is passive.[5] Like Dexter, Lawlor asserts that prose composition is the answer to this apparent classroom lethargy:

> In particular, as the authors … propose, the Latin GCSE should offer, as a clear examinable option, the opportunity to translate from English into Latin. Such an option would be welcomed by those teachers and pupils who find such work valuable and enriching.

Politeia 2013: 2

It is unlikely that anyone would object to a teacher teaching prose composition in the classroom (including myself). However, Lawlor associates the teaching of it with the promotion of the greater academic rigour which she proposes will match the Department for Education's demands. As we have seen, such an association is highly contested. If the aim of Latin teaching is to enable the student to comprehend and appreciate original Roman authors, evidence of the ability of prose composition as a tool to achieve this has been elusive. As a practice in itself, there is plenty of evidence historically that students have found prose composition hard work, to be sure (Sharwood Smith 1977; Brink 1962). Whether this is a result of the innate difficulty of the process, or because of the poor quality of the teaching or the inadequacy of resources, has never been clearly identified. It is very much debatable whether something should be included in an examination *simply because it is perceived as difficult*. Then, if prose composition is pedagogically useful, is the value obtained commensurate with the effort required? There is consensus that the GCSE Latin examination should test a student's ability to read, comprehend and appreciate original Roman authors. Prose composition is one of a set of tools to achieve that objective. It is not an objective in itself. To assess the means as well as the objective is surely wrong. We do know that the teaching of prose composition inevitably takes time away from the teaching of the very thing which other practices deliver much more efficiently – reading. If, therefore, we assume that prose composition has little value to add in the promotion of reading and takes up time that might be better spent on reading, then we are left with the idea that Lawlor was suggesting that prose composition should be assessed in a national examination *simply because some teachers like it.* Remember: teachers have the freedom to use all sort of means in the classroom (including communicative approaches, for example) which are never assessed in the examination, because the examiners rightly recognize that they are not in the business of assessing the performance of the teacher and their pedagogy, but the performance of the student at a given task.

Next, Lawlor commits an extraordinary U-turn. Recognizing that Latin, is not a National Curriculum subject and often suffers from a lack of teaching time, she suggests that prose composition will *not* form a compulsory component of the new GCSE after all (Politeia 2013). This immediately contradicts her own belief that it is *the thing* that can provide the academic rigour sorely lacking. If it was that unique *thing*, why should it now only be optional – unless academic rigour is somehow a thing reserved only for particular students? Another problem, more practical: we saw with the arguments put forward by Dexter (1973) that examination regulations would mean that if one part of the examination was optional, then there needed to be another part optional too, of *equal* difficulty. The necessity for inclusion of an option for prose composition at GCSE went on to provide a problem for the examination boards: how to find an equally challenging and pedagogically useful skill to offer as the alternative (a skill which would have to find a form of assessment that was manageable and would satisfy the Department for Education's demand for increased rigour) which had not *already* been tested in the same examination. Lawlor's arguments about the especial value (the 'high aspirations') that the teaching of prose composition conferred upon students would make the difficulty of finding a *comparably* challenging assessment even worse; when its very inclusion was purposed to provide *greater* challenge than anything else, the demand for optionality makes Lawlor's reasoning impossible.

The arguments put forward by the other presenters were much the same as those presented in the past, and are as equally clouded in misunderstanding and impracticability. For example, their assertion 'that real facility (let alone fluency) in a foreign language demands the ability to translate into it from one's native language, as well as to convert it into the mother tongue' (Politeia 2013:6) disclosed an understanding of fluency very much at odds with that of all researchers of second languages today. The authors appealed for an examination comparable with an MFL examination. This ignored the fact that the aims of learning a modern foreign language and those of Latin are not the same: for MFL, writing is one of the four communicative skills and is therefore worthy of assessment; for Latin, except in extremely rare circumstances,[6] writing must be *a facilitating skill for reading*. Therefore, the assessment should not be of the facilitating skill, but of the actual skill of reading. The familiar argument followed, of the supposedly special propensity of prose composition to develop reading skills more than can be achieved through actually reading, thereby showing a lack of knowledge of the research in foreign languages learning which indicates that there is very little transfer from one to another (see, for example, DeKeyser 2015).

Further arguments need hardly detain us: prose composition enables the writer to get beneath the skin of a Roman author, and it reveals the true nature of Latin as a concise and precise language – both of which can be taught through reading original Roman writing, surely, rather than second-guessing what they might have written. The argument that there needs to be alignment with prose composition at A level (where it still existed as an optional component of the examination) rather begs the question, bearing in mind the above, whether it should be at A level at all. Prose composition, apparently, would make teachers use terminology more carefully (an assumption – based on no evidence produced – that teachers were using terminology not very well or perhaps not at all when they were teaching their students by other means). In all, the case seemed to rest on arguments based more on personal interest than pedagogical necessity or practicality. Mercifully, more sensible counsels prevailed with a compromise: the examination officials decided that prose composition and grammar analysis questions (the 'permitted alternative') were both to be provided, of a very watered-down kind, so as not to make the examination too hard to pass, but so as to give the illusion that it met ministerial demands for greater rigour. The proposers' suggestions for the sort of English sentences which 16-year-old students should be told to translate into Latin were passed over as being far too difficult,[7] and more simple sentences provided instead.[8] And in order to accommodate these extra incursions into the examination, which was already felt to be too much to teach in the time available (OfQual 2015), the quantity of literature that was prescribed for study was reduced – a perverse decision if we remember that one of the original intentions for the introduction of prose composition was to enable students better to appreciate the writing skills of original authors. To date, the proportion of marks allocated for the prose composition or 'permitted alternative' elements is very small (10 per cent of the total for that section of the examination).

At A level, a similar demand to make prose composition compulsory was also rejected by university colleagues. However, preparation for success in this small part of the examination has a 'wash-back' effect through the rest of the curriculum, which is not to everyone's comfort.

In order to facilitate the teaching of the prose composition element in the GCSE and at A level, further books have been published, including *Latin to GCSE* and *De Romanis* for the GCSE examinations, and *Writing Latin* (Ashdowne and Morwood 2017) and *Latin Prose Composition* (Leigh 2019), for A level. They make the same arguments as heard before: 'The authors think that translating into English is invaluable for consolidating the language' (*Latin to GCSE*, Cullen and Taylor 2016: xiii); 'In the long term, by understanding the challenges faced even by the ancient writers in composing elegantly in the formal version of their language, students can come to appreciate better the style, artistry and literary qualities of the ancient authors, at least in so far as they can be seen in the choices made in their writing' (*Writing Latin*, Ashdowne and Morwood 2017: v); and '[P]rose composition gives a heightened appreciation of how Latin authors used the language to express themselves in their own particular styles' (*Latin Prose Composition*, Leigh 2019: back cover). The anonymous author of a blog post declared that, mysteriously, prose composition 'helps students become teachers; they learn grammar better' ('Sam' 2019), as if teachers (and pupils?) were not learning grammar effectively through other means.

These arguments are not sufficiently persuasive for the expenditure of so much time for so little gain. Surely, the best way to understand how to appreciate an original author is to read them, not try to convert some English into what we think they might have written if they had chosen to? Besides, even if composition has the value that the above authors say it has in language development, free composition is much more efficient and much more engaging, as we shall see below. Moreover, as an examination component, prose composition, which supposedly alerts students to the nuances of a given piece of English language (and how to turn it into Latin) clearly disadvantages those for whom English is not their first language.

Intermission: Prose composition to free composition

Commonly used modern coursebooks take different approaches to the teaching of prose composition. Tried-and-trusted models in which the grammar and vocabulary is built up step-by-step abound, differing only in the sequence of the presentation of new material. For the beginner and intermediate student, *Latin to GCSE, Ecce Romani, Oxford Latin Course, So You Really Want to Learn Latin?, Essential Latin* (Sharpley 2007), *Latin: A Clear Guide to Syntax* (Seigel 2009), *Variatio* (Clarke 2015) and *De Romanis* follow this pattern, drawing on the same vocabulary and grammar as the accompanying reading and translation materials. For the more intermediate to advanced students, publications show an increasing variety: *Writing Latin* (Ashdowne and Morwood 2017) follows the pattern set above; *Latin Prose Composition* (Leigh 2019) follows a straightforward Present-Practice-Feedback approach; *Wiley's Real Latin* (Maltby and Blecher 2014) takes an interesting diversion, asking students to translate translations from original Roman authors back into Latin (presumably for comparison with the originals); *Reading Latin* (Jones and Sidwell 1986) belies its name by providing matching prose composition exercises based on the supplementary grammar booklet; *Introduction to Latin* (Shelmerdine 2007) provides an unusual mixture of sentences to translate fully into Latin and sentences from which only phrases are to be translated; *Latin for Americans* (Ullman, Henderson and Henry 1997) provides intermittent sentences based on vocabulary and grammar from previous reading materials; *Latin for the New Millennium* (Minkova and Tunberg 2010) has a much wider variety of type of composition exercise (including alternate English–Latin/Latin–English dialogues, but not many of them. Perhaps the two most interesting books, for the advanced learner, are those which offer free composition. Introduction to *Latin Prose Composition* (Minkova 2009) suggests free composition activities based on typical Roman topics, recommending that the student models their writing on the example Latin passages provided. *Reading and Exercises in Latin Prose Composition* (Minkova and Tunberg 2004) provides students with Latin sentences, drawn from reading passages, which students are encouraged to modify. For example, the student is required to substitute words, rewrite sentences in indirect form, subordinate two clauses, compose a text from given sentences, as well as write free composition on given topics.

Models of practice

There has been very little research into students' practices in prose composition classes and it is methodologically uneven and very small scale. Nevertheless, even these investigations provide glimpses into the experiences of students in the classroom and should help refine classroom practice.

Davisson (2004) describes a number of case studies she has used in her university-level classes. In the first example (in preparation for composition exercises) she describes how her students write English paragraphs, as if written by a Roman visiting the modern world (and therefore on a modern topic). Each paragraph should contain up to five errors in English idiom which a Roman might make, with a footnote to explain to the teacher what and why. This practice, Davisson (2004) explains, serves to heighten students' awareness of how Latin expresses itself differently to English. In her second example, she discusses a writing project, in which students take their reading passages as the basis of their Latin composition and over a period of weeks, redraft and elaborate their initial simple sentences, by using increasingly sophisticated subordination, for example.

Beneker (2006) describes his own practice with intermediate students in the university. He suggests a step-by-step approach as follows:

Step 1: The student analyses the parts of a simple English sentence (subject–verb–adjective–object / subject–verb–object–adjective–indirect object) and notes the forms they would take.

Step 2: The student identifies the Latin vocabulary to match the English words.

Step 3: The student modifies each of the Latin words to the correct forms.

Step 4: The student rearranges the Latin words into more standard Latin word order.

At each step (or as required), the teacher discusses the choices made by the students. According to Beneker (2006), students should be able to internalize the steps after practice (although he notes that this seems not to happen as quickly as hoped).

Trego (2014) found that collaborative working groups, with students assigned specific roles, were a more successful as a classroom model for learning to translate sentences from the Latin coursebook *Wheelock's Latin* (Wheelock and LaFleur, 2011) than models where students worked independently and competitively.

Eales (2015) carried out a small-scale study of five advanced-level students of high attainment writing indirect statements. Recording students' discussions and comparing their translations, he noted that students frequently initially recalled Latin vocabulary correctly, but then changed their minds when they felt it did not match the English, and lacked knowledge of how to form the more irregular perfect passive and future active infinitives. Despite these significant problems in forming Latin sentences, they were able to comprehend original Latin satisfactorily. Eales (2015) suggested that prose composition was a useful tool for identifying student weaknesses in grammar knowledge.

Batchelor (2018) carried out a small-scale study of six intermediate-level students of mixed ability writing simple Latin sentences (subject–object–verb/subject–indirect object–object–verb). After various trials, the step method advocated by Beneker (2006) was found to be most effective (see above), although errors in understanding the precise meaning of the original English sentences continued to cause problems (for example, misinterpreting the continuous present 'is -ing' as an imperfect tense).

Holke (2019) evaluated the success of a small-scale class project using student-created versions of Roman political graffiti to reinforce the dative case with beginner students. Motivation and creativity were high and at the end, although students were still not confident in being able to form the correct dative endings for themselves, they were more able to identify a dative from any other tense when they saw it. Holke (2019) recommended the activity as an informal and engaging way of checking students' knowledge and understanding of the dative case.

Barrett (2020) carried out a small-scale study with thirteen beginner students, following Minkova's (2009) suggestion to base the composition around a pre-existing topic – in this case, the story of the eruption of Mount Vesuvius. Students built up, drafted and redrafted their own narratives, based on the vocabulary and sentence structures seen in their reading text. Errors were predominantly in finding the appropriate Latin vocabulary item for the sorts of idiomatic phrases the students wanted to express themselves in and in the formation of the correct persons for verb endings, the correct forms of singular/plurals nouns and adjectival agreement. As the writing became more elaborate, the number of errors increased. Nevertheless, feedback from students was generally positive, with students sharing their own stories with each other, leading to a broadly motivational effect. Barrett (2020) noted that the errors made by students served as a reminder to the teacher of what needed reinforcement in the class.

Smith and Conti (2016) recommend sentence builders as ways to help students practice writing in preparation for more complex tasks in MFL. Students select one word from each column to make a complete sentence. For very weak students, the English can be given as well. The words in each column should be from the same class and the whole selection should be semantically and grammatically related. The approach is transferable to Latin, as the two simple examples in the table show. Students choose one word from each column to complete a sentence of their own design.

Sentence builder: Example 1.

mater	est	in atrio
pater		in horto
filius		in culina
filia		in triclinio
soror		in cubiculo
frater		in via
amicus		in tablino

Sentence builder: Example 2.

neceese est	mihi	cenam	consumere.
difficile est	tibi	librum	parare.
facile est	nobis	pavimentum	lavare.
decorum est	vobis	vinum	amare.
commodum est	amico	leonem	agitare.
periculosum est	matri	coquum	legere.

Smith and Conti (2016) also recommend with the sentence builders that, in the preliminary stages, the meanings of individual words and phrases are given until a point is reached where students are sufficiently familiar with them.

Many coursebooks provide exercises where the student has to match the terminations of a Latin word to match an English sentence. These can easily be replicated on the board:

> *The girls were walking along the streets of the city.*
> *[Answer: puellae per vias urbis ambulabant.]*

Write in type: puell- per vi- urb- ambula-

Select type: puell- a/ae per vi- am/as urb- is/ium ambulaba- t/nt.

The number of alternatives should be kept initially to a minimum (singular/plural, for example), and irregular forms avoided, until students become proficient.

Free composition

In the US the early twentieth-century approach to Latin composition followed the British pattern. Articles in classical journals of the time show similar considerations. Prose composition, in the traditional manner, was said to render the learning of paradigms more meaningful (Barss 1906); to have helped with a student's understanding of English or a modern foreign language, because of its precision (Goodalf 1913); to have prevented students from thinking that there was a one-to-one correspondence of Latin and English vocabulary (Mitchell 1912); to have made the student think more about how Roman authors wrote (Duckett 1922). An interesting reflection of classroom practice can be deduced from a description given by Whitman (1926), a US Latin teacher: she notes that students made so many errors in prose composition assigned for home work that crucial class time was wasted in correcting mistakes rather than learning. Her solution, to assign them in class and to monitor and support students as they wrote, foreshadows more modern classroom techniques, where the teacher acts as a guide rather than a marker, and the assignment given is for practice rather than assessment.

The value of prose composition continued to be contested. The structural linguist Waldo Sweet (1956) made the usual arguments against it: the objective is reading; prose composition and its attendant learning of all possible inflections consumes time which might better be spent in actual reading; and the activity is dull and unrewarding to the student. Even he, however, felt that prose composition was an improvement over 'passive reading' (an argument we have already discounted above). Sweet's work with university students suggested a number of improvements, in his view, over the standard fare:

1 Selections – from Latin authors – arranged in a hierarchy of structure, beginning with single sentences and working up to continuous discourse.
2 Explanation of structure by constant contrast between English and Latin.
3 Memorization and overlearning of about 150 Latin quotations and mottoes.
4 Pattern practices based on these quotations.
5 Oral–aural work, both in class and in the language laboratory.
6 Writing of original Latin sentences which imitate Latin selections which they already know.

Sweet 1956: 9

Sweet's (1956) model released students from the burden of having to keep too many things in mind at once (a traditionally challenging aspect of prose composition) and kept them in reading Latin rather than struggling to understand underlying messages delivered in English. It also afforded them some autonomy: free to compose, but framed by models of original Latin writing. At the more advanced levels, he suggested students should study sentences from Latin which exhibit particular characteristics – such as word order or particular forms – where the signals are not English ones but Latin ones:

> This type of exercise would seem to have the following advantages over the traditional Prose Composition: a. It gives the student a sense of achievement. He has expressed his own thoughts in a foreign language. b. The emphasis is upon producing whole utterances rather than putting pieces together. c. There is little vocabulary burden; the student uses the words which he knows. d. Errors are few. e. The student *learns* something about the rhetorical. f. Reference is to a Latin model.
>
> Sweet 1956: 16

It is not known how much Sweet's ideas influenced US school classroom practice. At the US university level, prose composition seems to have continued its traditional path. In 1989, Ball and Ellsworth, two academics, in a much-read attack on the teaching of Latin Prose Composition, argued some familiar points:

1 Prose composition is a purely intellectual challenge.
2 It is elitist and scares off the less capable students.
3 Writing does not aid reading. Composition is not taught in small chucks.
4 Exercises should aid recognition of forms not their production.

Ball and Ellsworth 1989

Additionally, Ball and Ellsworth noted the apparent fallacy that prose composition enabled students to recreate an ancient author's style, adducing (like Sweet) that reading the original author was the best way of achieving it. Their statement ignited a passionate debate. Gilleland noting that in other fields of study the technique of composition was used to 'strengthen the student's knowledge', drew comparisons with a teacher of Shakespeare asking their students to compose sonnets:

> Does he expect his students to become Shakespeares? Of course not! He expects that his students will learn more about what a sonnet really is. Somehow the process of writing 'in the style of' makes the writer closer to the original author. But how can we possibly know what 'being closer' actually means? That they struggled to fit the words in metre? That they chose some words over other words? Or if a student is asked to hand in some iambic pentameter, do we expect Milton? Such nonsense is implied in the article by Ball and Ellsworth. In high school my Vergil class was occasionally asked to write dactylic hexameters, and by this personal involvement we learned a great deal about the technique of Vergil. Nor was the teacher a stereotypical elitist.
>
> Gilleland 1991: 216

But Gilleland's (1991) comparisons do not fit: the putative sonnet writers are using their own language to recreate their own thoughts in Shakespearean style. No one is assessing them on their ability to reverse-translate Latin, to find the best Latin words to represent another language, let alone recreate another author in their midst. Similarly, his schooldays' reminiscence of the occasional writing of dactylic hexameters suggests a classroom experience way beyond that of the vast majority of university students, let alone those still at school. As we have noted above, some commentators' views of the normalcy of their own experience in practice points up quite how unusual they were.

There are clearly other points to make about Ball and Ellsworth's (1989) claims. While there could be said that the process of writing into a foreign language might further develop students' knowledge of the language, in the case of Latin, as compared to a modern foreign language, the product itself has little or no practical use. The accusations of elitism probably hold, in that very few teachers today outside well-funded schools and universities are capable of it. No research exists to show whether it scares off students, but anecdotal evidence from the examinations boards themselves suggests that very many students choose the alternative to prose composition when one is available. We do know that reading and writing are separate skills, which need to be taught in different ways (DeKeyser 2015). The most-commonly adduced argument that prose composition helps reading is therefore not true. Free composition, by contrast, contributes to helping students develop better language skills of all sorts: language learning is a 'messy and unique experience' (Harris 2000: 221) and free composition is one of the practices which can provide the autonomy and opportunity for personalized expression conducive for a student to make progress at their own rate. What is more certain is that the short, disjointed sentences which students typically translate in Latin prose composition, are unlikely to promote the reading fluency that longer narratives achieve.

Although beliefs that prose composition helped students learn grammar and syntax better than through reading continued to persist (see, for example, Saunders 1993 and Pearcy 1998), the view that it was pedagogically valuable began to slip away as reading-comprehension courses began to be more frequently used in the US school classroom.

At the beginning of the twenty-first century, an increase in US Latin teachers' interest in SLA research and practices in modern foreign languages have prompted a shift from traditional prose composition to more creative forms of writing. Other factors may also have stimulated efforts to include more creative and student-centred practices, such as concern about falling enrolments (Kitchell 2015), and, in some schools, the need for Latin teachers to align with standards set by the ACTFL which pertain to modern languages. But there was also perhaps an underlying sense that traditional Latin teaching was insufficiently alluring to the modern student. Dugdale (2011), a Latin teacher, notes: '[The teacher's] obsession with traditional prose composition and the exclusion of other forms of writing, [...] hardly serve to expand students' sense of what it is possible to do with Latin' (Dugdale 2011: 3). Drawing on studies by Dörnyei and Csizer (1998) and Dörnyei and Cheng (2007), Dugdale (2011) reminds us that learner autonomy is one of the most motivational factors for language learning among students; and he adduces Swain's (1995) arguments that output (that is, written and spoken use of the language) is valuable because it pushes learners to process language 'more deeply and more consciously than is required during listening and reading' (Dugdale 2011: 2).

Free composition in practice

The experiences of teachers using free composition in the Latin class are generally in agreement that students need a great deal of practice, and that they should start learning to write very simply indeed. The British children's author and poet Michael Rosen talks about 'oral writing', that is, ways of writing down the things we say – not using elevated or heightened language: the teacher should 'release children's creativity and power' (Rosen 1989).

Researchers Kavanagh and Upton (1994) recommend a three-step process to developing pupils' writing abilities in foreign languages:

1 Writing to learn: copy-writing, note-taking, gap-filling.
2 Writing to a model: adapting a model text, working from one text type to another.
3 Learning to write: creating one's own texts suited to purpose and audience.

Kavanagh and Upton 1994

Scaffolding the writing

Several writers suggest the importance of scaffolding the topic for writing. Alison Hurrell (1999), writing in a teacher's guide for aimed at primary school students, gives some helpful hints in basic prose composition. These included writing post-storytelling activities with word banks providing the different parts of a sentence – nouns, verbs, prepositions, etc. Students were encouraged to build sentences using a different word from each pile. In this way their sentences were formed using the correct spelling and grammar before any attempt was made to write without any prompts (Hurrell 1999). Again, for MFL, Morgan (1994) suggested using images to start off – something to write about – and keeping the task short and manageable. In a study of collaborative free composition in Latin with university students, Davisson (2004) controlled for vocabulary and asked students to compare their writing with each other and share ideas with each other, thereby helping to expand knowledge of vocabulary and morphology. Again, for Latin at the university level, Kershner (2019) used culturally modern references as the starting place for writing in the style of the singer-songwriter Taylor Swift. From the university level come further reports of how scaffolded structures support students' critical awareness of Roman authors' styles.

Matz (1986) had students working on different versions of a translation from Cicero into English, translating back into back into Ciceronian style, and then comparing the different examples. They also saw if they could spot the original Cicero.

Lord (2006) had students writing Latin in the style of modern politicians. He justified this, saying:

> The requirements of students have changed: they tend to need more assistance in Latin grammar and syntax, even in the second year of language instruction, but on the other hand, they are likely to have a broader education in the sciences, humanities, and social sciences; in particular, they tend to possess a more sophisticated understanding of social history, as is consistent with overall trends in Classical Studies.
>
> Lord 2006: 2

Presumably students had a stronger personal investment in writing about someone they admired than with a piece of English prose of no particular interest to them.

Fogel (2002) developed a composition course broken into five thematic units rather than units based on grammatical constructs: (1) narrative, (2) prose rhythm, (3) rhetorical characterization of others and self, (4) ancient grammar and textual issues, (5) audience. The composition class allowed discussion about the nature and purpose of their writing, as well as developing students' technical performances.

In their research into how teachers taught fiction writing for young students of English, Wray and Lewis (1998) recommended the following scaffolding ideas:

1 Provide experience of a range of generic structures.
2 Offer a structure in which the given connectives maintain the cohesive ties of the text, helping students make sense of what they are writing about.
3 Offer a varied vocabulary of connectives and sentence beginnings, thus extending students' experience beyond the familiar and 'them'.
4 Encourage students to give a personal interpretation for the information they have gathered by the careful use of personal pronouns.
5 Ask students to select and think about what they have learnt, by encouraging them to reorder information and demonstrate understanding rather than just by copying out text.
6 Enable all student to achieve success of some, improving self-esteem and motivation.
7 Give students an overview of a writing task.

Wray and Lewis 1998: 1–2

Collaborative learning is ideal for writing projects. Riess (1909) reports how he allowed students to reuse the same vocabulary and ideas that they had been working on in translation class to extemporize on a scene from the story they have just read, in Latin, and on the board. Working with a partner or in a group leads to increased engagement and motivation, compared to on-the-spot questions in front of the class (Argetsinger 2006).

Variety of approaches

Students need to express themselves and the teacher needs to build in different sorts of opportunities to do so (Goleman 1996). Writing, therefore, does not have to be just prose. Pachler, Evans, Redondo and Fisher (2014), writing about MFL, suggest drawing or modelling with labels, instructions, composing music and songs, providing dance and commentary, poetry, programmes and posters.

Gruber-Miller (2006) describes a range of benefits that derive from writing in Latin: as well as reinforcing language skills in general and reading skills in particular, composition invites students to express their ideas, develop their writer's voice, and consider aspects such as invention, arrangement, diction, genre and perspective; it also requires effective communication with an audience. He recommends choosing an interesting subject to write about and providing several opportunities to revise what has been written. Pre-writing tasks include brainstorming ideas with the teacher on the whiteboard, collaborative working between the students, and an advisory and editing role played by the teacher (Gruber-Miller 2006). Suggestions for writing topics include:

1 Writing about things from a stimulus picture or inscription.
2 Writing a prequel or sequel for a previously read story.
3 Rewriting a passage in a different tense, or from another person's viewpoint (such as 1st person rather than 3rd), or into indirect statement.
4 Expanding sentences by elaboration (such as the addition of vocabulary or the use of subordination).
5 Writing for authentic audiences: guides, maps and charts, travel brochure, itineraries, comparisons, letters, descriptions of self or others.

After Gruber-Miller 2006

Dugdale (2011) gives further examples:

1 Creating cartoons with sentences, using vocabulary already learned; developing awareness of morphology; reinforced vocabulary; sense of achievement.
2 Writing a letter, based on an example from the Roman site of Vindolanda. Communication for real life has a motivating effect.
3 Latin haiku poetry – short and pithy, a genre-inspired puzzle.
4 Writing mottoes for each other or for an occasion.

5   Writing with a grammar point in mind (example given of comparison between two friends and their differing lives, requiring comparative adjectives).

6   Inscriptions writing – breaks habit of Subject-Object-Verb patterns.

Dugdale (2011) notes that creative writing assignments encourage more collaborative learning, as the students follow each other's compositions in and out of class. This encourages them in turn to refine and polish their work more frequently than would normally be the case when the piece is submitted to the teacher for marking. The compositions reflect their own interest in their own and the Romans' culture, and provide material for sharing with a wider audience (Dugdale suggests a school newspaper). Students take greater care over work that is seen by their peers and may be published. If the process of composition is one of multiple redrafts, error corrections can be as simple as the teacher underlining mistakes for the student to correct for themselves (Chandler 2003). Dubois (2015) suggests that underlining the correct parts of composition has a more motivating effect, but the principle of self-correction is the same. Experiences of collaborative writing in Latin suggests an increase in student creativity, engagement and motivation, which lead in turn to greater care for language accuracy.

Feedback

Although free composition does not often form part of national examinations, there is increasing interest in its use in the classroom as a tool to develop students' knowledge and understanding. Research on MFL teaching can usefully be applied to Latin. Teacher feedback can be written or oral and it should focus on a range of issues, including content, organization, language and style. It should be tailored the needs of the student at the time. Feedback should be on multiple drafts of papers, not just on the final one. Students should aim to receive feedback from several sources, including their peers, so they can benefit from different readers. The teacher needs to model the process of peer review so that everyone understands the parameters and respects the students who have produced the written work. One to one writing conferences may be more effective than written feedback; however, some students might prefer to have paired meetings with particular responsibilities (such as note-taking). Feedback should be specific and includes both encouragement and constructive criticism (Hyland and Hyland 2001). The student's text is important to them – the teacher should avoid turning it into their own. Questions should be used rather than commands, as they promote student autonomy. Content and organization should be commented on early in the writing process, leaving grammar for the end of writing. Teachers should be selective in error feedback to avoid overwhelming the student (and the teacher) with too many things to do. Indirect error correction promotes self-repair and is more beneficial than simply correcting (Lee 2008; Straub 2006; Ferris 2002, 2003).

A role for fan fiction?

The reading and writing of Latin fan fiction (fanfic) is a very small but emerging trend of interest. Fanfic is 'writing that continues, interrupts, reimagines, or just riffs on stories and characters other people have already written about' (Sawyer, Jamison and Grossman 2013: 17). This section is concerned primarily with the writing of fanfic as a pedagogical tool to develop students' knowledge and understanding of the second language.

Fanfic has a lengthy history, derivative of literature that draws from myths, oral traditions and folklore (Derecho 2006). Closer to home, Britanniae (2014) makes the same point, in a brief blog, about Ovid's *Heroides*: *even the Romans* wrote fanfic.

The author of a piece of fanfic is usually a fan of an original work of fiction. They extend a published story, using the original settings and characters, and sometimes adding in their own. The appropriation or deliberate 'misreading' of the original text enables the fan to build their own stories in the gaps within and between texts, to promote self-expression and alternate views, and to challenge its authority of the text (Jenkins 1992). The act of writing and rewriting, as well as rereading their own versions of the narrative, is central to the fan's aesthetic pleasure (Jenkins 1992). In online fan communities where fans share their own work, the negotiation of meaning, the choice of words and the negotiation of feedback through 'likes' and comments are appealing, encourage further participation and can boost self-esteem (Sauro 2020).

A number of established fan practices have been recognized:

1 Celebrating famous people or events – by the creation of collections of artefacts, building websites dedicated to the person, and participation by making contributions to websites.
2 Analysing events, stories and media – by discussion and debating.
3 Transforming and critiquing events, stories and media – through cosplay, making art, *filking* (rewriting music lyrics), *fanvidding* (editing videos), *scanlation* (fan translation of printed materials), and *fansubbing* (adding subtitles to video).

After Sauro 2020

Legal questions about copyright have meant publishers generally are not enthusiastic about this use (or abuse) of the original work. On the other hand, some publishers have welcomed fanfic as a way of maintaining interest in the original work and to establish a reading base, which can be commercially important for themselves.

For example, the *North American Cambridge Classics Project* were happy to publish Stan Farrow's *fabulae ancillantes* (NA-CCP 2007), stories based around what might be described as the alternative reality of the characters in the original *Cambridge Latin Course* book.

Much fanfic, however, exists outside the usual publications sphere of influence, and the internet has made it even more popular and widespread, with subsections of sites, such as Fanfiction.net (n.d.) and Archive of Our Own (n.d.), dedicated to the ancient world, and even to the familiar cast and settings of commonly used course textbooks, such as *Ecce Romani* and *Cambridge Latin Course* (without, one surmises, copyright permission). Many of them revolve around the standard *gen* (short for *general*) fictions, in which the fan writes alternate plotlines, characters, prequels and sequels to established storylines. I should, however, warn teachers about the sexually explicit nature of some these apparently innocuous Latin stories: the subgroups of *shipper* or relationship-based fictions and of *slash* fictions, including queer reading and transgressive fan fiction, would not be recommended for use in educational settings.

Writers of fanfic do gain knowledge through feeling and empathy (Wilson 2016). Fanfic lets fans reflect on and endorse community views, share experiences and occasionally putting themselves into the stories they write ('Susie Mays'). Fanfic written by adolescents tend to be quite simplistic, sharing jokes and experiences in the classroom rather than taking note of more serious political or historical concerns. From the limited number of works in Latin, based around the deposits in Archive of Our Own (n.d.), I briefly note the following characteristics:

1 Strongly character-driven (from a small range of 'faces' from the commonly used Latin coursebooks).
2 Simplistic plots (characters meet in the bar, street).
3 Brief historical and cultural details given, subservient to the characters and plot.
4 References to the coursebooks themselves ('insider knowledge').
5 Relationship plots, often of a transgressive kind, focusing on male–male, male–female and slave–master sexual relationships.
6 Anachronistic interpolation of modern contemporary material.
7 Mix of Latin and English languages.
8 Authorial asides.

Despite these somewhat unpromising beginnings, however, some teachers do consider fanfic to provide some glimmerings of pedagogical fruitfulness. In Black's (2006) study, fanfic writing encouraged high engagement and motivation as school-aged students discovered and developed their persona through writing and contributing. Sauro and Sundmark (2016) reported on a collaborative fanfic writing project in Sweden – 'The Hobbit Project'. Swedish university students learning

English as a Foreign Language wrote an alternative episode from *The Hobbit*, with each student taking a different character. The project developed the students' language knowledge and their appreciation of literature, as well as providing opportunities for them to engage critically with each other as they reviewed each other's contributions (Sauro and Sundmark 2016). Cormillie, Buendgens-Kosten, Sauro and Van der Veken (2021) described a similar, classroom-based collaborative fanfic writing project with school-aged students. Though the experience was generally felt to be a positive one, the authors concluded that the students' lack of knowledge of storytelling conventions, the open-endedness of the task, and lack of clarity from the teachers about the learning objectives which the activity was designed to meet, meant the project fell short of what it could have achieved. Their suggestion: more teacher scaffolding of the task, and a more obvious alignment with assessment given (Cormillie, Buendgens-Kosten, Sauro and Van der Veken 2021).

For Latin fanfic, no research is currently published. However, there are discussions of collaborative story-writing, which can broadly be described as fanfic. Some of these are loosely based on characters and events from stories in commonly used Latin coursebooks. For example, Buczek (2017) briefly describes how he develops Latin stories with his class, using familiar characters and scenes from the coursebook *Latin for the New Millennium* (Minkova and Tunberg 2010). Schwamm and Vander Veer (2021) describes something similar, with an online community of Latin leaners of school age. Meanwhile, Schwamm has developed an online community of Latin teachers who write what could be more closely described as fanfic, called 'Let's Build a Thing Together', the subject of which is derived from historical cultural events, such as Saturnalia, and which feature characters based on inscriptional evidence from original Roman tombstones (Schwamm n.d.). The apparent success of the projects suggests more widespread practice should be considered: aspects which seem to be appreciated by the participants include: writing for a real audience (for their peer group, rather than for their teacher); self-actualization; creativity and personalization; and the inclusion of personal and acquired knowledge and understanding of the ancient and modern cultural references. For example, the inclusion by students themselves of an intersex character based on Tiresias offered them opportunities not just to recall the ancient mythical references, but also to project and negotiate their own thoughts and ideas as young people of today (Schwamm and Vander Veer 2021). A number of other teachers are writing fanfic for their own students and encouraging them to write their own (see, for example, a Facebook post referring to fanfic about Grumio, a character from the *Cambridge Latin Course*, [NACCP-CLC 2020]). The team at the NA-CCP also offered a webinar on how to write fanfic based on the *Cambridge Latin Course* stories, encouraging teachers to experiment (NACCP-CLC 2019). It is clear, from the evidence of social media alone, that pedagogical uses of fanfic are – if not widespread – increasingly common.

Bahoric and Swaggerty (2015), two teachers of modern foreign languages, have suggested a number of fanfic-writing strategies of high pedagogic value for school-aged students. These could be applicable to the writing of stories in Latin, with some minor adaptations:

- Alternative universes:
    - In the coffee shop (characters interact in a coffee shop) [Latin version – in the *popina* / *taberna*].
    - Plot switch – the end of the familiar plot is different [Latin version – Hermogenes is let off and Caecilius goes to gaol (CLC, Book/Unit 1, Stage 4)].
    - Familiar characters are transplanted to a high school of college setting; good for interpersonal interactions, with potential for a 'fish-out-of-water' storyline.
- 5 x fiction: The character goes through one scene several times, slightly differently each way.
- Hurt/comfort: One of the characters is hurt or injured; the plot shows how they get healed or comforted or get better.
- Crossover: One or two characters from one story are transposed, or put into a scene from a different story.
- Alter a scene:
    - Emulate the format of the scene recently read, using your own words.
    - Rewrite the scene from a different character's point of view.
    - Rewrite the scene in a different genre type.
    - Identify stereotypical characters in the story and replace them with more respectful ones.
- Missing/deleted: Students write a scene that they think is missing from the main story or has been deleted.
- New adventure: Students write an entirely new adventure for several familiar characters; other characters of the students' own invention may be added.

After Bahoric and Swaggerty 2015

Bahoric and Swaggerty (2015) offer some cautionary recommendations: sites for fanfic, as mentioned above, are not curated and contain material which some parents and students may find offensive. The teacher, therefore, should provide a blog space for students to upload their fanfic, password-protected and accessible only to the students in the school. Similarly, if the teacher wishes students to have access to fanfic which is published online elsewhere, they should curate it and store it in the same protected blog space.

This latter area – the reading of fanfic for pedagogical reasons – has much to offer Latin teachers. Everyone agrees that input matters, and there is a wealth of fanfic in all languages for students to read, and through other sorts of digital literacies, including filking, fanvidding and fansubbing. The author is reminded of a conversation he had with his own daughter aged 14, who was so obsessed by the Harry Potter film franchise, that she watched endless loops of fansubbed slideshows of scenes edited from video because there were insufficient stories to satisfy her interest. While there are, to the author's knowledge, very few examples of digital Latin fanfic of this kind to use, the creation of examples for pedagogical use by or for students is not especially difficult. Thorne and Reinhardt (2008) suggested that schooling needed to make use of the multiple communicative channels which digital media had opened up, and acknowledge the salience it had for students and for learning. Teachers need to keep up with their students, provide and encourage the production of media which appeals to them. Perhaps it is now time for the subject community to develop a secure, curated website, where students could share fanfic in all its forms.

Notes

1. For details of the development, decline and fall of prose composition in Britain in the twentieth century, see Stray (2003, 2018), Story (2003) and Forrest (1996).
2. The O level examination (1951–87) was designed for entrants from the top 20 per cent of the ability range, with the CSE (1965–87) for the next 40 per cent (Waddell 1978). There were no Latin examinations available in CSE.
3. For details of the complaints about the curriculum and qualifications that the Department for Education felt necessitated change, see, e.g., the accounts by Woodhead (2009), Peal (2014) and Isaacs (2015). For details of the discussions between Government Coalition partners about measures to increase the challenge of existing qualifications, see Laws (2016: 210–22), Seldon and Snowdon (2015: 395–405) and Bennet (2019: 213–64). For more circumspect records of the period, see Ball (2017), Finn (2015), Seldon and Finn (2015) and Exley and Ball (2011).
4. I was present at the Politeia conference, 'Latin for Language Lovers', which explored the rationale for the reintroduction of Latin prose composition, among other topics. The Director of Politeia, Sheila Lawlor, asked by me, denied that the conference was funded by the Department for Education or its ministers. David Butterfield, one of the authors of the report circulated afterwards, said it was designed to 'catch the Minister's ear' (personal communication, 24 February 2021) at a time when, during the GCSE qualifications reforms, Latin risked not being included in the languages group of the EBacc (a group of academic subjects favoured by the minsters), which might result in further decline in state-maintained schools.
5. The misconception of reading as a passive activity is a recurrent theme for advocates of prose composition. See, e.g., Jones (2013) and 'Sam' (2019). For details of why reading is very much an active process, see, e.g., Nuttall (2005).
6. In my search for an occasion in which a person might *choose* to write Latin in order to communicate, I found an example of my own, in which I had a short

conversation in Latin with a Russian professor during an online international conference, through the Zoom chatbox function – the common language being Latin. Such occurrences are, it has to be said, rare, having occurred once in forty-five years in my own professional experience.

7. The exemplar sentences were: (a) After Troy had been captured, Ulysses was sailing home. (b) But a god sent fierce winds to kill all the sailors. (c) At last the ship reached an island on which a giant lived, called Polyphemus. (d) Polyphemus was so cruel that he wanted to eat Ulysses and his friends. (e) That night, while Polyphemus was sleeping, Ulysses ordered his men to put a stake into the giant's eye. (f) In this way Ulysses overcame Polyphemus and escaped to his ship (Politeia 2013).

8. The exemplar sentences from the OCR examination were: (a) The girls were walking to the forum. (b) The slave is able to work in the garden. (c) We greeted the son of the man.

References

Abbott, M. (1998). Trends in Language Education: Latin in the Mainstream. In R. LaFleur, *Latin for the 21st Century: From Concept to Classroom* (pp. 36–43). Glenview, IL: Scott Foresman -Addison Wesley.

Ancona, R. (2021, 25 Feb.). Some Evolving Ideas on Latin Pedagogy: Texts, Methods and Assessment. Unpublished Paper presented at the International Online Conference, 'Teaching Classical Languages in the 21st Century – *Vitae Discimus*'. Tblisi.

Argetsinger, K. (2006). Peer Teaching and Cooperative Learning in the First Year of Latin. In J. Gruber-Miller, *When Dead Tongues Speak: Teaching Beginning Greek and Latin* (pp. 68–85). Oxford: Oxford University Press.

Ashdowne, R. and J. Morwood (2017). *Writing Latin: An Introduction to Writing in the Language of Cicero and Caesar.* Bristol: Bristol Classical Press.

Bahoric, K. and E. Swaggerty (2015). Fanfiction: Exploring In- and Out-of-School Literacy Practices. *Colorado Reading Journal*, 26: 25–31.

Ball, R. and J. Ellsworth (1989). Against Teaching Composition in Classical Langauges. *Classical Journal*, 85 (1): 54–62.

Ball, S. (2017). *The Education Debate*, 3rd Edition. Bristol: Policy Press.

Balme, M. and J. Morwood (1996). *Oxford Latin Course. Part 1.* Oxford: Oxford University Press.

Balme, M. and J. Morwood (2003). The Oxford Latin Course. In J. Morwood, *The Teaching of Classics* (pp. 92–4). Cambridge: Cambridge University Press.

Bambrough, R. (1964). The Value of Prose Composition – II. *Didaskalos*, 1 (2): 26–7.

Barrett, G. (2020). An Experiment with Free Latin Prose Composition with a Year 10 Latin Class in a Non-Selective Girls' School. *Journal of Classics Teaching*, 41: 33–41.

Barss, J. (1906). The Teaching of Latin Prose Composition. *The New York Latin Leaflet*, 7 (158): 1–5.

Batchelor, D. (2018). Introducing Prose Composition to Year 9 Students: Strategies for Developing Confidence in English to Latin Translation. *Journal of Classics Teaching*, 38: 18–26.

Baty, C. (1962). Classics in the Schools: A Survey of the Position and Prospects. In The Classical Association, *Re-Appraisal* (pp. 10–14). Oxford: Clarendon Press.

Beneker, J. (2006). *Variations on a Theme: An Experiment in Latin Prose Composition.* Retrieved from CPL Online 3.1. Available at: https://camws.org/cpl/cplonline/files/Benekercplonline.pdf.

Bennet, O. (2019). *Michael Gove: A Man in a Hurry.* London: Biteback Publishing.

Black, R. (2006). Language, Culture, and Identity in Online Fanfiction. *E-Learning*, 3 (2): 170–84.

Board of Education (1938). *Report of the Consultative Committee on Secondary Education, with Special Reference to Grammar Schools and Technical High Schools.* London: His Majesty's Stationery Office.

Brink, C. (1962). Small Latin and the Classics. In The Classical Association, *Re-Appraisal* (pp. 6–9). Oxford: Clarendon Press.

Bristow, C. (2021). Reforming Qualifications: The How, the Why and the Who. *Journal of Classics Teaching*, 43: 60–3.

Britanniae, B. (2014, March 5). *Ovid's Heroides: The Original Fan Fiction.* Retrieved from Latin Language Blog, web blog. Available at: https://blogs.transparent.com/latin/ovids-heroides-the-original-fan-fiction/.

Brown, J. (1966). Prose Composition Again: The Case for Composing. *Didaskalos*, 2 (1): 175–81.

Buczek, C. (2017, 23 Jan.). *Building a Latin 1 Curriculum.* Retrieved from Hybrid Latin; Building Reading Proficiency. Available at: http://hybridlatin.blogspot.com/2017/01/building-latin-1-curriculum.html.

Chandler, J. (2003). The Efficacy of Various Kinds of Error Feedback for Improvement in the Accuracy and Fluency of L2 Student Writing. *Journal of Second Language Writing*, 12 (3): 267–96.

Clarke, E. (2015). *Variatio: A Scholarship Latin Course.* Unknown: Self-published.

Cormillie, F., J. Buendgens-Kosten, S. Sauro and J. Van der Veken (2021). 'There's Always an Option': Collaborative Writing of Multilingual Interactive Fanfiction in a Foreign Language Class. *CALICO Journal*, 38 (1): 17–42.

CSCP (1970). *Cambridge Latin Course*, 1st Edition. Cambridge: Cambridge University Press.

CSCP (2012). Changing Demands in Latin and Ancient Greek Examinations 1918–2021. Cambridge: Unpublished.

Cullen, H. and J. Taylor (2016). *Latin to GCSE: Part 1.* London: Bloomsbury Academic.

Davisson, M. (2004). *Prose Composition in Intermediate Lati: An Alternative Approach.* Retrieved from CPL Forum Online 1.1. Available at: https://camws.org/cpl/cplonline/files/DavissoncplFORUMonline.pdf.

DeKeyser, R. (2015). Skill Acquisition Theory. In B. VanPatten and J. Williams, *Theories in Second Language Acquisition* (pp. 94–112). London: Routledge.

Department of Education and Science (1977). *Classics in Comprehensive Schools: Matters for Discussion, 2*. London: Her Majesty's Stationery Office.

Department of Education and Science (1988). *Classics from 5 to 16*. London: Her Majesty's Stationnery Office.

Derecho, A. (2006). Archontic Literature: A Definition, a History, and Several Theories of Fan Fiction. In K. Hellekson and K. Busse, *Fan Fiction and Fan Communities in the Age of the Internet: New Essays* (pp. 61–80). Jefferson, NC: McFarland & Co.

Dexter, N. (1973). Changing Pattern of Examination. *Latin Teaching*, 35 (1): 8–16.

Dörnyei, Z. and H.-F. Cheng (2007). The Use of Motivational Strategies in Langugae Instruction: The Case of EFL Teaching in Taiwan. *Innovation in Language Learning and Teaching*, 1 (1): 153–74.

Dörnyei, Z. and K. Csizer (1998). Ten Commandments for Motivating Language Learners: Results of an Empirical Study. *Language Teaching Research*, 2 (3): 203–29.

Drake, G. (1966). The Classics in the Secondary Schools of the United States. In JACT, *JACT Pamphlet 3: Classics in the USA* (pp. 47–57). London: Joint Association of Classical Teachers.

Dubois, J. (2015, 8 Feb.). *How to Teach Writing*. Retrieved from A Witch in Agen, web blog. Available att: http://tprs-witch.com/how-to-teach-writing/?fbclid=IwAR0mEO6 21bOIeHc2PVMh9DyCAoMbk8xqMzTXQEruNPFRbv35MpWkCOXy6PM.

Duckett, E. (1922). 'Latin Prose' and Modern Learning. *The Classical Journal*, 17 (8): 430–7.

Dugdale, E. (2011). *Lingua Latina, Lingua Mea*: Creative Composition in Beginning Latin. *Teaching Classical Languages*, 1–23.

Eales, J. (2015). What Some Students Found Challenging about Indirect Statement in Prose Composition. *Journal of Classics Teaching*, 31: 19–31.

Exley, S. and S. Ball (2011). Something Old, Something New: Understanding Conservative Education Policy. In H. Bochel, *The Conservative Party and Social Policy* (pp. 97–117). Bristol: Policy Press.

Fanfiction.net (n.d.). *Fanfiction.net/community/latin*. Retrieved from Fanfiction.net. Available at: https://www.fanfiction.net/community/Latin/62046/.

Ferris, D. (2002). *Treatment of Error in Second Language Student Writing*. Ann Arbor, MI: University of Michigan Press.

Ferris, D. (2003). *Response to Student Writing: Research Implications for Second Language Students*. Mahwah, NJ: Lawrence Erlbaum.

Finn, M. (2015). *The Gove Legacy*. London: Palgrave Macmillan.

Fogel, J. (2002). Towards Beauty and Joy in Latin Prose Composition. *The Classical World*, 96 (1): 79–87.

Forrest , M. (1996). *Modernising the Classics: A Study in Curriculum Development*. Exeter: University of Exeter Press.

Gay, B. (2003). The Theoretical Underpinning of the Main Latin Courses. In J. Morwood, *The Teaching of Classics* (pp. 73–84). Cambridge: Cambridge University Press.

Gilleland, B. (1991). Elitist Professors and the Teaching of Prose Composition. *The Classical World*, 84 (3): 215–17.

Goleman, D. (1996). *Emotional Intelligence: Why It Can Matter More than IQ.* London: Bloomsbury.

Goodalf, G. (1913). Latin Prose Composition in College. *The Classical Weekly*, 6 (22): 170–4.

Grauberg, W. (1997). *The Elements of Foreign Language Teaching.* London: Multilingual Matters.

Gruber-Miller, J. (2006). Teaching Writing in Beginning Latin and Greek. In J. Gruber-Miller, *When Dead Tongues Speak: Teaching Beginning Greek and Latin* (pp. 190–214). Oxford: Oxford University Press.

Hardwick, M. (1960). *Brevitas.* London: University of London Press.

Harris, V. (2000). Towards Independence in Language Use and Language Learning. In K. Field, *Issues in Modern Foreign Languages Teaching* (pp. 220–36). London: Routledge Falmer.

Harrison, J. (1971). *Latin Reading Course.* London: G. Bell and Sons.

Hillard, A. and C. Botting (1913/2001). *Elementary Latin Exercises.* London: Gerald Duckworth and Co.

Holke, J. (2019). Graffiti on the Walls: An Action Research Plan on How Making Authentic Opportunities for Student Composition Helps Latin 1 Comprehension. *Journal of Classics Teaching*, 39: 101–4.

Hunt, S. (2013). 50 Years of Classical Civilization. In JACT, *Fifty Years of the Joint Association of Classical Teachers* (pp. 24–33). London: Joint Association of Classical Teachers.

Hunt, S. (2018). Getting Classics into Schools? Classics and the Social Justice Agenda of the UK Coalition Government, 2010–2015. In A. Holmes-Henderson, S. Hunt and M. Musié, *Forward with Classics: Classical Languages in Schools and Communities* (pp. 9–26). London: Bloomsbury Academic.

Hurrell, A. (1999). The Four Language Skills. In P. Driscoll and D. Frost, *The Teaching of Modern Foreign Languages in the Primary School* (pp. 67–83). London: Routledge.

Hyland, H. and K. Hyland (2001). Sugaring the Pill: Praise and Criticism in Written Feedback. *Jounral of Second Language Writing*, 10: 185–212.

Isaacs, T. (2015). Qualifications: What Constitutes Real Qualifications Reform? In R. Peal, *Changing Schools: Perspectives on Five Years of Education Reforms* (pp. 35–44). Woodbridge: John Catt Educational.

Jenkins, H. (1992). *Textual Poachers: Television Fans and Participatory Culture.* London: Routledge.

Jennings, A. (1976). The Copernican Revolution in Classics. *Didaskalos*, 5 (2): 296–309.

Joint Association of Classical Teachers (JACT) (1964). *Classics and the Reorgansiation of Secondary Schools. JACT Pamphlet 2.* London: Joint Association of Classical Teachers.

Jones, O. (1951). *Facilitas.* London: Blackie & Son.

Jones, P. (2013, 22 June). It's Vital that Children Translate English to Latin at GCSE. *The Spectator.*

Jones, P. and K. Sidwell (1986). *Reading Latin.* Cambridge: Cambridge University Press.

Kavanagh, B. and L. Upton (1994). *Creative Use of Texts: Pathfinder 21.* London: CILT.

Kershner, S. (2019). What Can Taylor Swift Do for Your Latin Prose Composition Students? Using Popular Music to Teach Poetry Analysis Skills. *Teaching Classical Languages*, 10 (2): 1–24.

Kitchell, K. (2015). 'Solitary Perfection?' The Past, Present and Future of Elitism in Latin Education. In E. Archibald, W. Brockliss and J. Gnoza, *Learning Latin and Greek from Antiquity to the Present* (pp. 166–83). Cambridge: Cambridge University Press.

Laws, D. (2016). *Coalition*. London: Biteback Publishing.

Leather, L. and A. Reynell (1964). Classics without Prose Composition. *Didaskalos*, 1 (2): 28–30.

Lee, A. (1964). The Value of Prose Composition – 1. *Didaskalos*, 1 (2): 22–5.

Lee, I. (2008). Understanding Teachers' Written Feedback Practices in Hong Kong Secondary Classrooms. *Journal of Second Language Writing*, 17 (2): 69–85.

Leigh, A. (2019). *Latin Prose Composition: A Guide from GCSE to A Level and Beyond*. London: Bloomsbury Academic.

Lloyd, M. and S. Hunt (2021). *Communicative Approaches for Ancient Languages*. London: Bloomsbury Academic.

Lord, K. (2006). *Imagining Nelson Mandela in Ancient Rome: A New Approach to Intermediate Latin Prose Composition*. Retrieved from CPL Online 3.1. Available at: https://camws.org/cpl/cplonline/files/Lordcplonline.pdf.

MacNaughton, E. and T. McDougall (1973). *A New Approach to Latin: 1*. Edinburgh: Oliver & Boyd.

Maltby, R. and K. Blecher (2014). *Wiley's Real Latin: Learning Latin from the Source*. Oxford: Wiley-Blackwell.

Matz, D. (1986). Cicero and His Imitators: A New Method of Teaching Prose Composition. *The Classical Journal*, 81: 352–4.

Melluish, T. (1966). Latin Prose Composition. *Latin Teaching*, 32 (2): 50–4.

Middleton, F. (2015, 2 Nov.). *Difficult Latin Risks Remaining a Qualification for Elite Pupils*. Retrieved from The Conversation. Available at: https://theconversation.com/difficult-latin-risks-remaining-a-qualification-for-elite-pupils-49987.

Minkova, M. (2009). *Introduction to Latin Prose Composition*. Mundelhein, IL: Bolchazy-Carducci Publishers.

Minkova, M. and T. Tunberg (2004). *Readings and Exercises in Latin Prose Composition*. Newburyport, MA: Focus Publishing.

Minkova, M. and T. Tunberg (2010). *Latin for the New Millennium*. Mundelein, IL: Bolchazy-Carducci Publishers.

Mitchell, B. (1912). The Teaching of Latin Prose Composition in the Secondary School. *The Classical Weekly*, 6 (4): 26–9.

Morgan, C. (1994). Creative Writing in Foreign Language Teaching. *Language Learning Journal*, 10 (1): 44–7.

Morris, S. (1966). Viae Novae: *New Techniques in Latin Teaching*. London: Hulton Educational Publications.

Mountford, J. (2006). *Bradley's Arnold Latin Prose Composition: Foreword and Updates*. Wauconda, IL: Bolchazy-Carducci.

NA-CCP (2007). fabulae ancillantes *(Units 1 and 2: North American Cambridge Latin Course).* Cambridge: London.

NACCP-CLC (2019, Dec.). *Cambridge Latin Course: Extensive Reading Using CLC Fan Fiction.* Retrieved from NACCP-Cambridge Latin Course. Available at: https://cambridge-events.webex.com/recordingservice/sites/cambridge-events/recording/e8aebe8bfb324c93a0a8c21b819e0c9e/playback.

NACCP-CLC (2020, 17 Dec.). Retrieved from NACCP-Cambridge Latin Course, Facebook update. Available at: https://www.facebook.com/groups/137750056237616/permalink/3951580424854541.

North, M. and A. Hillard (1960). *Latin Prose Composition for the Middle Forms of Schools.* London: Rivingtons.

Nuttall, C. (2005). *Teaching Reading Skills in a Foreign Language.* London: Macmillan Education.

OfQual (2015, June). *Analysis of Responses to Our Consultation on Conditions and Guidance for GCSE Ancient Languages.* Retrieved from OfQual. Available at: https://assets.publishing.service.gov.uk/government/uploads/system/uploads/attachment_data/file/433506/analysis-of-responses-to-our-consultation-on-conditions-and-guidance-for-gcse-ancient-languages.pdf.

Organization for Transformative Works (n.d.). *Archive of Our Own.* Retrieved from Archive of Our Own. Available at: https://archiveofourown.org/.

Oulton, N. (1999). *So You Really Want to Learn Latin: Book 1.* Tenterden: Galore Park Publishing.

Pachler, N., M. Evans, A. Redondo and L. Fisher (2014). *Learning to Teach Foreign Languages in the Secondary School.* London: Routledge.

Paterson, J. and E. MacNaughton (1953). *The Approach to Latin Writing.* Edinburgh: Oliver & Boyd.

Peal, R. (2014). *Progressively Worse: The Burden of Bad Ideas in British Schools.* London: Civitas.

Pearcy, L. (1998). Writing Latin in Colleges and Schools. *The Classical World*, 92 (1): 35–42.

Politeia (2013). *Latin for Language Lovers: Ancient Languages, the New Curriculum and GCSE.* London: Politeia.

Radice, K. (2020, May 1). *De Romanis.* Retrieved from Ckassics for All, Reading Room. Available at: https://classicsforall.org.uk/reading-room/ad-familiares/de-romanis.

Riess, E. (1909). Latin Prose in the High School. *The Classical Weekly*, 3: 161.

Rosen, M. (1989). *Did I Hear You Write?* London: Andre Deutsch.

'Sam' (2019, 5 Nov.). *Prose Comp: The Case in Favour.* Retrieved from Quinquennium. Available at: https://www.quinquennium.com/prose-comp-the-case-in-favour/.

Saunders, E. (1993). The Value of Latin Prose Composition. *The Classical Journal*, 88 (4): 385–92.

Sauro, S. (2020). Fan Fiction and Informal Language Learning. In M. Dressman and R. Sadler, *The Handbook of Informal Language Learning* (pp. 139–51). Chichester: Wiley Blackwell.

Sauro, S. and B. Sundmark (2016). Report from Middle-Earth: Fan Fiction in the EFL Classroom. *ELT Journal*, 70 (4): 414–23.

Sawyer, A., A. Jamison and L. Grossman (2013). *Fic: Why Fanfiction is Taking over the World*. Dallas, TX: Smart Pop.

Schools Council (1969). *Teaching Classics Today: A Progress Report*, Working Paper No. 23. London: Her Majesty's Stationnery Office.

Schwamm, J. (n.d.). *Let's Build a Thing Together*. Retrieved from Facebook. Available at: https://www.facebook.com/groups/1234021126973733.

Schwamm, J. and N. Vander Veer (2021). From Reading to World-Building: Collaborative Content Creation and Classical Language Learning. In M. Lloyd and S. Hunt, *Communicative Approaches for Ancient Languages* (pp. 47–54). London: Bloomsbury.

Seigel, M. (1999). *Latin: A Fresh Approach*. London: Anthem Press.

Seigel, M. (2009). *Latin: A Clear Guide to Syntax*. London: Anthem Press.

Seldon, A. and M. Finn (2015). *The Coalition Effect, 2010–2015*. Cambridge: Cambridge University Press.

Seldon, A. and P. Snowdon (2015). *Cameron at 10*. London: William Collins Books.

Sharpley, G. (2007). *Essential Latin*. London: Routledge.

Sharwood Smith, J. (1977). *On Teaching Classics*. London: Routledge and Kegan Paul.

Shelmerdine, S. (2007). *Introduction to Latin*. Newburyport, MA: Focus Publishing.

Smith, S. and G. Conti (2016). *The Language Teacher Toolkit*. CreateSpace Independent Publishing Platform. Self-published.

Story, P. (2003). The Development of the Cambridge Latin Course. In J. Morwood, *The Teaching of Classics* (pp. 85–91). Cambridge: Cambridge University Press.

Straub, E. (2006). *Key Works on Teacher Response*. Portsmouth, NH: Boynton/Cook Heinemann.

Stray, C. (2003). Classics in the Curriculum up to the 1960s. In J. Morwood, *The Teaching of Classics* (pp. 1–5). Cambridge: Cambridge University Press.

Stray, C. (2018). *Classics in Britain: Scholarship, Education, and Publishing*. Oxford: Oxford University Press.

Swain, M. (1995). Three Functions of Output in Second Language Learning. In G. Cook and B. Seidlhofer, *Principle and Practice in Applied Linguistics* (pp. 125–44). Oxford: Oxford University Press.

Sweet, W. (1956). *A Substitute for Prose Composition in the Teaching of Latin*. Retrieved from University of Michigan. Available at: deepblue.lib.umich.edu.

Taylor, J. (2009). *Latin Beyond GCSE*. Bristol: Bristol Classical Press.

Thorne, S. and J. Reinhardt (2008). 'Bridging Activities', New Media Literacies, and Advanced Foreign Language Proficiency. *CALICO Journal*, 25 (3): 558–72.

Trego, K. (2014). Composition, Competition, and Community: A Preliminary Study of the Use of Latin Composition in a Cooperative Learning Environment. *Teaching Classical Languages*, 5 (2): 70–85.

Tristram, D. (2003). Classics in the Curriculum from the 1960s to the 1990s. In J. Morwood, *The Teaching of Classics* (pp. 6–19). Cambridge: Cambridge University Press.

Ullman, B., C. Henderson and N. Henry (1997). *Latin for Americans*. Woodland Hills, CA: Glencoe/McGraw-Hill.

Waddell, J. (1978). *The Waddell Report: School Examinations.* London: Her Majesty's Stationery Office.

Wheelock, F. and R. LaFleur (2011). *Wheelock's Latin.* New York: Collins.

Whitman, D. (1926). An Experiment in Teaching Latin Prose Composition in Small Classes. *The Classical Weekly*, 19 (25): 210–13.

Wilding, L. (1949). *Latin Course for Schools: Part 1.* London: Faber and Faber.

Wilson, A. (2016). *The Role of Affect in Fan Fiction.* Retrieved from Transforamtive Works and Cultures, 21. Available at: https://journal.transformativeworks.org/index.php/twc/article/download/684/570.

Woodhead, C. (2009). *A Desolation of Learning.* Chippenham: Pencil-Sharp Publishing.

Wray, D, and M. Lewis (1998). An Approach to Scaffolding Children's Non-Fiction Writing: The Use of Writing Frames. In G. Shiel and N. Dhalaigh, *Developing Language and Literacy: The Role of the Teacher.* Dublin: Reading Association of Ireland.

6

Access, Diversity and Inclusion

The challenges

It is undeniable that in the recent past the Classics as a discipline have been utilized in ways which are to us now horrific and reprehensible.[1] Jacques Bromberg, Professor of Classics at the University of Pittsburgh, notes with distaste how 'fantasies about independent, yeoman farmers, soldier-citizens, amateur athletes, happy slaves, and avuncular slave-owners have whitewashed crueller realities' (2021: 8) and criticizes the dominance of elite perspectives, texts and orientations common in classics education. That white supremacists and misogynist groups in the US continue erroneously to use Classics to substantiate their beliefs has long been noted and deplored (Bostick 2021; Mackay 2021; Jackson 2020; Zuckerburg 2019; Bond 2018). Political groups, too, have often tried to validate their arguments with problematic references to the ancient world (Morley 2018; Wyke 2012; DuBois 2001). De Pourcq (2020) notes a continuing tendency for classical references to be more championed by conservative, usually populist and nationalist, politicians than others.[2] It is easy to get carried away finding ever more negative things to say.

On the other hand, the Classics has also long been an inspiration, both for rulers and for the ruled, from all social and educational backgrounds.[3] Many have used their knowledge of the Classics as a force for good in society (Beard 2021). As someone who has worked all my professional life in schools, in teacher training and in curriculum development, I see the emancipatory role that learning about the classical world and its languages performs for students in terms of subject knowledge, intercultural competence and subject knowledge – and I want to see more of them having that experience.

It is remarkable that for so long a time a subject which has as one of its raisons d'être the study of the people of the ancient world has been so myopic about the people it is being taught to. Latin's role as gatekeeper to an elite education is over. But turning Latin into a gateway to the riches and experiences of the ancient world that is open for all students remains a challenge. At the school level, there are three main challenges: to increase access, to attract and retain a more diverse body of students, and to improve the representation of the diversity of the ancient world itself in school resources. This chapter explores some of the problems that have been identified as disincentives for attracting students, and what actions have been set in train to improve the situation.

Access to Latin

The lack of access for students across the UK to Latin and classical subjects at the school level has been recently documented by Hunt and Holmes-Henderson (2021). They draw attention both to the geographical imbalance (with London and the South-East being the location of most schools where classical subjects are offered), and to the fact that most of the schools which provide Latin to examination level are fee-paying. In the recent past, a number of projects supported by the government have tried to improve matters (Hunt 2016a). Within the last decade, the Department for Education (DfE) has given Latin official recognition as a permitted language study at Key Stage 2 in primary schools, and has included Latin among the languages recommended for study at Key Stage 4 in secondary schools as part of the English Baccalaureate measure.[4] However, state-backed interventions have not always succeeded as well as they might where there is a mismatch between national policy directives and subject needs (Hunt 2018b).[5]

University outreach schemes, part of the widening participation sector, have been particularly effective in raising awareness of classical subjects at the university level for students who perhaps have not been not able (for reasons given above) to study them in school (Searle et al. 2018). Oxford University established an online digital leaning platform for teaching Latin to students from local state-maintained schools (Searle 2019). The University of Warwick, through its Warwick Classics Network,[6] provides a hub for schools in Coventry and surrounds. Linked with the Coventry City of Culture event of 2021, Warwick is being hugely successful in attracting ethnically diverse and socially mixed state-maintained schools to introduce classical subjects, including Latin, on their curricula, using a wide-ranging set of activities, based on the archaeology of Roman Coventry, Virtual Reality pedagogy, an annual festival of classical drama, and professional development events (Grigsby 2020). State-independent school partnerships, encouraged by the DfE since 1988 to share resources and expertise, have been successful in helping students from state-maintained schools access specialist teaching for Latin.[7]

To accommodate growth in schools, the need for more Latin teachers becomes increasingly strong. DfE policies have varied over the last eight years resulting in a boom-and-bust supply model: numbers of training places on traditional PGCE course have been reduced, capped and then uncapped, causing uncertain provision; while school-centred training routes have been encouraged, not without some success.[8] However, the total number of training places is never certain from one year to the next, teacher bursaries for training fees have ranged wildly, and the complicated routes by which one can qualify as a teacher have led to a distinct problem for growth in schools where there has never been a Latin teacher before. There is still a shortfall in qualified Latin teachers each year.

A number of non-governmental organizations have stepped in to fill the gap. The charity Classics for All has taken by far the biggest role and since 2010 has supported teacher training, resources and curriculum development in 429 primary and 390 secondary schools, many in areas where there has been no previous provision of any classical subject (CfA 2020).[9] It achieves this through tailored support programmes, an annual summer school for teachers, online continuing professional development through seminars provided by eminent academics, and advocacy work.

Advocating a Classical Education (ACE), a project led by Edith Hall and Arlene Holmes-Henderson, encourages state-maintained schools to offer non-linguistic classical studies through professional development events and advocacy. At the primary level, The Iris Project, Classics in Communities and the Primary Latin Project have all raised the profile of Latin in various ways, with resources and teacher training support (see, for example, Bell 2018; Wing-Davey 2018; Maguire 2018; Robinson 2018; Bracke 2013, 2016, 2018). While the dedication of numerous individuals in developing numerous small-scale programmes is to be praised, a single, coherent, age-suitable Latin programme for these, the earliest stages of learning, has not yet been agreed upon, meaning that numerous small-scale projects often fail to reach sustainability. This is all the more incredible if one considers that this is the only point at which the DfE legitimizes the study of any classical subjects.

While such projects are clearly of benefit to students, there is a risk that what is offered to students at Key Stage 2 is more of a language study in which Latin plays a part, rather than the beginning of the study of Latin itself.

In the US, there is a similar mix of providers, although the lack of nationally agreed qualifications and a curriculum provide their own challenges. The American Classical League,[10] which provides Latin teachers with resources and professional development, plays an important advocacy role with national government and education departments. The Society for Classical Studies has an *Ancient Worlds, Modern Communities* programme, for which it offers grants to organizations to develop community-led projects which promote critical discussions of or creative responses to ancient Mediterranean studies. There is a thriving network of local subject associations, usually university-based, which promote classics and help to provide pedagogical insight and support. There has been a long tradition of Latin for literacy projects in schools in areas of social and economic disadvantage (see, for example, Polsky 1998; Masciantonio 1984; Mavrogenes 1977). Building on these, a number of organizations have continued to develop programmes to introduce younger students to the classical world, often with a Latin for literacy angle. These include the Aequora programme, run by The Paideia Institute in New York, the Ascanius Youth Classics Institute, and the National Junior Classical League. Service education (whereby, for example, university students visit local schools to provide curriculum enhancement through inspirational talks and extra-curricular lessons) is a popular course of action undertaken in both the US and the UK. The lack of alignment between school and university terms and the lack of continuity can be practical difficulties for both partners and, as Butterworth points out, service education can easily fall into 'a rhetoric of helping disadvantaged groups which often undermine the very goals of equal collaboration and social change that [they] aim to achieve' (Butterworth 2017: 5). Service education is attractive to universities, it provides employment experience for their students; it is appealing to students – many of whom commence teacher training after graduation. I see it as a step towards a more long-term solution, in which schools themselves take on the responsibility of teaching classical subjects for themselves.

Diversity and inclusion

In the US, Bostick (2020c) notes the long-standing under-representation of black students on Latin programmes at high school, a result of discriminatory practices not just at the individual school level but also, she claims, by the subject associations themselves, when they seem to promote Latin for the more privileged rather than for everyone. In the UK, records of student numbers enrolled in Latin classes are not kept and it is not possible to discern what proportion of them are from ethnic minority backgrounds; however, where Latin is offered in schools, it tends to be that it is a subject studied by all students across the school for at least one or two years, before it becomes optional. My personal observations are that the number of students from ethnic minority backgrounds starting Latin is becoming more representative of the local communities which schools serve.[11] However, teachers should not be complacent – indeed, the recent testimony of Princeton Classics Professor Dan-el Padrilla Peralta (Poser 2021), of British Indian student Yaamir Badhe (2020) at Oxford and of Zhao Gu Gammage (2021), a seventh-grade American Asian student, bear witness to the continuing perception among some BIPOC students that the study of classics on either side of the Atlantic may not be for them. Part of the problem must lie in the fact that many teaching resources insufficiently represent the diversity of ancient world. Latin is not alone. In the UK, for example, the Royal Historical Society deplored the 'lack of diversity and inclusion in narrow school and university curricula has resulted in fewer BME students choosing to engage in non-compulsory study of history' (2018) and called for sweeping changes. Priggs, writing in *Teaching History*, notes:

> [Students] need to learn about communities which are very different from themselves. They need to learn about communities that feel far from their own ancestry. They need to learn about matters of race, ethnicity, culture, class or religion that broaden their experience rather than mirror it.
>
> Priggs 2020: 11

Simply put, students need to see themselves in the textbooks, and they also need to see the other – the marginalized, the little heard and little seen. The study of classical subjects suffers a similar problem – and a similar opportunity. In a thought-piece in the *Times Literary Supplement*, Professor Josephine Quinn asks for a reconsideration of what is studied at the university level:

> 'Ancient History' courses are still almost exclusively concerned with Greek and Roman topics, and the notion of the Greeks and Romans as the founders of Western civilization remains fashionable. It comes in progressive versions where Athens provides us with models for participatory politics, philosophy and public discourse, and which tend to ignore the slaves, the veiled women, their male guardians, and the restriction of political participation to ethnically pure Athenian citizen men.
>
> Quinn 2020

Quinn's comments may equally be applied to schools: Latin textbooks have tended to pay insufficient attention to the range of people and experiences in the ancient world, focusing mostly on the 'Great Deeds' and 'Famous Men' of traditional Roman history. This is despite much research carried out over the last fifty years to uncover the hidden lives and silenced voices of women, children, enslaved people and others. Sawyer (2016) observes how few people of colour and women there are in commonly used Latin coursebooks, and how much gender-stereotyping; even the exemplar stories drawn from history often reinforce stereotypes. In the same vein, Bostick notes:

> Secondary teaching materials reinforce [...] exclusionary narratives. The majority of secondary textbooks provide an unnecessarily narrow – and often inaccurate – glimpse into ancient Roman life by centering the experience of elite, fair-skinned people.
>
> Bostick 2019a

But the purpose of a history curriculum is to help broaden students' horizons, not narrow them. Priggs suggests that when students develop an understanding of the diversity of the past, they gain 'the necessary substantive and disciplinary grounding to make sense of diverse narratives [and] to develop historical perspectives and dispositions to challenge narratives that might conceal certain voices' (Priggs 2020: 11). Priggs concludes:

> Students should 'see themselves' in the curriculum, while also building their knowledge and understanding of a diverse past that takes them into the unfamiliar.
>
> Priggs 2020: 11

However, many Latin coursebooks reflect the idea of the distant past as a kind of nostalgic, golden age – a kind of *retrotopia* in which all that was in the imagined past was somehow for the good (Bauman 2017). Bostick notes how school Latin coursebooks still present the values of Rome as a model for living today; but the Rome they present is 'an imaginary place constructed from manipulations and omissions' (Bostick 2020c: 291). She goes on:

> The nostalgic myth of 'the golden past' requires the creation of a world where rape is romance and enslavement [is] a benign work arrangement.
>
> Bostick 2020c: 291

In their ground-breaking book, *From Abortion to Pederasty: Addressing Difficult Topics in the Classics Classroom*, Rabinovitz and McHardy (2014) describe a number of experiences and make recommendations for discussing difficult, emotive and sensitive issues in the university classroom. School students deserve no less. The choice of texts for study are a case in point. It is easy to skim through the more uncomfortable aspects of teachers' favourite reading material or texts selected for public examination: Caesar's *De Bello Gallico* is the story of what we would today describe as a crime against humanity (Bostick 2020a); Ovid's *Metamorphoses* are rape narratives dressed up as romances (Raaflaub 2021; Bostick 2020b). While teachers see themselves as capable of handling such texts sensitively, time is often lacking and they often lack the experience and confidence (Hunt 2016b). This begs the question whether they should be set at the school level in the first place.

The representation of the ancient world in commonly used beginner coursebooks is of as much concern. The inaccurate and unsympathetic representation and stereotyping of women in commonly used Latin coursebooks have long been criticized (Joffe 2019; Churchill 2006). The impact on students' perceptions of Roman women is not insignificant, often maintaining incorrect understandings of their role in ancient society and reinforcing contemporary stereotypes (Amos 2020; Upchurch 2014). Another area of concern is the misrepresentation of enslaved people. Bostick has drawn attention to the past errors of judgement made by institutions such as the US Junior Classical League in their trivializing of slavery and oppression through the promotion of events such as mock Roman slave-auctions (Bostick 2019b, 2020d). But the representation of Roman slavery in commonly used Latin textbooks has also been of concern for making slavery seem harmless and even humorous (Bostick 2018; Di Giulio 2020). Supplementary materials for the *Cambridge Latin Course* invited its readers to play a game of chance and write a 'Diary of a Slave', in which the successful outcome was to be set free for having completed a good deed for the master. Parodi (2020) has shown the deleterious impact coursebook materials can have on students' understanding of a complex and difficult issue. Such events and materials have rightly come under increasing criticism and have been discontinued (Bostick 2018, 2019b, 2020d).

The problem is more than just the overt imagery and storylines and choice of cultural materials which form the majority of the coursebooks. The choice of words which a coursebook or teacher uses to represent the ancient world also makes a difference to students' perceptions of it (Dugan 2020). Even the Latin vocabulary used to exemplify grammar can be problematic (for example, the use of the noun *servus [enslaved person]* as a common chart form for the 2nd declension; the problematic translations of *servus* as *slave* and *ancilla* as *slave-girl/maid*; and the tropes of the 'happy slave' and of the Roman enslaver as one who is kind when they use their power of manumission to reward 'good acts' (Dugan 2019, 2020; Robinson 2017).

Take, for example, the story *venalicius [The slave dealer]* from Stage 3 of the first book of the *Cambridge Latin Course* (UK 4th Edition), which students typically encounter after a few weeks into a beginners' Latin course. It exemplifies many of the difficulties together. Joffe (2019) has discussed this passage in detail, but a few points here draw out the theme: Melissa, a foreign-born enslaved woman, is sold by the slave dealer Syphax, depicted in the accompanying illustration as a racial stereotype, is bought by Caecilius, the fair-skinned male Roman, and is shown off serially to the family, including two males (the son and another enslaved person) and another, passive female – Metella, Caecilius' wife. A 'joke' at the end of the story – designed originally by the authors to add salience to a grammatical feature – reinforces the prejudices on several levels: *Melissa Grumionem delectat. Melissa Quintum delectat. eheu! ancilla Metellam non delectat [Melissa pleases Grumio. Melissa pleases Quintus. Oh dear! The enslaved woman does not please Metella].*

I am now horrified to confess that I have taught this passage perhaps a hundred times since I started teaching 30 or more years ago, with barely a thought about the objectification of the women, the casual stereotyping of the non-Romans, and the blind acceptance of a financial transaction in which one human being is sold to another. As a beginning teacher, I was focused on the language – the accusatives, the new vocabulary *(habet [has], venit [comes], ridet [laughs])*. As I became a more confident teacher, I became more interested in the way the story was structured so that the new vocabulary was introduced in a way that was logical and which supported the meaning of the story. Focused as I was on the language as intended, the story provided an opportunity to practice recognition of the accusative singular and its function in the sentences, conveniently repeated one after the other. As I became a more skilful teacher, in recognizing the centrality of the story as the medium for language learning rather than as an accessory, I began to realize that the narrative itself was deeply problematic: the buying and selling of a young, enslaved woman, a transaction between two enslavers, made supposedly palatable by some 'jokes'. While the accompanying image has been slightly redrawn in the most recent editions, the narrative itself, reminiscent of the slightly risqué, British sitcom era of the 1970s when it was first authored, has not changed at all.[12] In retrospect, one can say that this passage was 'not right' when it was originally written; more, that I was something of an ingenu when I started teaching it and should have known better. In the early twenty-first century, however, it ought not have a place in a school coursebook, and I now advise against its use in the classroom – although it provides a notable cautionary tale for teacher trainees. In response to a rise in complaints, the publishers have recognized the highly problematic nature of this and other passages in the book and has undertaken a rewriting of the whole course.

Teachable moments

Latin texts, whether in the coursebook or elsewhere, often contain challenging material. But it is the subject matter's very difficulties that make them worthwhile objects of study (Rabinovitz and McHardy 2014). The teacher should not hide them –their silence about brutal acts (such as rape narratives) can signal acquiescence (Hunt 2016b). Teachable moments arise all the time and the teacher should be encouraged to make use of them, within the bounds of decorum, institutional protocols and personal confidence (Sawyer 2016; Hunt 2016b). A number of teachers have written in more detail about their own practices. Barnes (2018) directed a discussion of Graeco-Roman colonization narratives from the Alexandria stories of the *Cambridge Latin Course* to help students develop their understanding of multicultural societies. Other teachers have used a contrastive approach to develop students' more nuanced understandings of the ways in which narratives choose to represent and misrepresent events for their intended audiences: Dutmer (2020), using a modern account of slavery as a corrective to its representation by an ancient source; Ancona using a contrasting pair of Latin narratives – one from a surprising source:

> I paired Cornelius Nepos' Life of Hannibal with a simple-to-read Latin novella called *Cloelia* by Ellie Arnold based on comprehensible input's limited word count. We looked at views of patriotism, importance of family, loyalty, and heroism through the *juxtaposed lenses* of a Roman enemy man (Hannibal) and a young Roman girl (Cloelia).
>
> Ancona 2021

It is possible to go further. In the teaching of modern history, Westerlund (2018) has shown how students and teachers can explore how the textbook itself manipulates their perspective. In the case of Latin textbooks, Di Giulio (2020) suggests that the students' exploration of the ways in which textbooks choose to represent the ancient world can help them develop racial competency. According to De Giulio, five aspects should be considered:

1 The choice of illustrations.
2 The use of loaded vocabulary.
3 The presentation of the storyline.
4 The presentation of the heroes of the piece.
5 The authors' perspectives.

After Di Giulio 2020

In a paper presented at the CSCP Annual Conference in 2020, Latin teacher Lottie Mortimer detailed similar practices with her beginning Latin students with the *Cambridge Latin Course* (Mortimer 2020). The practice has considerable potential, but I note that it requires a high level of sophistication that may be beyond students at this early stage who have been learning Latin for only a few weeks. There is a danger that the practice, meant entirely well, serves to undermine the authority of the rest of the coursebook and therefore contributes to the kind of feelings of exclusion in the students that the teacher is trying to avoid.

In sum, if the coursebook itself becomes the problem and gets in the way of helping students to understand an historical issue, then changes need to be made to it.

Improving Latin coursebooks

It is generally agreed, then, that the subject matter of school Latin coursebooks needs to be broadened to include more diverse voices, and to be deepened to encourage students to develop more sophisticated critical and analytical skills. The Latin coursebook is for many students the first view into the ancient world: getting it right is essential.

The development of the *Cambridge Latin Course* has been well documented (Story 2003; Forrest 1996). Its rich and sophisticated narrative made use of cutting-edge scholarship into the Roman sites of Pompeii, Aquae Sulis, Fishbourne and other sites. It is still a model in Latin coursebooks for its integration of archaeological realia and language. Its digital resources have led the way in improving access to Latin (Lister 2015; Griffiths 2008). Without losing any of the things which makes it a distinctive beginner–intermediate coursebook, however, CSCP has had to respond to valid criticism of the way that the *Cambridge Latin Course* represents women, enslaved people and ethnic diversity. The addition in the US 5th Edition of more female characters with their own storylines met with general approval that the publishers were starting to move in the right direction. However, that the new female character Lucia was killed off at the end of the first book and a failure to attend to some of the bigger problems of the coursebook's representation of enslaved people was not felt by teachers to have gone far enough, and it has meant a systematic rewriting and redrawing of the course, for the UK 5th Edition, still in progress. This includes the removal of the word *servus [enslaved person]* from the demonstration charts in favour of *amicus [friend]*; the separation of the authentic voices of the Romans themselves from the authorial voice of the publishers (thereby providing students and teachers the critical distance needed to test Roman attitudes more effectively); the development of more and stronger female characters, including the 'survival' of the female character Lucia beyond Book 1; and the complete rewriting or removal of the more offending storylines. The story *venalicius [the slave dealer]* mentioned above has been entirely rewritten as *ornatrix [the hairdresser]*, in which the more obviously lascivious attentions of the male characters have been replaced with the enslaved female character Melissa's feelings about her new surroundings in Caecilius' family's house: *Caecilus Metellam vocat. Metella ancillam intente spectat et Caecilium laudat. Melissa villam circumspectat. Melissa est anxia. [Caecilius calls Metella. Metella looks closely at the enslaved girl and praises Caecilius. Melissa looks around the house. Melissa is worried.]* Such changes are an improvement over what went before; whether they will meet teachers' expectations is currently not known.

Hands-Up Education have recently published a new Latin course for beginners: *Suburani*. A reading-comprehension based course, the continuous narrative contains a number of appealing features for a modern audience: a strong female lead from a lower-class non-nuclear family unit; a multi-ethnic supporting cast; a no-holds barred exploration of the riches, poverty and degradation of Roman society in the first century CE (Delaney, Smith, Tims, Smith and Griffiths 2021).

Other resources which more fully diversify the Latin curriculum are in progress: Maria Haley's *Ancient Herstories* blog aims to introduce younger students to narratives in which women of all sorts take centre stage (Haley and Cosgrave 2020). The Latin coursebook *De Romanis* contains a number of passages which feature strong female characters. A number of recently published Latin novellas feature LGBTQ+ themes, as we have seen above (for details of resources, see Appendix 2). Others are interested in making fuller use of neo-Latin authors, amongst whom more female writers are represented, and the subject matter is varied. Leite (2021) uses Joseph de Anchieta's natural history writing to engage and motivate her students in Brazil, with tales of local beasts such as armadillos and anteaters. Hendrickson (2018) advocates a new range of school texts of neo-Latin authors, along the lines of the traditional standard commentaries, to bring them easily to the notice of teachers and curriculum designers. He notes a number of neo-Latin books for school use, including *Latin of New Spain* (Williams 2016) and *The Neo-Latin Reader* (Riley 2016). Hendrickson argues:

> While few would advocate dumping Vergil, it is perhaps time for Classics to rethink the chronological narrowness of its Latin canon, or at least to assess the value of including more non-canonical authors in the curriculum. A re-evaluation is particularly in order given that our field's emphasis on the Latin of ancient Rome has a lot to do with assumptions inherited from those Neo-Latin authors that we don't value enough to teach.
>
> Hendrickson 2018

Arguments about pedagogy

Debates over teaching approaches in modern foreign languages is criticized by Lockey (2020), who argues that a discussion of whether one teaching approach or another is more or less equitable distracts from the bigger narratives about resources. But a number of practitioners have suggested that in the case of Latin, where the traditional approaches, such as grammar-translation, survive, pedagogy does need to change. Pearcy notes 'it is no surprise that most people, especially adults, who study Latin in this way develop no fluency in the language' (Pearcy 2005: 93). In a blog, US Latin teacher John Bracey suggests that the traditional, analytical approach of grammar-translation actively dissuades students from continuing their studies:

> Unfortunately, far too many Latin programs have embraced exclusivity rather than seeking to counteract it. Often this takes the form of making pedagogical choices that advantage a select few students and disadvantage the rest. I am not saying that all, or even most, of these teachers are *trying* to create homogenous classes. I am saying that certain practices have and will continue to create exclusive programs, regardless of intent.
>
> Bracey 2017

These views are echoed by US Latin teachers, Lance Piantaggini (2020a–b) and Rachael Ash (2019) who argue that teaching approaches which use comprehensible input are likely to be more equitable in the classroom because they are centred on the student's understanding which develops from their personal experience. In a 2018 article in the Canadian journal *Ceres*, teacher Jade Wells suggested Latin enrolments in schools could increase if more use was made of TPRS approaches to learning Latin, saying:

> Though Latin is naturally a difficult language to master, it is made unnecessarily more difficult by [the] Grammar-Translation Method [GTM]. The lack of participation opportunities and predominantly the lack of practice in Latin is the main cause of such difficulty. Grammar-based language courses have been condemned by experts in SLA due to their lack of inclusivity of different learning styles since there are few opportunities for participation and even fewer opportunities for variation of activities. It is an elitist view that if a student cannot survive Latin in its current state (GTM), then that student is not suited to learn Latin. Instead, this is hindering Latin study as a whole, when the field can be made much more accessible at the introductory and intermediate level.
>
> Wells 2018: 51

Nadhira Hill, a US BIPOC graduate student of archaeology, posits the de-centring of the teacher in the classroom:

> Sure, it may be comfortable to continue to do what you feel has worked in the past. But keep in mind that what works and may be convenient for you, as the instructor, may not work for your students. Absence of complaint does not necessarily mean that nothing is wrong.
>
> Hill 2021

It seems to me that the teacher's role is very much moulded by the demands of the pedagogical approach. Grammar-translation, and, to a lesser extent, reading-comprehension, place the teacher at the front: the source of knowledge and expertise and the provider of guidance. But, as Reay (2017) and Hammond (2015) have shown, formalized, teacher-centred lessons may not often be conducive to the learning habits of many students from culturally or linguistically diverse or deprived socio-economic backgrounds. Hammond argues that traditional learning methods in which 'knowledge is taught and processed through story, song, movement, repetitive chants, rituals and dialogic talk' still work, even in 'today's print-heavy and tech-savvy society' (Hammond 2015: 127). To this point, active approaches, for which the language provides the means of the joyful exchange of information about and for each other, may be more likely to shape teacher and student into engaged, motivated and enthusiastic co-learners. How students develop sufficient linguistic knowledge to cope with reading the sort of complex original Latin texts routinely set for examination, however, needs further investigation.

Usualizing diversity

Teachers need to make the school curriculum full of diverse characters. *Teacherhead* blogger and ex headteacher Tom Sherrington (2020) describes this as 'usualizing diversity', where the characters just fit into the everyday classroom rather than are pointed out as special or extraordinary cases. Kaufman (2020), arguing for a campaign for getting more Black History into the classroom, makes the case for a complete and thorough investigation where it is represented in the curriculum already, and then for getting it into the specifications and into teacher training, for developing and using better resources, for linking with community activists' work, and for getting university historians and schools to work together. I have to say that in the UK, at least, in the field of classics education, much of this is already happening.[13] Examination specifications include a wider range of authors and topics for study; university teacher training courses explicitly address the issue of diversity in the ancient world and how to teach it; and university–school links (many accessed via social media) have become common and well used.

Conclusion

Latin – more than a language – is getting its house in order. All school subjects have to be more than just academics. Pike noted the real value of Latin in helping students learn something about themselves as well as something about others:

> We can study the people who used the language as a means to interact with each other, so that we can better understand how we interact within our own communities, building empathy, active listening skills, and our own creativity in the process.
>
> Pike 2016: 7

Teachers know that students bring much to the class as well as take away from it. What will they find there? Will it turn them away? Will it attract them and keep them? Will they feel they can make a contribution and come away knowing they have made a difference?

Resources
Further reading

Akala (2018). *Natives: Race and Class in the Ruins of Empire*. London: Two Roads.

Hammond, Z. (2015). *Culturally Responsive Teaching and the Brain*. Thousand Oaks, CA: Corwin.

Kara, B. (2020). *A Little Guide for Teachers: Diversity in Schools*. Thousand Oaks, CA: Corwin.

Olusoga, D. (2017). *Black and British: A Forgotten History*. Macmillan.

Olusoga, D. (2020) *Black and British*, child-friendly version of the 2017 book. London: Macmillan Children's Books.

Reay, D. (2017). *Miseducation: Inequality and the Working Class and Education*. Bristol: Policy Press.

Sobel, D. and S. Alston (2021). *The Inclusive Classroom: A New Approach to Differentiation*. London and New York: Bloomsbury Educational.

Emdin, C. (2016). *For White Folks Who Teach in the Hood, and the Rest of Y'all Too*. Boston, MA: Beacon Press.

Useful websites

ACL Commitment to Change. Available at: https://www.aclclassics.org/Commitment-to-Change/Commitments-to-Change (ACL n.d.).

CSCP set of web blogs for teachers of classics. Available at: https://www.cambridge.org/gb/education/blog/.

Talking about Hard Things in the Latin Classroom, Benjamin Joffe (2020).

Building Equitable Relationships in the Latin Classroom, John Bracey (2020).

Power in Representation: Teaching Classical Women in the Latin Classroom, Maureen Lamb (2020a).

Uplifting Student Voice and Empowering Student Choice in the Latin Classroom, Maureen Lamb (2020b).

6 Questions with Skye Shirley, Founder of Lupercal, Skye Shirley (2020).

Combatting Ableism in the Latin Classroom, Jen Jarnagin (2020a).

Latin is for Everyone: 7 Ways to Incorporate Inclusive Images in Your Classroom, Jenn Jarnagin (2020b).

CSCP BLM statement. Available at: https://www.cambridgescp.com/black-lives-matter-statement-cscp (CSCP n.d.).

Five Tips for Teaching Racial Competency with *Racially Biased Textbooks: A 21st Century Skill for Classicists*, Tom Di Giulio (2020).

Multicultural Classics website resources. Available at: https://multiculturalclassics.wordpress.com/teaching-resources-for-all-levels/ (MRECC n.d.).

NLE Statement on Diversity and Inclusion. Available at: https://www.nle.org/News-Announcements/ArtMID/433/ArticleID/34/The-National-Latin-Exams-Statement-on-Diversity-and-Inclusion (NLE 2019).

The **Our Voices** conference provided a space for members of traditionally marginalized groups to share not only their research and pedagogy, but also their personal experiences in academia (Our Voices Conference 2020).

The **Pharos** website has three purposes: to document appropriations of Greco-Roman culture by hate groups online; to expose the errors, omissions and distortions that underpin these groups' interpretations of ancient material; and to articulate a politically progressive approach to the study of Greco-Roman antiquity. See: http://pages.vassar.edu/pharos/ (Pharos n.d.). Pharos has recently published a set of teacher resources.

SCS resources for further reading of antiracist articles and links, related to the study of the ancient world. Available at: https://classicalstudies.org/education/antiracist-resources-links-and-lists (SCS 2020).

Syke Shirley's website lists women Latinists throughout history. Available at: https://www.skyeshirley.com/women-latinists.

Towards a More Inclusive Classics (online conference held through the Institute of Classical Studies in 2020). Available at: https://ics.sas.ac.uk/events/towards-more-inclusive-classics (Institute of Classical Studies 2020); report at: https://cucd.blogs.sas.ac.uk/files/2020/09/GOFF-AND-PETSALIS-DIOMIDIS-Inclusive-Classics-Report.pdf (Goff and Petsalis-Diomidis 2020).

Writing about Slavery/Teaching about Slavery: *This Might Help*, P. Gabrielle Foreman et al. community-sourced document: https://docs.google.com/document/d/1A4TEdDgYslX-hlKezLodMIM71My3KTN0zxRv0IQTOQs/mobilebasic (Foreman n.d.).

Notes

1. See, e.g., the ways in which classical ideas and motifs were appropriated and used in repellent ways by, among others, European colonizers (Bradley 2010) and the Nazi leadership (Chapoutot 2016). More recently, nationalists from European countries continue to draw erroneous inspiration from the ancient world. Koo (2000) describes an extraordinary attempt by the French National Front spokeswoman to defend the teaching of ancient languages and use ancient precedent to argue for modern discriminatory immigration policies:

   > Plus grave, des membres du Front national <<défendent>> à leur manière les langues anciennes: le 2 mai 1990, un discours de Marie-France Stirbois, alors membre du FN, prônait à l'Assemblée nationale l'example d'Athènes pour ses lois discriminatoires à l'égard des métèques. [More seriously, some members of the National Front 'defend' the ancient languages in their own way: on 2nd May 1990 a speech by Marie-France Stirbois, then a member of the National Front, delivered to the National Assembly the example of Athens for its discriminatory laws against resident foreigners.]

   > Koo 2000: 5

2. This can cut both ways. For example, in the UK, Prime Minister Boris Johnson's use of Latin and ancient Greek tags encourages in the media a negative association of Classics with an elite education: a stick with which to beat him (Moore 2020). Johnson (2000) himself disavows this: his opportunity to learn the Classics is something he says he would like everyone to have, and in his former patronage of the UK charity Classics for All, which works to introduce classical subjects into state-maintained schools across the UK, he lent visible and financial support. It

should also be pointed out that, in the UK at least, the formal study of classical subjects, has not always been restricted to those in elite, private schools: under the grammar school system, many working-class children had access to formal Latin teaching – myself included (see Mandler 2020, for a recent historical overview of the changes in UK education policy towards grammar schools).

3. For example, for the impact of Classics on the ideas of the Founding Fathers of the US, see Winterer (2002) and Richard (1995, 2008); for its positive impact on the education of the British working classes, see Hall and Stead (2020) and Hall (2018).

4. Examples of the positive impact of these measures for establishing Latin in state-maintained schools can be seen in Holmes-Henderson, Hunt and Musié (2018); the experiences of secondary school teachers reintroducing Latin can be read in Hunt (2018a, 2020b), and those of primary school teachers in Reynard (2020) and Maguire (2012). The sudden and unexpected announcement of a £4,000,000 fund to establish more Latin in state-maintained schools indicates a more positive attitude from the Department for Education (DfE 2021). Practical details are awaited at the time of writing.

5. In particular, the demands of the UK national eximnation system for classical subjects and its fitness for purpose, have recently come into question (Bristow 2021; Hunt 2021; Hodgkinson 2021).

6. Warwick Classics Network, available at: https://warwick.ac.uk/fac/arts/classics/warwickclassicsnetwork/.

7. The policy started in 1988 and has undergone numerous changes, including being abolished. It was resurrected in 2019; see, e.g., Schools Together (2021). The York ISSP (n.d.) has been highly successful in enabling students from local state-maintained schools to learn Latin in local independent school weekend classes.

8. The Harris Academy ITE, Liverpool College ITE and the new Coventry online PGCE are gradually increasing the number of established routes into teaching Latin. The traditional PGCE courses at the University of Cambridge, King's College London and the University of Sussex continue to provide the highest number of teacher trainees in Classics (Hunt 2020a).

9. Disclaimer: I am a trainer and consultant for Classics for All.

10. American Classical League, available at: https://www.aclclassics.org/.

11. See, e.g., the successful introduction of Latin and classical studies in multiethnic schools in Leicester (Reynard 2020) and in North-East London (Hogg 2017). I also draw evidence from the schools with which my university teacher training course is partnered and those with which I have worked directly to introduce Latin through the charity Classics for All.

12. It should be noted that, in the UK at least, many of the BBC sitcoms presented for 'family viewing' in the 1970s are no longer released on terrestrial TV due to their stereotyping of women and people from minority ethnic backgrounds.

13. The Welsh Government has added learning about the the stories of Black, Asian and minority ethnic people into guidance for the new Welsh school curriculum to start in September 2022 (Welsh Government 2021).

References

ACL (n.d.). *Commitments to Change.* Retrieved 11 March 2021, from American Classical League. Available at: https://www.aclclassics.org/Commitment-to-Change/Commitments-to-Change.

Akala (2018). *Natives: Race and Class in the Ruins of Empire.* London: Two Roads.

Amos, E. (2020). A Case Study Investigation of Student Perceptions of Women as Seen in the Cambridge Latin Course in a Selective Girls Grammar School. *Journal of Classics Teaching,* 42: 5–13.

Ancona, R. (2021, 25 Feb.). *Some Evolving Thoughts on Latin Pedagogy: Texts, Methods and Assessment.* Tblisi: Unpublished Paper presented at the International Online Conference, 'Teaching Classical Languages in the 21st Century – *Vitae Discimus'.*

Ash, R. (2019). Untextbooking for the CI Latin Class: Why and How to Begin. *Journal of Classics Teaching,* 39: 65–70.

Badhe, Y. (2020, 8 July). *'Fancy an Indian Studying Greek!' How I Found My Place in the Classical Tradition as a British Indian.* Retrieved 11 March 2021, from *The Oxford Student.* Available at: https://www.oxfordstudent.com/2020/07/08/fancy-an-indian-studying-greek-how-i-found-my-place-in-the-classical-tradition-as-a-british-indian/?fbclid=IwAR2YzusvjWR6j4FXpewSSIvlQW2_uNeBX0CMsYQUf6n1-t-G-RiLCRmmnBk.

Barnes, J. (2018). Developing Students' Ideas of Diversity in the Ancient and Modern Worlds through the Topic of Alexandria in the Cambridge Latin Course, Book II. *Journal of Classics Teaching,* 37: 1–9.

Bauman, Z. (2017). *Retrotopia.* Cambridge: Polity.

Beard, M. (2021). *Is Classics Toxic?* Retrieved 11 March 2021, from *Times Literary Supplement.* Available at: https://www.the-tls.co.uk/articles/is-classics-toxic/?fbclid=IwAR1k4rh1-ezeldU_2lYLCnDwKLjz1UDQU-Ez4Ea_5-SyGMJDT10cVKpYXYM.

Bell, B. (2018). Delivering Latin in Primary Schools. Minimus – The Mouse that Made Latin Cool. In A. Holmes-Henderson, S. Hunt and M. Musié, *Forward with Classics: Classical Languages in Schools and Communities* (pp. 111–16). London: Bloomsbury Academic.

Bond, S. (2018, 30 August). *The Misuse of an Ancient Roman Acronym by White Nationalist Groups.* Retrieved from *Hyperallergic.* Available at: https://hyperallergic.com/457510/the-misuse-of-an-ancient-roman-acronym-by-white-nationalist-groups/.

Bostick, D. (2018, 28 Feb.). *Teaching Slavery in the High School Latin Classroom.* Retrieved 11 March 2021, from *in medias res.* Available at: https://medium.com/in-medias-res/teaching-slavery-in-the-high-school-latin-classroom-ce4146827abe.

Bostick, D. (2019a, 14 March). *The Future of Classics, From 'Below'.* Retrieved 11 March 2021, from *Sententiae Antiquae.* Available at: https://sententiaeantiquae.com/2019/03/14/24043/.

Bostick, D. (2019b, 29 Oct.). *The Shame of Mock Slave Auctions in Secondary Classics.* Retrieved 11 March 2021, from *Sententiae Antiquae.* Available at: https://sententiaeantiquae.com/2019/10/29/the-shame-of-mock-slave-auctions-in-secondary-classics/.

Bostick, D. (2020a, 9 Feb.). *Is It Still 'Too Soon' to Tell the Truth about Julius Caesar?* Retrieved from *ad meliora*. Available at: https://medium.com/ad-meliora/is-it-too-soon-to-tell-the-truth-about-julius-caesar-2ba5e19f25c7.

Bostick, D. (2020b, 14 Feb.). *Latin Teachers: Rape is Not Romantic, So Stop Describing it that Way.* Retrieved from *ad meliora*. Available at: https://medium.com/ad-meliora/latin-teachers-rape-is-not-romantic-so-stop-describing-it-that-way-9a84a08d5e28.

Bostick, D. (2020c). Not for All: Nostalgic Distortions as a Weapon of Segregation in Secondary Classics. *American Journal of Philology*, 141 (2): 283–306.

Bostick, D. (2020d, 12 May). *Revisiting Rent-a-Roman: An Interview with Jermaine Bryant about Junior Classical League Slave Auctions.* Retrieved 11 March 2021, from *ad meliora*. Available at: https://medium.com/ad-meliora/revisiting-rent-a-roman-an-interview-with-jermaine-bryant-on-junior-classical-league-slave-7a398d8e4fb7.

Bostick, D. (2021). *The Classical Roots of White Supremacy.* Retrieved 11 March 11 2021, from *Learning for Justice*. Available at: https://www.learningforjustice.org/magazine/spring-2021/the-classical-roots-of-white-supremacy?fbclid=IwAR18w4ZpCkQ553EwfLH-u_SB9N1I4RTX6fnrnmIvusZQUyM5Wiwb_vgNhCo.

Bracey, J. (2017, 12 Oct.). *Why Students of Color Don't Take Latin.* Retrieved 11 March 2021, from *Eidolon*. Available at: https://eidolon.pub/why-students-of-color-dont-take-latin-4ddee3144934.

Bracey, J. (2020, 1 Dec.). *Building Equitable Relationships in the Latin Classroom.* Retrieved 11 March 2021, from *Brighter Thinking*, web blog. Available at: https://www.cambridge.org/gb/education/blog/2020/12/01/building-equitable-relationships-in-the-latin-classroom/?fbclid=IwAR0aINEu-nNOev-jBPl_gq2Fx-cnlhgQtNUQt7mQYY3qXjNrP_ouZbRdt0I.

Bracke, E. (2013). Literacy through Latin in South Wales: MFL Approaches to Primary Latin Teaching. *Journal of Classics Teaching*, 28: 43–6.

Bracke, E. (2016). The Role of University Student Teachers in Increasing Widening Participation to Classics. *Journal of Widening Participation and Lifelong Learning*, 18 (2): 111–29.

Bracke, E. (2018). Taking Classics into Communities: Latin in the Park: Catullus and Conjugations in the Sunshine. In A. Holmes-Henderson, S. Hunt and M. Musié, *Forward with Classics: Teaching Classical Languages in Schools and Communities* (pp. 198–203). London: Bloomsbury Academic.

Bradley, M. (2010). *Classics and Imperialism in the British Empire.* Oxford: Oxford University Press.

Bristow, C. (2021). Reforming Qualifications: The How, the Why and the Who. *Journal of Classics Teaching*, 43: 60-63.

Bromberg, J. (2021). *Global Classics.* London: Routledge.

Butterworth, E. (2017). Latin in the Community: The Paideia Institute's Aequora Programme. *The Classical Outlook*, 92 (1): 1–8.

CfA (n.d.). Retrieved from Classics for All. Available at: https://classicsforall.org.uk/.

CfA (2020, 7 July). *Classics for All Impact Report 2010–2019.* Retrieved from Classics for All. Available at: https://s3-eu-west-1.amazonaws.com/client-system/classicsforall/2020/06/CfA-Impact-Report_2010-19_screen.pdf.

Chapoutot, J. (2016). *Greeks, Romans, Germans.* Oakland, CA: University of California Press.

Churchill, L. (2006). Is there a Woman in this Textbook? Feminist Pedagogy and Elementary Latin. In J. Gruber-Miller, *When Dead Tongues Speak: Teaching Beginning Greek and Latin* (pp. 86–112). Oxford: Oxford University Press.

CSCP (n.d.). *Black Lives Matter: Statement from CSCP.* Retrieved 11 March 2021, from CSCP. Available at: https://www.cambridgescp.com/black-lives-matter-statement-cscp.

De Pourcq, M. (2020). The Costly Fabric of Conservatism: Classical References in Contemporray Public Culture. In E. Richardson, *Classics in Extremis* (pp. 170–83). London: Bloomsbury Academic.

DfE (2021). Thousands More Students to Learn Ancient and Modern Languages. £4million new scheme to give opportunity for all to study Latin. Available at: https://www.gov.uk/government/news/thousands-more-students-to-learn-ancient-and-modern-languages.

Delaney, C., H. Smith, L. Tims, T. Smith and W. Griffiths (2021). Keeping the Ancient World Relevant for Modern Students with Suburani. *Journal of Classics Teaching,* 43: 64–7.

Di Giulio, T. (2020, 10 Jan.). *Five Tips for Teaching Racial Competency with Racially Biased Textbooks: A 21st Century Skill for Classicists.* Retrieved 11 March 2021, from *ad meliora.* Available at: https://medium.com/ad-meliora/five-tips-for-teaching-racial-competency-with-racially-biased-textbooks-708706aa04cc.

DuBois, P. (2001). *Trojan Horses: Saving the Classics from Conservatives.* New York: New York University Press.

Dugan, K. (2019). The 'Happy Slave' Narrative and Classics Pedagogy: A Verbal and Visual Analysis of Beginning Greek and Latin Textbooks. *New England Classical Journal,* 46 (1): 62–87.

Dugan, K. (2020). Antiracism and Restorative Justice in Classics Pedagogy: Race, Slavery, and the Function of Language in Beginning Greek and Latin Textbooks. Unpublished dissertation, University of Georgia.

Dutmer, E. (2020, 21 Sept). *Using New Social History to Teach Culture in High School Latin.* Retrieved 11 March 2021, from JHIBlog, web blog. Available at: https://jhiblog.org/2020/09/21/using-new-social-history-to-teach-culture-in-high-school-latin/.

Emdin, C. (2016). *For White Folks Who Teach in the Hood . . . and the Rest of Y'all Too. Reality Pedagogy and Urban Education.* Boston, MA: Beacon Press.

Foreman, G. (n.d.). *Writing about Slavery/Teaching about Slavery: This Might Help.* Retrieved from Writing about Slavery/Teaching About Slavery: This Might Help. Available at: https://docs.google.com/document/d/1A4TEdDgYslX-hlKezLodMIM71My3KTN0zxRv0IQTOQs/mobilebasic.

Forrest, M. (1996). *Modernising the Classics: A Study in Curriculum Development.* Exeter: University of Exeter Press.

Gammage, Z. G. (2021, 26 May). *The Future of Classics: A High Schooler's Perspective.* Retrieved from *ad aequiora.* Available at: https://medium.com/ad-meliora/the-future-of-classics-a-high-schoolers-perspective-12b5a5ddc9e1.

Goff, B. and A. Petsalis-Diomidis (2020). *Inclusive Classics Initiative: Report on 'Towards a More Inclusive Classics' Conference, 25–26 June 2020*. Retrieved from *CUCD Bulletin*, 49. Available at: https://cucd.blogs.sas.ac.uk/files/2020/09/GOFF-AND-PETSALIS-DIOMIDIS-Inclusive-Classics-Report.pdf.

Griffiths, W. (2008). Increasing Access to Latin in Schools. In B. Lister, *Meeting the Challenge: International Perspectives on the Teaching of Latin* (pp. 71–90). Cambridge: Cambridge University Press.

Grigsby, P. (2020). Bringing Classics to the State Schools of the Midlands: A Year in the Life of the WCN. *Journal of Classics Teaching*, 42: 88–91.

Haley, M. and E. Cosgrave (2020). Ancient Herstories. *Journal of Classics Teaching*, 42: 95–6.

Hall, E. (2018). Classics in our Ancestors' Communities. In A. Holmes-Henderson, S. Hunt and M. Musié, *Forward with Classics: Classical Languages in Schools and Communities* (pp. 244–61). London: Bloomsbury Academic.

Hall, E. and H. Stead (2020). *A People's History of Classics: Class and Greco-Roman Antiquity in Britain and Ireland 1689 to 1939*. London: Routledge.

Hammond, Z. (2015). *Culturally Responsive Teaching & the Brain*. Thousand Oaks, CA: Corwin.

Hendrickson, T. (2018, 18 May). *Why so Few of Us Teach Neo-Latin*. Retrieved from *Eidolon*. Available at: https://eidolon.pub/why-so-few-of-us-teach-neo-latin-3f85eb1984b6.

Hill, N. (2021, 17 June). *5 Things We Need to Sacrifice in Classical Studies*. Retrieved from *Notes from the Apotheke*. Available at: http://notesfromtheapotheke.com/5-things-to-sacrifice-in-classics/#more-444.

Hodgkinson, D. (2021). Classics for the Future. *Journal of Classics Teaching*, 44: 106–8.

Hogg, D. (2017). Latin and Greek in London E17. *Journal of Classics Teaching*, 36: 11–14.

Holmes-Henderson, A., S. Hunt and M. Musié (2018). *Forward with Classics: Classical Languages in Schools and Communities*. London: Bloomsbury Academic.

Hunt, S. (2016a). *Starting to Teach Latin*. London: Bloomsbury Academic.

Hunt, S. (2016b). Teaching Sensitive Topics in the Secondary Classics Classroom. *Journal of Classics Teaching*, 34: 31–43.

Hunt, S. (2018a). Getting Classics into Secondary Schools: Three Case Studies. *Journal of Classics Teaching*, 37: 64–70.

Hunt, S. (2018b). Getting Classics into Schools? Classics and the Social Justice Agenda of the UK Coalition Government, 2010–2015. In A. Holmes-Henderson, S. Hunt and M. Musié, *Forward with Classics: Classical Languages in Schools and Communities* (pp. 9–26). London: Bloomsbury Academic.

Hunt, S. (2020a). Editorial. *Journal of Classics Teaching*, 42: 1–4.

Hunt, S. (2020b). Introducing Latin: Non-specialist Latin Teachers Talk. *Journal of Classics Teaching*, 42: 36–42.

Hunt, S. (2021). *Where Have All the Exams Gone?* Retrieved from *Classics for All: Classics Matters*. Available at: https://classicsforall.org.uk/sites/default/files/uploads/CM%20newsletters/ClassicsMatters-Spring21_Screen%20with%20links.pdf.

Hunt, S. and A. Holmes-Henderson (2021, Feb.). *A Level Classics Poverty: Classical Subjects in Schools in England: Access, Attainment and Progression.* Retrieved from *CUCD Bulletin*, 50. Available at: https://cucd.blogs.sas.ac.uk/files/2021/02/Holmes-Henderson-and-Hunt-Classics-Poverty.docx.pdf.

Institute of Classical Studies (2020, 25–26 June). *Towards a More Inclusive Classics.* Retrieved from Institute of Classical Studies. Available at: https://ics.sas.ac.uk/events/towards-more-inclusive-classics.

Jackson, P. (2020, 11 June). *Fight or Die: How to Move from Statements to Actions.* Retrieved from Eidolon. Available at: https://eidolon.pub/fight-or-die-a5613e249d9a.

Jarnagin, J. (2020a, 4 Dec.). *Combating Ableism in the Latin Classroom.* Retrieved 11 March 2021, from Brighter Thinking, web blog. Available at: https://www.cambridge.org/gb/education/blog/2020/12/04/combating-ableism-in-the-latin-classroom/?fbclid=IwAR0ZhS-IgQWe4znar_OigluB7d9XnvogO2OPUz0lluRLkktTTzX0hijfwB0.

Jarnagin, J. (2020b, 3 Dec.). *Latin is for Everyone: 7 Ways to Incorporate Inclusive Images in Your Classroom.* Retrieved 11 March 2021, from Brigher Thinking, web blog. Available at: https://www.cambridge.org/us/education/blog/2020/12/03/7-ways-to-incorporate-inclusive-images-in-latin-classroom/.

Joffe, B. (2019). Teaching the Venalicius Story in the Age of #MeToo: A Reconsideration. *The Classical Outlook*, 94 (3): 125–38.

Joffe, B. (2020, 1 Dec.). *Talking about Hard Things in the Latin Classroom.* Retrieved 11 March 2021, from Brighter Thinking, web blog. Available at: https://www.cambridge.org/gb/education/blog/2020/12/01/talking-about-hard-things-in-the-latin-classroom/?fbclid=IwAR1TxW-P-cT9AITp-hdphphkEOAQeVMVmvElgbZDXCKEONGjilD9laH_5sY.

Johnson, B. (2020, 30 April). *The Real Reason to Study the Classics.* Retrieved from *The Economist*. Available at: https://www.economist.com/books-and-arts/2020/04/30/the-real-reason-to-study-the-classics.

Kara, B. (2020). *A Little Guide for Teachers: Diversity in Schools.* London: Sage Publications.

Kaufman, M. (2020, 19 Dec.). *Black History Matters: Changing What Happens in our Classroom, Part 2.* Retrieved 11 March 2021, from Miranda Kaufman, web bog. Available at: http://www.mirandakaufmann.com/blog/black-history-matters-changing-what-happens-in-our-classrooms-part-2.

Koo, M. (2000). *Enseigner les langues anciennes.* Paris: Hachette Education Didactiques.

Lamb, M. (2020a, 2 Dec.). *Power in Representation: Teaching Classical Women in the Latin Classroom.* Retrieved 11 March 2021, from Brigher Thinking, web blog. Available at: https://www.cambridge.org/gb/education/blog/2020/12/02/classical-women-in-the-latin-classroom/?fbclid=IwAR3o28ayaMgrtjbjZSg7oJ2gyf-bdQzOpwwXNhZ4wJaRLDBaxbKm3JGmvq4.

Lamb, M. (2020b, 1 Dec.). *Uplifting Student Voice and Empowering Student Choice in the Latin Classroom.* Retrieved 11 March 2021, from Brighter Thinking, web blog. Available at: https://www.cambridge.org/gb/education/blog/2020/12/01/uplifting-

student-voice-and-empowering-student-choice-in-the-latin-classroom/?fbclid=IwA
R1aPlnS8PxzRHUQH0AWoDehvegtFeHEx2PsmQgpHNJIAF7584e3S4xEhLQ.

Leite, L. (2021). Active Latin in the Tropics: An Experience with Neo-Latin in Brazil.
In M. Lloyd and S. Hunt, *Communicative Approaches for Ancient Languages*
(pp. 91–100). London: Bloomsbury Academic.

Lister, B. (2015). Exclusively for Everyone: To What Extent has the Cambridge Latin
Course Widened Access to Latin? In E. Archibald, W. Brockliss and J. Gnoza,
Learning Latin and Greek from Antiquity to the Present (pp. 184–97). Cambridge:
Cambridge University Press.

Lockey, I. (2020, 10 March). *Can't We Work Together? Reframing Inclusivity in
Classics*. Retrieved 11 March 2021, from *ad meliora*. Available at: https://medium.
com/ad-meliora/cant-we-work-together-reframing-inclusivity-in-classics-
d52e4f0fbf89.

Mackay, J. (2021, 25 June). *The Whitewashing of Rome*. Retrieved from *Aeon*. Available
at: https://aeon.co/essays/colonialism-is-built-on-the-rubble-of-a-false-idea-of-
ancient-rome?fbclid=IwAR0bu6HodxFMHG-
2mNhI9ybn51n2YlSJsfh3OgKlXaC0R_FLMnuXdPRKRrQ.

Maguire, J. (2012). North Walsham Cluster Latin Project: The First Year (2011–12).
Journal of Classics Teaching, 26: 17–18.

Maguire, J. (2018). Latin in Norfolk: Joining Up the Dots. In A. Holmes-Henderson, S.
Hunt and M. Musié, *Forward with Classics: Teaching Classical Languages in Schools
and Communities* (pp. 129–36). London: Bloomsbury Academic.

Mandler, P. (2020). *The Crisis of the Meritocracy: Britain's Transition to Mass Education
Since the Second World War*. Oxford: Oxford University Press.

Masciantonio, R. (1984). New Curriculum Materials for a Course on English Vocabulary
Development through Latin. *The Classical Journal*, 79 (3): 251–5.

Mavrogenes, N. (1977). The Effect of Elementary Latin Instruction on Language Arts
Performance. *The Elementary School Journal*, 4: 268–71.

Moore, M. (2020, 14 July). *Mary Beard Gets Accusative over Boris Johnson's Latin*.
Retrieved from *The Times*. Available at: https://www.thetimes.co.uk/article/mary-
beard-gets-accusative-over-boris-johnsons-latin-prrblh86r.

Morley, N. (2018). *Classics: Why it Matters*. Cambridge: Polity Press.

Mortimer, L. (2020, 17 Oct.). Developing Racial Competence Using the Cambridge
Latin Course. CSCP Autumn Conference. Cambridge: Unpublished Conference
Paper.

MRECC (n.d.). *Multiculturalism, Race and Ethnicity in Classics Consortium (MRECC)*.
Retrieved 1 March 2011. Available at: https://multiculturalclassics.wordpress.com/
teaching-resources-for-all-levels/.

NLE (2019, 15 April). *The National Latin Exam's Statement on Diversity and Inclusion*.
Retrieved 11 March 2021, from National Latin Exam: https://www.nle.org/News-
Announcements/ArtMID/433/ArticleID/34/The-National-Latin-Exams-Statement-
on-Diversity-and-Inclusion.

Olusoga, D. (2017). *Black and British: A Forgotten History*. London: Pan.

Olusoga, D. (2020). *Black and British*. London: Macmillan Children's Books.

Our Voices Conference (2020, February). *Our Voices for Inclusive Classics Pedagogy.* Retrieved 11 March 2021. Available at: https://ourvoicesinclassics.com/conference-materials-and-resources/.

Parodi, E. (2020). A Critical Investigation of Y7 Students' Perceptions of Roman Slavery as Evidenced in the Stories of the Cambridge Latin Course. *Journal for Classics Teaching*, 42: 43–54.

Pearcy, L. (2005). *The Grammar of Our Civility.* Waco, TX: Baylor University Press.

Pharos (n.d.). *Pharos: Doing Justice to the Classics.* Retrieved 11 March 202. Available at: http://pages.vassar.edu/pharos/.

Piantaggini, L. (2020a, 25 June). *CI, Equity, User-Error & Inequitable Practices.* Retrieved 11 March 2021, from Magister P, web blog. Available at: https://magisterp.com/2020/06/25/ci-equity-user-error-inequitable-practices/.

Piantaggini, L. (2020b). Grammar-Translation: What is It – Really – For Students? *Jounral of Classics Teaching*, 42: 92–4.

Pike, M. (2016). Latin in the 21st Century. *Journal of Classics Teaching*, 33: 6–7.

Polsky, M. (1998). Latin in the Elementary Schools. In R. LaFleur, *Latin for the 21st Century: From Concept to Classroom* (pp. 59–69). Glenview, IL: Scott Foresman-Addison Wesley.

Poser, R. (2021, 2 Feb.). *He Wants to Save the Classics from Whiteness: Can the Field Survive?* Retrieved 11 March 2021, from *The New York Times Magazine.* Available at: https://www.nytimes.com/2021/02/02/magazine/classics-greece-rome-whiteness.html?smid=tw-share&fbclid=IwAR0ZxgSQfrb2k2jQgX-sETWakFrnl_z-h_vIf5JL8cI5DmbDbJNIC4_4lJQ.

Priggs, C. (2020). No More 'Doing' Diversity. *Teaching History*, 179: 10–19.

Quinn, J. (2020, 10 July). *Time to Move On: Arguing Against Traditional Definitions of Classics.* Retrieved from *Times Literary Supplement.* Available at: https://www.the-tls.co.uk/articles/time-to-move-on/#.

Raaflaub, K. (2021). Caesar and Genocide: Confronting the Dark Side of Caesar's Gallic Wars. *New England Classical Journal*, 48 (1): 54–-80.

Rabinovitz, N. and F. McHardy (2014). *From Abortion to Pederasty: Addressing Difficult Topics in the Classics Classroom.* Columbus, OH: Ohio State University Press.

Radice, K., A. Cheetham, S. Kirk and G. Lord (2020). *De Romanis.* London: Bloomsbury Academic.

Reay, D. (2017). *Miseducation: Inequality, Education and the Working Classes.* Bristol: Policy Press.

Reynard, A. (2020). Classics at Lionheart Trust. *Journal of Classics Teaching*, 41: 84–5.

Richard, C. (1995). *The Founders and the Classics: Greece, Rome, and the American Enlightenment.* Cambridge, MA: Harvard University Press.

Richard, C. (2008). *Greeks and Romans Bearing Gifts: How the Ancients Inspired the Founding Fathers.* Lanham, MD: Rowman and Littlefield Publishers.

Riley, M. (2016). *The Neo-Latin Reader: Selections from Petrarch to Rimbaud.* Sophron Editor.

Robinson, E. (2017, 25 Sept.). *'The Slaves Were Happy': High School Latin and the Horrors of Classical Studies.* Retrieved 11 March 2021, from Eidolon. Available at:

https://eidolon.pub/the-slaves-were-happy-high-school-latin-and-the-horrors-of-classical-studies-4e1123649916.

Robinson, L. (2018). Creation and Impact of Regional Centres of Excellence for Classics: The Iris Classics Centre at Cheney. In A. Holmes-Henderson, S. Hunt and M. Musié, *Forward with Classics: Teaching Classical Languages in Schools and Communities* (pp. 149–54). London: Bloomsbury Academic.

Royal Historical Society (2018, October). *Race, Ethnicity & Equality in UK History: A Report and Resource for Change.* Retrieved from Royal Historical Society. Available at: https://files.royalhistsoc.org/wp-content/uploads/2018/10/17205337/RHS_race_report_EMBARGO_0001_18Oct.pdf.

Sawyer, B. (2016). Latin for All Identities. *Journal of Classics Teaching*, 33: 35–9.

Schools Together (2021). *Schools Together.* Retrieved from Schools Together. Available at: https://www.schoolstogether.org/.

SCS (2020, 2 Aug.). *Antiracist Resources: Links and Lists.* Retrieved 11 March 2021, from: https://classicalstudies.org/education/antiracist-resources-links-and-lists.

Searle, E. (2019). Using Virtual Learning Environments for Classics Outreach. In B. Natoli and S. Hunt, *Teaching Classics with Technology* (pp. 93–106). London: Bloomsbury Academic.

Searle, E., L. Jackson and M. Scott (2018). Widening Access to Classics in the UK: How the Impact, Public Engagement, Outreach and Knowledge Exchange Agenda Have Helped. In A. Holmes-Henderson, S. Hunt and M. Musié, *Forward with Classics: Classical Languages in Schools and Communities* (pp. 27–46). London: Bloomsbury Academic.

Sherrington, T. (2020, 23 Nov.). *Towards an Anti-Racist Curriculum: Step 2. 'Usualise Diversity'.* Retrieved 11 March 2021, from Teacherhead, web blog. Available at: https://teacherhead.com/2020/11/23/towards-an-anti-racist-curriculum-step-2-usualise-diversity/.

Shirley, S. (2020, 2 Dec.). *6 Questions with Skye Shirley, Founder of Lupercal.* Retrieved 11 March 2021, from Brigher Thinking, web blog. Available at: https://www.cambridge.org/us/education/blog/2020/12/02/6-questions-with-skye-shirley-founder-of-lupercal/?utm_source=hootsuite&utm_medium=twitter&utm_campaign=MNE_campaign&fbclid=IwAR0v7xPHH1b42Ux8_FSGD1erPzEi_w1ft01S5b3zg3Y2PJxZ3MkPMM4aab0.

Sobel, D. and S. Alston. (2021). *The Inclusive Classroom: A New Approach to Differentiation.* London: Bloomsbury Education.

Story, P. (2003). The Development of the Cambridge Latin Course. In J. Morwood, *The Teaching of Classics* (pp. 85–91). Cambridge: Cambridge University Press.

Upchurch, O. (2014). How Do Students Perceive Women in Roman Society as a Result of Studying the Cambridge Latin Course? A Case Study of a Year 9 Class at an Urban Comprehensive School. *Journal of Classics Teaching*, 29: 30–6.

Wells, J. (2018). *The Dead Elephant in The Room: The Current State of Latin in the Canadian Latin Classroom.* Retrieved from Ceres IV. Available at: https://www.queensu.ca/classics/sites/webpublish.queensu.ca.clswww/files/files/Graduate/CERES%20Vol%20IV%20June2018.pdf#page=47.

Welsh Government (2021). *Press Release: Learning of Black, Asian and minority ethnic histories included in new Welsh Curriculum.* Retrieved 7 October 2021, from Llyw. Cymru / Gov.Wales. Available at: https://gov.wales/learning-black-asian-and-minority-ethnic-histories-included-new-welsh-curriculum.

Westerlund, R. (2018, 1 March). *Slaves or Workers: 'Grammatical Choices as Moral Choices' in History Textbooks.* Retrieved 11 March 2021, from Reclaiming the Language for Social Justice, web blog. Available at: https://reclaimingthelanguage. wordpress.com/2018/03/01/slaves-or-workers-grammatical-choices-as-moral-choices-in-history-textbooks/.

Williams, R. (2016). *Latin of New Spain.* Mundelein, IL: Bolchazy-Carducci Publishers.

Wing-Davey, Z. (2018). Delivering Latin in Primary Schools: The Story of the Latin Programme – Via Facilis. In A. Holmes-Henderson, S. Hunt and M. Musié, *Forward with Classics: Classical Languages in Schools and Communities* (pp. 117–27). London: Bloomsbury Academic.

Winterer, C. (2002). *The Culture of Classicism: Ancient Greece and Rome in American Cultural Life 1780–1910.* Baltimore, MD: Johns Hopkins University Press.

Wyke, M. (2012). *Caesar in the USA.* Berkeley, CA: University of California Press.

York ISSP (n.d.). *York ISSP.* Retrieved from York ISSP. Available at: https://yorkissp.org/ about-us/#:~:text=York%20Independent%20State%20School%20Partnership%20 (ISSP)%20is%20an,shared%20activities%20between%20all%20of%20the%20 City%E2%80%99s%20schools.

Zuckerburg, D. (2019). *Not All Dead White Men: Classics and Misogyny in the Digital Age.* Cambridge, MA: Harvard University Press.

7

The Future

Is It Digital?

CALL and AL-CALL

I have written most of this book during the third of the Covid-19 lockdowns imposed across England by the British government. Schools have recently opened for face-to-face teaching – the first time since the year began. No teacher would have expected to have to turn to online teaching as suddenly as many of them have since the pandemic closed schools first back in March 2020. Initial anxiety amongst teachers and students was huge and not helped by contrary official guidance given by the DfE (Hunt 2021). Further consultation and advice given by stakeholders, such as the examination boards, did little to help (Dixon 2020; Imrie 2020). More positively, lockdown forced teachers to use educational technology more than they might otherwise have done, and the author believes that in the long term they will add their newly learnt skills and practices to their normal classroom repertoire. When Bartolo Natoli and I put together the book *Teaching Classics with Technology* (Natoli and Hunt 2019), we knew that any book on educational technology risked becoming quickly dated. We tried, therefore, to include forward-thinking contributions, grounded in research, practicable in the classroom, and which dealt with bigger pedagogical themes than just a description of the latest fad. Teachers and students have access to multiple forms of ways of learning: e-learning, blended learning, hybrid learning or mixed learning, web-enhanced learning, distance learning and m-learning. In this vein, I conclude this book with some emerging trends in Latin pedagogy which educational technology may be able to deliver.

In the MFL classroom, Computer-Assisted Language Learning (CALL) has been the subject of much research. Following an interactionist approach to learning, modern languages CALL tends to emphasize social interaction between the user and others as they negotiate mutual comprehension of their message meaning. Even though computers are not 'others' in the human sense, the interactions between students and the computer are typical of interactions in real life. Latin teachers, however, may have other aims in the teaching of the language, which is much less concerned with social interaction – with humans or computers. In order, therefore, to distinguish it from modern foreign languages CALL, I propose the name AL-CALL (Ancient Languages CALL), because, although some of the practices may be the same, the ends to which it is put mostly differ (that is, the first language is routinely used in the classroom, and interactive communication in Latin is not the main aim)

In the early years of CALL, educational technology was seen as a means of improving efficiency: drill and practice programmes could be faster, repeated as often as required, and taken outside the classroom, thereby freeing up time in the classroom for more meaningful learning activities; databases and the internet meant that texts and images could be easily accessed, manipulated, stored and supplied to students. Warscahuer (1996) refers to this as behaviouristic CALL based on the notion of computer as tutor. Early users of AL-CALL similarly saw the potential for turning standard classroom fare (and, perhaps, the more tedious elements of it) into something the computer took care of: the focus was on testing grammar and vocabulary knowledge (Goodhew 2003; Latousek1998). The CSCP digital resources, developed from 1999, were a game-changer for Latin teaching in the UK, and opened up a range of different activities for the teacher to deploy not just for testing but also for learning.[1] The widespread deployment of computers, data projectors and interactive whiteboards in schools in the UK at the beginning of the twenty-first century provided further impetus to experiment in the classroom with novel and innovative teaching methods. AL-CALL has offered a challenge to teachers: to adapt their old ways of working or to replace them entirely? After the events of 2020–1, teachers and students were forced to use technology and practice has become increasingly experimental. The rest of this chapter looks to what the future might hold for AL-CALL.

Collaborative digital learning

Past case studies have indicated the value of technology-enhanced collaborative learning in Latin: Hunt (2008) described the collaborative annotation of projected text for teaching literature; Smith (2012) used a digital space for encouraging students to discuss Latin literature at GCSE; Paterson (2012) used the interactive whiteboard as a place of common reference for discussions about Cicero, saved for subsequent reworking; Lewis (2019) found collaborative discussion through online Microsoft OneDrive documents encouraged even the most reticent students to contribute discussion points on Latin literature. Schwamm (2019) has described how his online learning community co-creates Latin stories, how it includes multiple learners' personal interests, and how it enables learners to develop Latin language skills through peer-review and rewriting. In the pandemic, the common use of breakout rooms and chat functions in online teaching has alerted teachers to the need to provide opportunities for students even in face-to-face teaching to work together without direct teacher instruction, and to encourage every voice to be heard. Some of these practices which have taken place in online teaching are sure to strengthen face-to-face classroom teaching.

Flipped classrooms: Has their time come?

Computer-assisted flipped learning allows teachers to provide information for students to process prior to class, thereby making class time more effective for higher level planning, discussions, drafting and redrafting activities. Some studies have shown the success of this approach for classical studies in the university level classroom (Natoli 2014; Gilliver 2019) and at the school level (Baddeley 2021). In the past, there have been challenges with this model of teaching, as students have not always primed themselves with the information prior to class, or because they have misunderstood it and the teacher needed to reteach the material. Nevertheless, evidence drawn from threads on social media suggest that Latin teachers made much use of the flipped classroom model in pandemic-inspired asynchronous teaching. Baddeley (2021) noted that students are sufficiently motivated to watch a pre-lesson video on an historical topic, which freed up lesson time to develop and elaborate their understanding through higher-order thinking and task-setting. A further advantage of pre-recorded materials is that students may review them as many times as they wish, before, during and after the lesson. In the pandemic many teachers have experimented with screencasting and simple animations to record presentation resources for students.[2] The increasing use of recorded audio-visual materials at home and live materials in school blur the boundaries of where learning takes place, and course designers need to consider how to optimize existing resources for multiple technologies as well as develop new ones which take advantage of them.

Making it multimodal: The end of the book?

The *Cambridge Latin Course* and *Suburani* both have extensive interactive resources aligned with the coursebook material, of considerable sophistication, available online, for free or for subscription. These include text analysers, interactive dictionaries, audio dictionaries, lists of derivations, vocabulary testers, drag-and-drop exercises, digital cloze exercises, audio and video files, teacher guides and hyperlinks to outside websites and resources. Several other coursebooks have accompanying websites of materials, such as downloadable worksheets. While course leaders at the university level have experienced challenges in tailoring their own materials to online learning platforms (Moore 2021; Furman 2021), school teachers have been able to access their usual courses already online, and have for the most part only had to refine their pedagogical practices rather than create new resources. Numerous enterprising teachers have made full use of YouTube, for example, and devoted considerable time and effort in building collections of videos to help students with coursebook material, grammar and set text literature such as Caesar and Virgil.[3] A number of websites also provide exchanges for teachers to share such resources. The coursebooks often also have thriving online affinity groups who share resources and tips and ask questions. Crowd-sourcing of materials not only saves teachers time, but also helps to develop a community understanding of the coursebook's pedagogical approach which goes beyond the teachers' notes. There may, however, be issues of curatorship and quality-control and there is also the risk that crowd-sourced materials might not align with the pedagogical approaches of the coursebooks themselves, despite receiving apparent authentication by inclusion on the website.

The centrality of the coursebook does not appeal to some teachers, who prefer to use a range of resources which match their own students interests and their personal teaching preferences (Ash 2019). Freely accessible texts, images and videos on the internet make self- or collaboratively created, multimodal, personalized, and fully interactive courses possible. The internet can provide almost unlimited images, text, video and audio. Websites such as *Latinitium* (Pettersson and Rosengren 2021) provide multiple ways of accessing Latin through visual, written and spoken means, thereby providing greater comprehensible input. Jessie Craft's YouTube channel offers a range of videos, in Latin, with or without subtitles, using *Minecraft* (Craft 2019). A small number of Latin movies exist, professionally made, which can show Latin as a spoken language and which is often sufficiently comprehensible for students. Teachers have experimented with students watching videos before the lesson, submitting their own audio or video presentations, and creating their own interactive texts, images, and webpages. Many of these activities have been undertaken as a respite against too much passive reception in front of the computer during lockdown. It is perhaps worth considering how much these forms of student outputs might be considered appropriate for more formal assessment in the future. A novel trend in other subject areas, for example, is the use of video essays as a form of assessment rather than the written word, which may provide a more inclusive and creative approach to showing student knowledge and understanding (see, for example, the website *Learning on Screen* 2021). I am unaware of any use of the video essay in the Latin classroom at present, but I am sure that it will come in due course.

Interactive books are beginning to appear for classical studies. The Archive of Performances of Greek and Roman Drama (2021) has produced two well-received open-access multimedia books on the performance histories of the Greek tragedies *Agamemnon* and *Medea*: high quality publication values, interactive resources (such as maps, images and text), built-in video and audio and hyperlinks to external resources all showcase their potential for helping students learn about the ancient world and make it evident that the printed word can only get us so far. The Getty Museum's interactive web-book *Faces of Roman Egypt* demonstrates the attractive power of combination of text, image and movement.[4] Anna Willi's open-access digital *Manual of Everyday Roman Writing* (2021) shows how much can be achieved with off-the-shelf e-publishing. Teachers and students could make more interactive materials using simple programmes such as Sway[5] and derive the benefits of multimodality in language learning.

Digital translations, assessment and feedback

The prevalence of online translations of commonly used texts from Latin coursebooks has spread some alarm among teachers: students routinely copy and paste the 'answers' or use *Google Translate* (mostly unsuccessfully). The effect of this is that many teachers are reconsidering the assignment of written translations for students to complete at home. In the search for 'uncheatable' online assignments it is easy for teachers to replicate traditional testing for recall and retrieval of vocabulary and grammar: however, while a convenient tried-and-tested approach has much to commend it, there is a danger that teaching practices might stagnate unless teachers utilize the special affordances of digital learning to create better and more sophisticated ways of assessing students' understanding. The authors of *Suburani* have developed a tracking tool which provides instant feedback to students on assessments and reports to the teacher's mark book. Teachers have experimented with apps, such as Peardeck and PowerPoint, as a means of presenting information and tracking students' progress by their annotations of text and images. However, examples seen online by me suggest that the limited amount of information which can be conveyed and assessed by this means may offer only a small indication of a student's progress; worse, the atomizsation of a lengthy text into small chunks in order to fit on the screen goes against the principles established earlier in this book for developing reading fluency which depend on whole texts rather than short sentences, phrases or words.

Academics at the university level have published a number of articles and blogs to challenge the assessment orthodoxy of translation exercises and vocabulary tests (see, for example, CUCD 2020 and Ryan 2020). These ideas have yet to percolate down to the school level, where the twin pressures of traditional coursebooks and traditional examinations continue to squeeze out such innovatory and perhaps better practices. For example, current national examinations in the UK have barely changed format in fifty years (CSCP 2012). One of the problems with the UK system, at least, is that everyone studies the same original Roman authors without any regard given for the length of study: those who have studied longest are likely to be the best prepared and the system probably gives an advantage to students already privileged because they often have access to Latin for longer through the private preparatory/ senior school route. The Advanced Placement examinations in the US, drawing on original authors such as Caesar and Virgil, similarly expect a period of study, with specialist teachers, that few schools are able to provide. The ALIRA (2021) Latin assessment, by contrast, is a computer-adaptive assessment of Latin students' ability to read for comprehension a variety of Latin-language texts, including not only texts from ancient Rome, but also texts from the modern Latin-users' community, and even Wikipedia, social networks and online publications. The adaptive technology means that the student receives a grade based on what they are able to do at the stage of learning they have reached: successful performance at one level means the assessment tasks increase in difficulty until a point is reached which determines the student's proficiency. The language tasks vary from simple words and phrases – essentially starting with a vocabulary test – through to passages which are first supported and then unsupported by images, and on to lengthier texts of fabricated and then original Latin. The grading bands align with ACTFL proficiency guidelines (novice – intermediate – advanced), and is therefore directly comparable with those of modern foreign languages. For this reason, some US schools are using the ALIRA assessments to determine the seal of biliteracy for their students.

Personalization and student voice

Walden's experiences as a distance-learning teacher of Latin demonstrate the importance of the teacher's (virtual) presence – a source of familiarity and comfort for most students (Walden, 2019). Many teachers who have used online conferencing apps like Zoom or Microsoft Teams have established classroom-style 'routines' to support students: greetings, enquiries after the students' wellbeing, the usual jokes and repartee of the classroom, and a final wave goodbye at the end of the lesson. Taking care matters (Maslow 1943). And the feeling is reciprocated: students bring their pets to show, introduce their favourite video links, and showcase what they have found on the internet that is relevant (or sometimes not so!). Teachers have started to utilize the various affordances of PowerPoint, for example, to include their own voiceovers, to record themselves reading Latin or English translations, and to provide audio instructions as well as written ones. The increasing use of audio as an accompaniment to written texts (in English and Latin) and for providing instructions on PowerPoint presentations could provide a breakthrough for improving the comprehension for all students, not just those who struggle to read.

Innovation or replication?

Infromation Technology provides opportunities to teach and learn in different, potentially better ways. The surge in the use of the interactive whiteboard seems to have stalled: I note that while the projection of text and its annotation are common practice in the Latin classroom (Hunt 2019), other functionalities are more rarely used. In other cases, I have watched whole classes on iPad or computer workbooks slavishly copying and pasting information from one document to another. While there is evidence that the student making choices and selecting information develops important skills for learning, the use of technology here delivers little more than a more efficient process of transcription. Online vocabulary testers have proved popular and effective and are widely used; however, the immediate classroom appeal of quiz apps like Kahoot! and Quizlet has to be balanced against the potential superficiality of learning that takes place. A small-scale study of the spaced-repetition vocabulary tester Memrise showed its effectiveness for Latin vocabulary learning (Walker 2015). The Padlet app and handheld voting devices have been shown to be effective for student engagement and participation both online and in the classroom

(Cleary 2022, forthcoming; Lovatt 2020, 2019). Programs such as Socrative, in which student responses are collated and compared on screen, offer good opportunities for teacher-guided peer review which could not be easily achieved by traditional means (Hay 2019). Many teachers still teach dictionary skills, and yet it could be said that learning to use online analysis tools effectively might be a better option: many teachers use such tools themselves to prepare texts in advance of teaching them.[6] Laufer and Hill's (2000) study of MFL students' use of online dictionaries for reading comprehension showed their use differed according to a number of factors, including training transfer, but that overall multiple dictionary entries (including first language, morphological explanations and audio) seemed to benefit students' incidental vocabulary learning for recognition purposes. The *Cambridge Latin Course Explorer Tool* language analyser was originally developed by the University of Cambridge to speed up undergraduate students' reading of original Latin texts (Lister 2007) and is in common use in the school classroom. Studies have shown mixed perceptions of the value of its use: some report that teachers and students lack a clear rationale for using it and consequently distrust it (Titcombe 2022, forthcoming; Hunt 2018; Laserson 2005); others have shown that its success is dependent on the way it is put to use: as a demonstration for the modelling of vocabulary and grammar, as a diagnostic tool for checking students' understanding, and as a means to support students' reading of a text *before* translation, analysis or class discussion (Titcombe 2022, forthcoming; Hunt 2016). An audio component might further help students improve retention of vocabulary (if that is what is desired). Away from the classroom, mobile language learning – through online resources that can be accessed on a mobile device and e-learning which is through electronic tools and resources – is still much untapped. Students could be learning across multiple contexts, through social and content interactions, using the same personal devices that they use every day at home, in the street, with friends and family. All could be put to use to provide a ready stream of resources and activities to provide formal and informal learning opportunities. More importantly, such multi-modal learning could provide the multiple sorts of comprehensible input that SLA research indicates is necessary for developing language proficiency.

Visualizations, computer games and virtual worlds

No more do students have to peer at small, black-and-white photographs or line drawings in the textbook. The interactive whiteboard, data projectors and personal computers provide multiple ways of showing the ancient world to today's students and are standard features of almost every lesson I see. The internet, and particularly

YouTube, provides an almost endless supply of audio and video clips. Increasingly, 3D digital visualizations are being created, which provide students with a more visual and potentially immersive experience of the ancient world. The opportunity for 3D models to be viewed from different angles and manipulated can help students visualize the ancient world more effectively than through seeing maps and plans (Nicholls 2019a). For example, *Liquid's Roma* guides students through a 3D Rome reconstructed through Minecraft (Liquid's Roma n.d.); and Nicholl's (2016) digital reconstruction of Rome in *SketchUp* allows students to find their own way through the 'city', thereby helping them to understand how it fits together, the arrangement and size of buildings, and give an impression of how its population lived their lives and interacted with each other.[7] *Flyover Zone* (2021), a commercial organization, offers several 3D walk-thrus of famous Roman sites and a competitive chariot-racing video game.[8] *The Forgotten City* is a mystery adventure game, set in Ancient Rome, boasting historically accurate scenes and actions.[9] More simply, teachers can use Google Earth to virtually walk-through Roman sites such as Pompeii and Rome, and Stanford's *Orbis*[10] website to calculate the distance, time and expense of travel between Roman cities in the ancient world (for uses of the latter, see Arcenas 2019 and Morrice 2021).

The UK is the sixth-largest video-game market in the world, with more female than male participants, and an increase in the use of gaming on mobile phones and iPad than at personal computers (Statista 2019). Moshell and Hughes (2002) distinguish between three types of learning that virtual environments can support: constructivist learning, through the exploration of prebuilt virtual words; constructionist learning, through students creating or modifying virtual words; and situated learning, through interactive role play in shared or collaborative environments. Studies have shown the value of video games as an important means to engage young people and develop their historical knowledge and understanding through situated and embodied experiences (Politopoulos et al. 2019; Kee 2017; Kee and Compeau 2019; Chapman 2016; Kappell and Elliott 2013; Gee 2008). Canatella (2022, forthcoming), in a small-scale study of boys in a school in a socially deprived area of London, found that a learning sequence into which the video game *Rome: Total War* was embedded seemed to improve cohesive relationships in the class and to motivate students to continue with their formal studies both inside and outside school.

There is enormous potential for stimulating students' learning about the ancient world and perhaps its languages through these media. While traditional texts and images must not be abandoned, they have their limits. McCall says:

> [A]ll interested in the past, every shade of historian or game player included, need to be aware that a richer understanding of the past can be gained through the employment of a variety of media to understand historical phenomena.
>
> McCall 2020: 121

Questions remain, nevertheless, whether teachers should worry about the 'realism' of the portrayal of the ancient world and the institutions and actions of the characters within (for a detailed look at such debates, see Rollinger 2020, Clare 2021 and Brown 2015). In a review of studies of the use of video games in education, Young et al. (2012) note how teachers tend to use them simply to deliver historical content – a challenging task when so much in them seems to be unhistorical. Gilbert (2017) suggests there is more potential in the social studies classroom: using video games for questioning authorial decision-making, representation and diversity. Moreover, the tendency for video games to promote warlike activities and the prevalence of slang might not be to everyone's taste. What ideologies are represented in the games? For classical subjects more generally, the video games *Assassin's Creed Odyssey* and *Rome: Total War* have received some notice, mostly again with reference to the accuracy of their historical content. For examples of these, see Ghita and Andrikopoulos (2009), Lowe (2009), Vanderwalle (n.d.) and Oxford University's YouTube series, *Let's Play Assassin's Creed Odyssey* (Faculty of Classics, University of Oxford 2020).

While there has been some research into the role of games-based learning for modern foreign language learning (see Blake 2013 for an overview), there has been little yet specifically for ancient languages. It should not be impossible to switch languages in the more commonly used video games to Latin; but this would require a move to a more interactionist communicative approach to language acquisition which might sit uneasily with many currently used methods for learning Latin. A further problem arises in that such games are not *designed* to be instructional in themselves – attractive as they are. Only two are known to me: Craft's (2021) Latin language Minecraft-based game *quisnam id fecit? [Who did it?]* and the Pericles' Group's *Operation LAPIS* (Slota and Ballestrini 2019), which are both interactive adventure games with the aim of learning Latin. It is good fortune that these games are written by educators who put historical thinking and language learning at the forefront of the design. Luke Ranieri's entertaining but thoughtful analysis of the gobbledegook of the spoken Latin in episodes of *Assassin's Creed Origins* demonstrates the learning confusion that results when ancient languages are interpolated by non-specialist games developers (Ranieri 2021). In addition, if lesson objectives and the means of achieving them are not deeply embedded in the activities, there is a risk that students will learn how to play the game but they will not learn desired language or historical skills (Compeau and MacDougall 2014). Another thought: do students *need* to have an ancient historical setting to learn Latin? Might one repurpose existing games with Latin as the user language?

Augmented Reality (AR) and Virtual Reality (VR)[11] technologies have huge potential to engage students. Although not widespread in schools, some museums and archaeological sites are using the technology effectively (Kee, Poitras and Compeau 2019). Site-specific examples in Rome have been described by Nicholls (2019b). Grigsby (2020) attests to students' excitement when they first donned VR goggles at an event organized by the Warwick Classics Network. At the time of writing, the University of Bristol is developing a so-called *Virtual Reality Oracle*, which aims to replicate the religious experience of an ancient visit to the Oracle at Dodona.[12] It is planned that analysis of the impact on the visitors will help guide future research into VR in educational and museum/heritage settings. The commercial organization *Lithodomos VR*[13] has developed virtual reality apps based on archaeologically accurate scenes from ancient Athens and Rome, which have huge potential in the classroom of the future. Students might interact with the virtual world through a computer or an app on a mobile phone, or they may take part in an immersive experience, either with a VR headset (with or without a data glove) or in a classroom set up with wall-sized projection screens. While such apparatus might seem far-fetched, I am convinced that they will become standard features of the classroom for the next generation.

Online affinity groups

Numerous specialist groups have developed a strong online presence. Some are devoted to particular teaching approaches (such as the Teaching Latin Traditionally[14] and the Latin Best Practices: The Next Generation in Comprehensible Input[15] Facebook groups); some are devoted to particular Latin coursebooks or to particular examinations qualifications. Twitter, too, is a source of information and personal blogs provide outlets for classroom experiences and personal observations outside the mainstream academic publications: in common use are *#latinteach* and *#classicstwitter*. Opportunities for teachers to network in person even pre-lockdown have been difficult due to the lack of funds for participation. Many Latin teachers are the sole classicist in their schools and social media provide an easy venue for sharing ideas, professional learning and making friends and colleagues. Social media also provide opportunities for members of affinity groups to participate regardless of age, maturity or experience: there is generally common ground between all (Carpenter, Tani, Morrison and Keane 2020).

However, there are some caveats. The UK government is known to monitor the success of its educational policies and in promoting supporters through social media (Old 2015). Some researchers suggest a deliberate move on the part of the New Right to push populist rhetoric into education policy environments and denigrate a supposedly liberal education elite comprised of university academics, local authorities and teacher unions (Watson 2020; Watson and Barnes 2021). Less political, some participants in affinity groups may over-dominate, drown out and eventually drive away contrary or exploratory members. In the other hand, Robson (2018) suggests that social media enable teachers to develop their own professional identities, such as expert teacher, politically aware, advisory and mentoring roles, which may in turn develop individuals' agency within the group and also outside it. We have already seen how social media facilitated the sorts of discussion which forced changes to the representation of Roman enslaved people in the *Cambridge Latin Course*. Social media may ultimately provide the forum to argue for changes to other commercially made resources and for curriculum and qualification development. Even more positively, there are now many social groups for reading and speaking Latin. These include such groups as Latin and Lattes (Berardelli 2020), a Latin speaking group for high-school students, the reading group Lupercal (2020), a Latin reading group that is 'dedicated to fostering community, practicing spoken Latin, and celebrating herstory', and an increasing number of online Latin *conventicula* and study groups.

Publications, conferences and blogs

Online publishing has become the norm for articles about the teaching of classical languages, literature and civilization. Classics education, including Latin teaching, has received little funding to carry out the sort of research which has been devoted to second language acquisition, for example; and there is a dearth of personnel to carry it out. The decline and near loss of classical subjects from state-maintained schools in both the UK and the US has meant attention has rightly been spent on shoring up the subjects, developing modern resources, supporting teacher training, and undertaking endless advocacy work with newspapers, politicians, parents and school boards. Nevertheless, the amount of small-scale, practitioner research in classics teaching has increased in recent years and, in my view, provides a valuable contribution to the body of professional knowledge. For example, the Initial Teacher Education programmes in the UK, all at Masters level, produce around thirty small scale practitioner research projects per year. It is also worth noting how much more permeable the interface has become between formal publications such as books and journal articles and informal blogs, websites, YouTube videos, Facebook and Twitter posts (as evidenced in the References list, for example). Increasing cross-referencing is facilitated by the use of metadata and hyperlinks; images, graphs and charts can all be included in full colour; the inclusion of supplementary materials such as audio and video is nearing standard practice. Appendix 2 provides a list of the major Anglophone journals and web blogs which are useful for Latin teachers.

What the lockdown has made abundantly clear is that online conferences are here to stay. If anything, there has been such a wealth of talks, discussions, webinars and online conferences that the interested teacher will have found little time to take it all in. A teacher can 'visit' conferences in two or three countries in a single sitting. The tendency for participants to live-tweet to their social media networks is a further dimension: new ideas (and bad ones!) get round very fast. But conferences for students, too, are possible: a number of UK universities happily supply an academic for an hour to live-call into the classroom.[16] The presentation of two or more different points of view, projected into the classrooms of several schools, could be a game-changer in helping to define the subject for young people – questioning, arguing, and constructing knowledge, rather than blindly memorizing 'known' facts. Online conferences in schools could have a big part to play in demystifying the university experience, and in empowering students and teachers to take control of their own learning by hearing and perhaps participating in real 'live' debate.

Conclusion

In many ways in the UK the teaching of Latin at the beginning of the twenty-first century follows Victorian patterns: printed text, vocabulary lists, formal grammar, with the teacher (*per pro* the examinations board) as ultimate authority. Textbooks and approach are still often based around a 1950s format, designed to prepare students in competitive examinations and essentially restrict access to a small number of highly privileged students. They contained sequential, piece-by-piece learning, which was heavily grammar-focused, using lexically dense and aesthetically complex texts (in English and Latin). Ultimately, students' aptitude for university study was supposedly shown through translation of Latin into idiomatic and highly accurate English.

Today, the A level and AP Latin exams, the gatekeepers of entry to traditional Classics courses at the university level, still expect a similar training of many years in the classroom – one that is getting harder to achieve for students in most of the existing schools which have the capability to offer it, and almost impossible for those in schools which have no track record, limited timetable and non-specialist teachers. Many of the commonly used coursebooks provide the means for students to have a reasonable chance at passing through the gateway, focusing on just the right vocabulary and just the right syntax to enable the student to squeeze through to the other side. They innocently suppose that by providing neat sets of resources and promoting the corresponding pedagogies, they will provide access to Classics for any who start it. In the process, they end up maintaining the gateway rather than breaking it down. Tim Brighouse, writing in 1993 of the English National Curriculum, deplored the 'unfortunate backwash effect of higher education on the schooling system as a whole and by inference on the methods deployed in the education of those for whom higher education will always remain inaccessible'. In 2010, the Minister of State for Education Michael Gove's consultation of university representatives rather than of primary and secondary school teachers, made the same error, by developing curriculum reforms with the interests of the minority of selective 'Russell Group' universities first, rather than with the teachers of the supply chain itself – the school-aged students. While the university contributors to the Classics consultation provided thoughtful and measured responses, they opted for the status quo. To me, that was an opportunity missed for curriculum development and reform in a manner which would suit the needs of school students for the twenty-first century. In the UK, the continued decline in the numbers of students, especially in state-maintained schools, taking Latin at A level is now at last concentrating the minds of university academics, as it has teachers' for many years. For the US, a decline to just under 4,900 students taking the AP Latin examination in 2021 has also been ringing alarm bells.

If teachers want Latin teaching to grow – and the only area where it can grow is in the state-maintained sector – they need to find more ways to engage students and help them realize success. For example, teaching does not have to be slavishly following a coursebook from beginning to end, as I hope that this book has shown. Indeed, I hope that technology will improve the coursebook into something more like a course programme which draws on the affordances of digital technology to provide students with a more rounded and holistic approach to learning the language. There will always be need of a teacher. Bayne et al., in their book, *The Manifesto for Teaching Online*, argues that: 'teaching is a complex bringing together of people, texts, images, sounds, locations, discourses, technologies, and modalities, by which we are able to open up difference and critique' (Bayne et al. 2020: 39). Technology provides the means to learn in many different ways, perhaps not yet considered. Are teachers ready to grasp the opportunities or do they prefer to stick to familiar routines? Online teaching forced on them by the lockdown has encouraged experimentation. Will teachers start to do different things now back in the classroom? Why use technology merely to replicate the Victorian classroom, with paper, pen, dictionary and commentary, if those things were only used because there was no alternative at the time?

Sorensen (2009) noted that online teaching stripped the teacher of the control they had through the hard-copy textbook and worksheets, with the students instead browsing through hyperlinks and following their own interests. Are teachers ready to allow students that degree of freedom? Are they threatened by it? From personal experience, in the university classroom, where trainee teachers habitually sit with laptop at the ready to download resources and make their notes, I still find it slightly disconcerting when they browse for information as I speak, to contribute to class what they have found and sometimes challenge something I have said. I am beginning to welcome it, not feel threatened by it, value it as an addition it to my teaching. But it is hard. Teaching is complex: there are many ways to do it, and technology adds yet more, perhaps unchartered experiences. Dare we loosen (or lose) control?

In the UK, the number of state-maintained schools which are beginning to offer Latin again shows an upward trend, with the charity Classics for All announcing it has helped its 1,000th school with the development of classical languages and civilization (Classics for All 2021). In the US, a large number of Magnet Schools, which have specialized curricula, have developed in the public school system in areas of socioeconomic deprivation, thereby giving access to Latin for marginalized students. But, if we are to make Latin more inclusive and accessible, the subject community needs to find ways to connect more with students out of the classroom – even setting up online-learning communities for those students who do not have access to a specialist teacher in their school. Latin has been available to be taught online for a long time and continues to thrive (Walden 2019; Daugherty 1998); perhaps, counterintuitively, the lack of a communicative element makes it pedagogically easier to assign – a 'language no-one has to speak'. Stephen Fry, the British writer and TV presenter, recently expressed his sadness to 'think how many great untried Hellenists and Latinists, how many potentially joyous lovers of the Classics have lived and died without ever having been exposed to Ancient Greece and Rome?' (2021) because of a lack of access to Latin and classical studies in the majority of schools today. But today, teachers do not have to rely totally on schools to provide instruction. The rap artist and archaeology enthusiast M. C. Hammer recently initiated an online debate about the repatriation of African cultural artefacts (Grove 2021). Hammer has a huge Twitter following among young African Americans, and the success of the debate and continuing online discussion has pushed Oxford academics to reconsider their traditional approaches for engaging the public – and potential students. The subject community for Latin might learn from him: if we truly want Latin to be available for everyone, not just those lucky ones in the few schools which provide it, technology at home, on the screen in the living room, on the wall in the bedroom and especially on the smartphone in the hand, surely has a much larger part to play.

Notes

1. See Lister (2007) for an account of the development of the CSCP digital resources; their impact on teaching in schools is described by Griffiths (2008).
2. See Schrock's website *Screencasting and Screen Recording* website for multiple examples and ideas, available at: https://www.schrockguide.net/screencasting.html. A simple program for screen recording is available at: https://www.screencastify.com/; for simple animations, see: https://goanimateforschools.github.io/.
3. See, e.g., Patrick Yaggy's YouTube channel, available at: https://www.youtube.com/user/patrickyaggy/videos. Also Ben Johnson's *Latin Tutorial* website, available at: https://latintutorial.com/about.
4. Faces of Roman Egypt, available at: https://artsandculture.google.com/story/YQVRtpUvIK_TtA?hl=en.

5. *Sway*, available at: https://sway.office.com/my.
6. Examples of language analysis tools include Alpheios (available at: https://alpheios. net/) and Perseus 4.0 (available at: http://www.perseus.tufts.edu/hopper).
7. For more details, see: https://research.reading.ac.uk/virtualrome/about/.
8. The website of *Flyover Zone* (2021) currently contains reconstructions of the Temple of Baalbek, parts of Hadrian's villa at Tivoli, and parts of Ancient Rome, including the Forum and the Pantheon (www.flyoverzone.com). The authors stress the historical accuracy of the representations of the sites. For a demonstration video, see Frischer (2021).
9. *The Forgotten City*, available at: https://forgottencitygame.com/.
10. *Orbis: The Stanford Geospatial Network Model of the Roman World*, available at: https://orbis.stanford.edu.
11. Augmented reality is a technology that superimposes a computer-generated image on a user's view of the real world; Virtual Reality is a simulated experience that can be similar to or completely different from the real world.
12. *Virtual Reality Oracle*, available at: http://www.vroracle.co.uk/.
13. *Lithodomos VR*, available at: https://www.lithodomosvr.com/.
14. *Teaching Latin Traditionally*, available at: https://www.facebook.com/ groups/1451944284859288.
15. *Latin Best Practices: The Next Generation in Comprehensible Input*, available at: https://www.facebook.com/groups/122958344965415/?multi_permalinks= 809703882957521.
16. See, e.g., the University of Oxford's 'Classical Conversations' program, available at: https://clasoutreach.web.ox.ac.uk/classical-conversations.

References

ALIRA (2021, 24 March). *ACTFL Latin Interpretive Reading Assessment® (ALIRA)*. Retrieved from LTI. Language Testing International. Available at: https://www. languagetesting.com/actfl-latin-interpretive-reading-assessment.

Arcenas, S. (2019). Teaching Ancient Geography with Digital Tools. In B. Natoli and S. Hunt, *Teaching Classics with Technology* (pp. 165–80). London: Bloomsbury Academic.

Archive of Performances of Greek and Roman Drama (2021). *Publications*. Retrieved from Archive of Performances of Greek and Roman Drama. Available at: http://www. apgrd.ox.ac.uk/about-us.

Ash, R. (2019). Untextbooking for the CI Latin Class: Why and How to Begin. *Journal of Classics Teaching*, 39: 65–70.

Baddeley, S. (2021). Online Teaching: A Reflection. *Journal of Classics Teaching*, 44: 109–16.

Bayne, S., P. Evans, R. Ewins, J. Knox, J. Lamb, H. MacLeod, C. O'Shea, J. Ross, P. Sheail and C. Sinclair (2020). *The Manifesto for Teaching Online.* Cambridge, MA: The MIT Press.

Berardelli, A. (2020, 20 July). *Latin and Lattes*. Retrieved from Latin and Lattes. Available at: https://www.lupercallegit.org/post/latin-lattes.

Blake, R. (2013). *Brave New Digital Classroom: Technology and Foreign Language Learning*. Washingto,n DC: Georgetown University Press.

Brown, H. (2015). *Videogames and Education*. London: Routledge.

Cannatella, P. (2022, forthcoming). Student and Teacher Perceptions of the Value of Total War: Saga in Motivating KS3 Students. *Journal of Classics Teaching*, 45.

Carpenter, J., T. Tani, S. Morrison and J. Keane (2020). Exploring the Landscape of Educator Professional Activity on Twitter: An Analysis of 16 Education-Related Twitter Hashtags. *Professional Development in Education*, April.

Chapman, A. (2016). *Digital Games as History*. London: Routledge.

Clare, R. (2021). *Ancient Greece and Rome in Videogames: Representation, Play, Transmedia*. London: Bloomsbury.

Classics for All (2021, 25 June). *Classics for All*. Retrieved from Classics for All, Twitter. Available at: https://twitter.com/classicsforall/status/1404793892915056641.

Cleary, C. (2022, forthcoming). An Investigation of Year 8 Students' Experiences with Online Learning through the Padlet App. *Jounral of Classics Teaching*, 45.

Compeau, T. and R. MacDougall (2014). Tecunseh Lies Here: Goals and Challenges for a Pervasive History Game in Progress. In K. Kee, *Pastplay: Teaching and Learning History with Technology* (pp. 87–110). Ann Arbor, MI: University of Michigan Press.

Craft, J. (2019). Bridging the Gap between Students and Antiquity: Language Accquisition Videos with Minecraft and CI/TPRS. In B. Natoli and S. Hunt, *Teaching Classics with Technology* (pp. 181–92). London: Bloomsbury Academic.

Craft, J. (2021). *Magister Craft:* quisnam id fecit? Retrieved 24 March 2021, from: https://www.magistercraft.com/quisnam-id-fecit.

CSCP (2012). *Changing Demands in Latin and Ancient Greek Examinations 1918–2021*. Cambridge: Unpublished.

CUCD (2020, 3 April). *Language (and Other) Assessments in the Time of COVID-19*. Retrieved 24 March 2021, from Teaching Classics and Ancient History in HE. CUCD Education Committee blog, web blog. Available at: https://cucdeducation. wordpress.com/2020/04/03/language-and-other-assessments-in-the-time-of-covid-19/.

Daugherty, C. (1998). Latin Distance Learning and the Electronic Classroom. In R. LaFleur, *Latin for the 21st Century: From Concept to Classroom* (pp. 251–62). Glenview, IL: Scot Foresman-Addison Wesley.

Dixon, J. (2020). Covid-19, Classical Subjects and the Classroom: Teachers' Feedback from Summer 2020. *Journal of Classics Teaching*, 42: 60–5.

Faculty of Classics, University of Oxford (2020). *Let's Play Assassin's Creed Odyssey with Oxford University*. Retrieved from YouTube. Available at: https://www.youtube.com/playlist?list=PLN_RX1AjtckBdnEBLlcukbe41TmOd9y5p.

Flyover Zone (2021). *Flyover Zone*. Retrieved from Flyover Zone. Available at: https://www.flyoverzone.com/.

Frischer, B. (2021, 27 May). *Virtual Field Trips to Ancient Rome*. Retrieved from Paideia Institute Public Lectures, YouTube. Available at: https://www.youtube.com/watch?

app=desktop&d=n&feature=youtu.be&fbclid=IwAR1xdJTnqCqlYa_
rtIlc3l0oQMDqMb-DFPzHtAfcE9fCX7yac_mjKLNqAnw&v=HYWNBi-rWsU.

Fry, S. (2021). *The Ghost of Classics Yet to Come.* Retrieved from *Antigone Journal.*
Available at: https://antigonejournal.com/2021/05/the-ghost-of-classics/.

Furman, M. (2021). Surviving to Thriving: Supporting Graduate Student Instructors
and Teaching Assistants during the Transition to Online Teaching. *Teaching Classical
Languages,* 11 (2): 81–9.

Gee, J. (2008). *What Video Games Have to Teach Us about Learning and Literacy.*
London: Palgrave Macmillan.

Ghita, C. and G. Andrikopoulos (2009). Total War and Total Realism: A Battle for
Antiquity in Computer Game History. In D. Lowe and K. Shahabudin, *Classics for
All: Reworking Antiquity in Mass Culture* (pp. 109–27). Newcastle Upon Tyne:
Cambridge Scholars Publishing.

Gilbert (2017). 'The Past is Your Playground': The Challenges and Possibilities of
Assassin's Creed: Syndicate for Social Education. *Theory and Research in Social
Education,* 45 (1) 145–55.

Gilliver, K. (2019). Flipping Romans: Experiments in Using Technology for Teaching in
Higher Education. In B. Natoli and S. Hunt, *Teaching Classics with Technology*
(pp. 9–18). London: Bloomsbury Academic.

Goodhew, D. (2003). Using ICT in Classics. In J. Morwood, *The Teaching of Classics*
(pp. 136–44). Cambridge: Cambridge University Press.

Griffiths, W. (2008). Increasing Access to Latin in Schools. In B. Lister, *Meeting the
Challenge: International Perspectives on the Teaching of Latin* (pp. 71–90). Cambridge:
Cambridge University Press.

Grigsby, P. (2020). Bringing Classics to the State Schools of the Midlands: A Year in the
Life of the WCN. *Journal of Classics Teaching,* 42: 88–91.

Grove, J. (2021, 16 March). Hammer Time Professor: For Diverse Audiences, Try New
Platforms. *Times Higher Education Supplement.*

Hay, L. (2019). In the Classroom with Multi-Modal Teaching. In B. Natoli and
S. Hunt, *Teaching Classics with Technology* (pp. 229–38). London: Bloomsbury
Academic.

Hunt, F. (2018). Teaching and Learning Latin in the Key Stage 3 Classroom: Using the
Cambridge Latin Course Explorer Tool. *Journal of Classics Teaching,* 38: 42–9.

Hunt, S. (2008). Information and Communication Technology and the Teaching of
Latin Literature. In B. Lister, *Meeting the Challenge: International Prespectives on the
Teaching of Latin* (pp. 107–20). Cambridge: Cambridge University Press.

Hunt, S. (2016). *Starting to Teach Latin.* London: Bloomsbury Academic.

Hunt, S. (2019). On Stage and Screen: 'Big Book' Latin and Dialogic Teaching. In
B. Natoli and S. Hunt, *Teaching Classics with Technology* (pp. 193–205). London:
Bloomsbury Academic.

Hunt, S. (2021). Sight Unseen: Visible and Invisible Teachers in Online Teaching.
Teaching Classical Languages, 11 (2): 33–66.

Imrie, A. (2020). The Coronavirus Pandemic, Exams Crisis and Classics in Scottish
Schools. *Journal of Classics Teaching,* 42: 55–9.

Kappell, M. and A. Elliott (2013). *Playing with the Past: Digital Games and the Simulation of History.* London: Bloomsbury.

Kee, K. (2017). *Pastplay: Teaching and Learning History with Technology.* Ann Arbor, MI: University of Michigan Press.

Kee, K. and T. Compeau (2019). *Seeing the Past with Computers: Experiments with Augmented Reality and Computer Vision for History.* Ann Arbor, MI: University of Michigan Press.

Kee, K., E. Poitras and T. Compeau (2019). History All Around Us: Towards Best Practices for Augmented Reality for History. In K. Kee and T. Compeau, *Seeing the Past with Computers: Experiments with Augmented Reality and Computer Vision for History* (pp. 207–23). Ann Arbor, MI: University of Michigan Press.

Laserson, T. (2005). The Cambridge Latin Course Online - the Learner's Perspective. In B. Lister, *Meeting the Challenge: European Perspectives on the Teaching and Learning of Latin.* Cambridge: Cambridge University Press.

Latousek, R. (1998). *Computamus!* We Compute! In R. LaFleur, *Latin for the 21st Century: From Concept to Classroom* (pp. 263–75). Glenview, IL: Scott Foresman-Addison Wesley.

Laufer, B. and M. Hill (2000). What Lexical Information Do L2 Leaners Select in a CALL Dictionary and How Does it Affect Retention? *Language Learning & Technology*, 3 (2): 61–81.

Learning on Screen (2021). *Introductory Guide to Video Essays.* Retrieved from Learning on Screen, British Universities and Colleges Film and Vision Council. Available at: https://learningonscreen.ac.uk/guidance/introductory-guide-to-video-essays/.

Lewis, E. (2019). VLEs, Latin Literature and Student Voice. In B. Natoli and S. Hunt, *Teaching Classics with Technology* (pp. 53–66). London: Bloomsbury Academic.

Liquid's Roma (n.d.). *Liquid's Roma.* Retrieved from Liquid's Roma, YouTube. Available at: https://www.youtube.com/channel/UC9TCpDe7Ch6_SimXxAvQIDw.

Lister, B. (2007). *Changing Classics in Schools.* Cambridge: Cambridge University Press.

Lovatt, H. (2019). 'Just-in-Time Learning': Using Hand-Held Voting Devices in the Undergraduate Lecture Room. In B. Natoli and S. Hunt, *Teaching Classics with Technology* (pp. 153–64). London: Bloomsbury Academic.

Lovatt, H. (2020, 1 Dec.). *Using Padlet in Online and Blended Classics Teaching.* Retrieved 23 March 2021, from Teaching Classics and Ancient History in HE. CUCD Education Committee Blog, web blog. Available at: https://cucdeducation.wordpress.com/2020/12/01/using-padlet-in-online-and-blended-classics-teaching/?fbclid=IwAR0IFxd0vrrJmbLu2ol_q9b5IQgVbKCMFpRPUgO93NxeuozOCO4kPQLbfLA.

Lowe, D. (2009). Playing with Antiquity: Videogame Receptions of the Classical World. In D. Lowe and K. Shahabudin, *Classics for All: Reworking Antiquity in Mass Culture* (pp. 64–90). Newcastle Upon Tyne: Cambridge Scholars Publishing.

Lupercal (2020). *Lupercal: A Latin Reading Group.* Retrieved from Lupercal. Available at: https://www.lupercallegit.org/.

Maslow, A. (1943). A Theory of Human Motivation. *Psychological Review*, 5 (4): 370–96.

McCall, J. (2020). Digital Legionaries: Video Game Simulations of the Face of Battle in the Roman Republic. In C. Rollinger, *Classical Antiquity in Video Games: Playing with the Ancient World* (pp. 107–26). London: Bloomsbury Academic.

Moore, D. (2021). Lessons from Online Modern Foreign Language Classes for the Classical Language Instructor. *Teaching Classical Languages*, 11 (2): 67–78.

Morrice, A. (2021). Using 'ORBIS' Software to Explore Ancient Geography: An action research project with a Year 8 class in an independent school. Journal of Trainee Teacher Education Research. Available at: https://jotter.educ.cam.ac.uk/volume12/643-668morricea/643-668morricea.pdf.

Moshell, J. and C. Hughes (2002). Virtual Environments as a Tool for Academic Learning. In K. Stanney, *Handbook of Virtual Environments, Design, Implementation and Applications* (pp. 893–910). Mahwah, NJ: Lawrence Erlbaum Associates.

Natoli, B. (2014). Flipping the Latin Classroom: Balancing Educational Practice with the Theory of eLearning. *Journal of Classics Teaching*, 30: 37–40.

Natoli, B. and S. Hunt (2019). *Teaching Classics with Technology.* London: Bloomsbury Academic.

Nicholls, M. (2016). Digital Visualisation in Classics Teaching and Beyond. *Journal of Classics Teaching*, 33: 27–30.

Nicholls, M. (2019a). SketchUp and Digital Modelling for Classics. In B. Natoli and S. Hunt, *Teaching Classics with Technology* (pp. 131–44). London: Bloomsbury Academic.

Nicholls, M. (2019b, 30 July). *The Digital Reconstructions Bringing Roman Ruins to Life.* Retrieved 24 March 2021, from *Apollo Magazine.* Available at: https://www.apollo-magazine.com/the-digital-reconstructions-bringing-roman-ruins-to-life/.

Old, M. (2015). Social Media: Did Blogs Break the Blob? In R. Peal, *Changing Schools: Persepctives on Five Years of Education Reform* (pp. 55–65). London: John Catt Educational.

Paterson, C. (2012). Ancient Texts and Modern Tools: Cicero and Interactive Whiteboards. *Journal of Classics Teaching*, 25: 14–16.

Pettersson, D. and A. Rosengren (2021). The Latinitium Project. In M. Lloyd and S. Hunt, *Communicative Approaches for Ancient Languages* (pp. 195–210). London: Bloomsbury Academic.

Politopoulos, A., C. Ariese, K. Boom and A. Mol. (2-19). *Romans and Rollercoasters: Scholarship in the Digital Playground.* Journal of Computer Applications in Archaeology, 2 (1): 163–75.

Ranieri, L. (2021, 18 June). *Latin Teacher Gets Trolled for 8 minutes by Video Game: Assassin's Creed Origins Spoken Latin.* Retrieved from PolyMathy. Available at: https://www.youtube.com/watch?v=ESwCNJEpihA.

Robson, J. (2018). Performance, Structure and Ideal Identity: Reconceptualising Teachers' Engagement in Online Social Spaces. *British Journal of Educational Technology*, 49 (3): 439–50.

Rollinger, C. (2020). *Classical Antiquity in Video Games: Playing with the Ancient World.* London: Bloomsbury.

Ryan, C. (2020, 25 March). *Assessing Languages Remotely – Part 1.* Retrieved 24 March 2021, from Cressida's Commenets – Learning by Playing, web blog. Available at:

https://cressidaryan.wordpress.com/2020/03/25/assessing-languages-remotely-part-1/?fbclid=IwAR0zBAirwccfee_ME0ZSSWbLh_aJk_5c-yfuGD3fQG_2e3utnkV30Vs2UI0.

Schwamm, J. (2019). *Auream Quisquis Mediocritatem Diligit*: The Joyful Learning Community Model for Learning Latin Online. In B. Natoli and S. Hunt, *Teaching Classics with Technology* (pp. 19–28). London: Bloomsbury Academic.

Slota, S. and K. Ballestrini (2019). *Una Vita*: Exploring the Relationship between Play, Learning Science and Cultural Competency. In B. Natoli and S. Hunt, *Teaching Classics with Technology* (pp. 81–92). London: Bloomsbury Academic.

Smith, A. (2012). The Use of Collaborative e-Learning Technology for GCSE Latin. *Journal of Classics Teaching*, 26: 3–8.

Sorensen, E. (2009). *The Materiality of Learning: Technology and Knowledge in Educational Practice.* New York: Cambridge Univerity Press.

Statista (2019, 16 Sept.). *Video Gaming in the United Kingdom – Statistics & Facts.* Retrieved 21 March 2021, from Statista. Available at: https://www.statista.com/topics/1763/gaming-in-the-united-kingdom/.

Titcombe, D. (2022, forthcoming). Cheating or Learning? An Investigation into Students' Perceptions of the Value of the CLC Explorer Tool. *Jounral of Classics Teaching*, 45.

Vanderwalle, A. (n.d.). *Assassin's Creed Odyssey: A Playable Version of Classical Greece.* Retrieved 21 March 2021, from Antiquipop. Available at: https://antiquipop.hypotheses.org/eng/8994eng.

Virtual Reality Oracle (2021). *Virtual Reality Oracle.* Retrieved from Virtual Reality Oracle. Available at: http://www.vroracle.co.uk/?fbclid=IwAR33Y3Fi2vjCwB2MyQNNzB6lzEz8X2QU8W9-sKee--Rvh-v_bcDHGlQzLXw.

Walden, V. (2019). Distance Learning and Technology: Teaching Latin, Greek and Classical Civilisation at a Distance from the UK. In B. Natoli and S. Hunt, *Teaching Classics with Technology* (pp. 29–38). London: Bloomsbury.

Walker, L. (2015). The Impact of Using Memrise on Student Perceptions of Learning Latin Vocabulary and on Long-Term Memory of Words. *Journal of Classics Teaching*, 32: 14–20.

Warschauer, M. (1996). Computer Assisted Language Learning: An Introduction. In S. Fotos, *Multimedia Language Teaching* (pp. 3–20). Tokyo: Logos International.

Watson, S. (2020). New Right 2.0: Teacher Populism on Social Media in England. *British Educational Research Journal*, 47 (2): 299–315.

Watson, S. and N. Barnes (2021). Online Educational Populism and New Right 2.0 in Australia and England. *Globalisation, Societies and Education.*

Willi, A. (2021, 14 June). *Writing Equipment, Manual of Roman Everyday Writing, Vol. 2.* Retrieved from LatinNow ePubs. Available at: https://latinnowepubs.github.io/WritingEquipmentVol2/mobile/index.html.

Young, M., S. Slota, A. Cutler, G. Jalette, G. Mullin, B. Lai and Z. Simeoni (2012). Our Princess Is in Another Castle: A Review of Trends in Serious Gaming for Education. *Review of Educational Research*, 82 (1): 62–89.

Appendix 1
Abbreviations

ACE	Advocating Classical Education
ACL	American Classical League
ACTFL	American Council for the Teaching of Foreign Languages
A level	Advanced level
AL-CALL	Ancient Languages – Computer Assisted Language Learning
ALIRA	ACTFL Latin Interpretive Reading Assessment
AP	Advanced Placement
AQA	Assessment and Qualifications Alliance examination board
AR	Augmented Reality
ARLT	Association for the Reform of Latin Teaching, now known as the Association for Latin Teaching
AS level	Advanced Subsidiary level
BBC	British Broadcasting Corporation
BIPOC	Black and Indigenous People of Colour, used to refer to members of non-white communities in the US
BME	Black and Minority Ethnic, used to refer to members of non-white communities in the UK
CA	The Classical Association
CALL	Computer-Assisted Language Learning
CfA	Classics for All
CI	Comprehensible Input
CPD	Continuing Professional Development
CSCP	Cambridge School Classics Project
CSE	Certificate of Secondary Education

CUCD	Council of University Classics Departments
DfE	Department for Education
EBacc	English Baccalaureate
GCSE	General Certificate of Secondary Education
HE	Higher Education
ISSP	Independent-State School Partnership
IT	Information Technology
ITE	Initial Teacher Education
IWB	Interactive Whitebaord
MFL	Modern Foreign Languages
MRECC	Multiculturalism, Race and Ethnicity in Classics Consortium
NACCP	North American Cambridge Classics Project
NJCL	National Junior Classical League
NLE	National Latin Examination
O level	Ordinary Level
OCR	Oxford and Cambridge and Royal Society of Arts (RSA) examinations board
PGCE	Postgraduate Certificate in Education
PQA	Personalized questioning and answers
SCS	Society for Classical Studies
SLA	Second Language Acquisition
SLD	Second Language Development
TESL	Teaching English as a Second Language
TPR	Total Physical Response
TPRS	Teaching Proficiency through Reading and Storytelling
VLE	Virtual Learning Environment
VR	Virtual Reality
WCN	Warwick Classics Network
WJEC	Welsh Joint Examinations Council examinations board

Appendix 2
Resources

The resources listed below are mentioned in the text of this book. The author bears no responsibility for the content of any of the websites listed. To ensure that the links do not go out of date, the author's companion website contains the same (and more) material: www.stevenhuntclassics.com.

Journals: Pedagogy focused

Council of University Classics Departments Bulletin (Higher Education focus). Available at: https://cucd.blogs.sas.ac.uk/bulletin/.
Euroclassica (pan-European). Available at: https://www.euroclassica.eu/portale/latein/euroclassica/publications.html.
Journal of Classics Teaching. Available at: https://www.cambridge.org/core/journals/journal-of-classics-teaching.
Prima. Available at: https://www.etclassics.org/PRIMA.
Teaching Classical Languages. Available at: https://tcl.camws.org/.
The Classical Outlook. Available at: https://www.aclclassics.org/Publications/The-Classical-Outlook.
The Classical World. Available at: https://www.press.jhu.edu/journals/classical-world-quarterly-journal-antiquity.

Books: Pedagogy focused

Changing Classics in Schools. B. Lister (2007). Cambridge: Cambridge University Press.
Classics Teaching in Europe. J. Bulwer (ed.) (2006). Bristol: Bristol Classical Press.
Communicative Approaches for Classical Languages. M. Lloyd and S. Hunt (eds) (2021). London: Bloomsbury Academic.
Forward with Classics: Classical Languages in Schools and Communities. A. Holmes-Henderson, S. Hunt and M. Musié (eds) (2018). London: Bloomsbury Academic.
Latin: How to Read It Fluently: A Practical Manual. D. Hoyos (1997). New England: CANE Press.

Latin for the 21st Century: From Concept to Classroom. R. LaFleur (ed.) (1998). Glenview, IL: Scott Foresman-Addison Wesley.

Meeting the Challenge: International Perspectives on the Teaching of Latin. B. Lister (ed.) (2008). Cambridge: Cambridge University Press.

Starting to Teach Latin. S. Hunt (2016). London: Bloomsbury Academic.

Teach the Latin, I Pray You. P. Distler (1962). Chicago, IL: Loyola University Press.

Teaching Classics with Technology. B. Natoli and S. Hunt (eds) (2019). London: Bloomsbury Academic.

The Teaching of Classics. J. Morwood (ed.) (2003). Cambridge: Cambridge University Press.

When Dead Tongues Speak: Teaching Beginning Greek and Latin. J. Gruber-Miller (ed.) (2006). Oxford: Oxford University Press.

Coursebooks

Cambridge Latin Course. UK 4th Edition. Cambridge School Classics Project (1998). Cambridge: Cambridge University Press.

Cambridge Latin Course. US 5th Edition. Cambridge School Classics Project (2016). Cambridge: Cambridge University Press. Available at: www.cambridgescp.com. Facebook: *TLA Cambridge*. Facebook: *NACCP: Cambridge Latin Course*. Twitter: @Caecilius_CLC. Cambridge School Classics Project (CSCP) blog, at: https://blog.cambridgescp.com/ and Cambridge Education at: https://www.cambridge.org/gb/education/blog/subject/latin/.

De Romanis. K. Radice, A. Cheetham, S. Kirk and G. Lord (2020). London: Bloomsbury Academic.

Ecce Romani. Scottish Classics Group (1971). London: Oliver and Boyd. Facebook: *Ecce Romani Teacher Exchange* Facebook group.

Latin Beyond GCSE. J. Taylor (2009). London: Bloomsbury.

Lingua Latina per se Illustrata. H. Øerberg (2011) London: Hackett Publishing. Facebook: *Lingua Latin per se Illustrata*.

Latin through Mythology. J. Hanlin (1991). Cambridge: Cambridge University Press.

Latin to GCSE. H. Cullen and J. Taylor (2016). London: Bloomsbury.

Minimus. B. Bell (1999). Cambridge: Cambridge University Press. Facebook: *Minimus Latin*.

Oxford Latin Course. M. Balme and J. Morwood (2003). Oxford: Oxford University Press. Facebook: *Teachers of Oxford Latin Course*.

So You Really Want to Learn Latin? N. Oulton (1999). Tenterden: Galore Park Publishing.

Suburani. Hands-Up Education (2020). Haverhill: Hands-Up Education. Available at: https://hands-up-education.org/suburani.html. Facebook: *Suburani Teachers – Worldwide*.

Telling Tales in Latin. L. Robinson (2013). London: Souvenir Press.

Wheelock's Latin. F. Wheelock and R. LaFleur (1956). London: Harper Collins.

Web blogs and online Journals

Many of the following have a mixture of commentary and pedagogy.

ad aequiora. Available at: https://medium.com/ad-meliora.
Antigone journal. Available at: https://antigonejournal.com/.
eidolon (now archived) . Available at: https://eidolon.pub/.
in medias res. Available at: https://www.paideiainstitute.org/in_medias_res.
sententiae antiquae. Available at: https://sententiaeantiquae.com/ .

Organizations for the study and promotion of classical subjects in schools

Advocating a Classical Education (ACE). Available at: http://aceclassics.org.uk/.
Association for Latin Teaching (ARLT). Available at: http://www.arlt.co.uk/.
Classical Association (CA). Available at: https://classicalassociation.org/.
Cambridge School Classics Project (CSCP)/North American-Cambridge Classics
    Project (NA-CCP). Available at: www.cambridgescp.com.
Classics for All (CfA). Available at: https://classicsforall.org.uk/.
Classics in Communities (CiC). Available at: https://www.classicsincommunities.org/.
Iris Project. Available at: http://irisproject.org.uk/index.php.
Paideia Institute. Available at: https://www.paideiainstitute.org/.
Primary Latin Project. Available at: https://www.primarylatinproject.org/.
Roman Society. Available at: https://www.romansociety.org/.
Society for Classical Studies (SCS). Available at: https://classicalstudies.org/ (also
    contains links to US classics sub-communities, at: https://classicalstudies.org/
    world-classics/classics-associations-and-research-institutes).

Social media: Twitter and Facebook

There are numerous social media outlets for classical subjects, many of which are pedagogical. #classicstwitter and #latinteach are popular hashtags. A complete list of Facebook pages is impossible. The most commonly used are:

- AP Latin Teachers
- Dr Illa Flora's Latin in the Real World
- IB Latin Teacher Idea Exchange
- Latin Best Practices: The Next Generation in Comprehensible Input

- Latin Teacher Community
- Latin Teacher Idea Exchange
- Learning Latin
- Salvete: Latin in Primary schools (LIPS)
- Social Justice in Secondary Latin
- Teaching Latin for Acquisition
- Teaching Latin Online
- Teaching Latin Traditionally

Latin study groups

There are far too many online study groups for learning Latin to list here. For details, see: www.stevenhuntclassics.com.

Latin speaking groups

For a list, see A. Gratus Avitus, Spoken Latin: Learning, Teaching, Lecturing and Research, *Journal of Classics Teaching*, 37, available at: https://www.cambridge.org/core/journals/journal-of-classics-teaching/article/spoken-latin-learning-teaching-lecturing-and-research/ED66CC496B5BD893A4C519ABF6A257F3; and relevant chapters in Lloyd and Hunt, *Communicative Approaches for Ancient Languages* (2021).

Video games set in ancient Rome

For a list, see: https://en.wikipedia.org/wiki/Fiction_set_in_ancient_Rome#Video_games.

Films set in ancient Rome

For a list, see: https://en.wikipedia.org/wiki/List_of_films_set_in_ancient_Rome.

Latin novellas

For a list, see Dan Conway's site: https@//latinnovelladatabase.blogspot.com/.

Ellie Arnold maintains the *mille noctes* website, a repository for many Latin stories, as well as advice on teaching. Available at: http://www.latinteachertoolbox.com/mille-noctes-texts.html.

Jocelyn Demuth runs the Latina Hilaria website, with an online repository of many short Latin stories. Available at: http://www.latinahilara.com/stories-not-in-your-textbook.

Daniel Pettersson and Amelie Rosengren's Latinitium website. Available at: https://www.latinitium.com/.

Lance Piantaggni's website *Magister P* showcases numerous interconnected novellas based around his *Piso* series. Available at: https://magisterp.com/novellas/.

John Piazza's website has a section on, 'Building and Using a Latin FVR Library'. Available at: http://johnpiazza.net/latin/fvr-library/.

Dan Stoa maintains the Comprehensible Antiquity website, which has a section on Free Voluntary Reading. Available at: https://comprehensibleantiquity.com/free-volunteer-reading/.

For further discussions of Latin novellas for use in the school and college classroom, see also The Classical Outlook, Volume 96, 3 (2021).

Appendix 3
UK/US Education Systems Compared

UK school types

State Schools are free, maintained by the state and open to anyone. State secondary schools (for ages 11–18) and primary schools (for age 4–10) may be run by the Local Authority, or by other groups ('Free Schools' and 'Academies') on behalf of the state. Most secondary schools are non-selective by intake ('secondary moderns' and 'comprehensives') and a few are academically selective by examination ('grammar schools'). They are all funded by general taxation. Some Academies link together into Multi-Academy Trusts (MATs). Free Schools and Academies are allowed to vary their curriculum beyond the national curriculum.

Independent Schools, including Public Schools (of ancient lineage) and other private schools, are fee-paying and often academically selective by examination. These and preparatory schools are not bound by any national curriculum or standards.

Preparatory Schools are private, fee-paying schools for students up to age 11 or 13, whose purpose is to prepare them for the entrance examinations of specific independent secondary schools.

For details of the UK examination system, see *School Qualifications in Classical Subjects in the UK* (Hunt 2020). Available at: https://cucd.blogs.sas.ac.uk/files/2020/01/HUNT-School-qualifications-in-classical-subjects-in-the-UK-3.pdf.

US school types

Public Schools are free, maintained by the local government, and are funded by local, state, federal government funds. Public schools are required to abide by certain state and federal standards, and teachers must have appropriate licensure. Students attend a public school based upon where they live.

Magnet Schools are public schools that specialize in certain areas (e.g. technology, arts or science). As public schools, magnet schools are free, but are operated by school districts. Students are admitted into magnet schools either based upon academic achievement or via random lottery.

Private Schools are private, fee-paying schools, and receive no government funding. Because *private schools* do not receive any government funding, they are not bound by any national curriculum or standards. Students are admitted by application.

Charter Schools are a hybrid between *public* and *private* schools. Like public schools, charter schools are free. However, like private schools, students are admitted via application. Any organization can apply to the state government to open a charter school. If the application is accepted, the charter school can receive government funding for a specified period of time. However, if the state government is dissatisfied with the charter school, their charter can be revoked and the school is closed.

	UK				**US**		
Age of student (years)	**School Year name**	**Key stage name**	**School type**	**National examination**	**School Year name**	**School type**	**National examination**
4–5	Reception		Primary		Pre-Kindergarten (PreK)		
5–6	Year 1	KS1			Kindergarten (K)	Primary / Elementary School	
6–7	Year 2				First Grade		
7–8	Year 3	KS2			Second Grade		
8–9	Year 4				Third Grade		
9–10	Year 5				Fourth Grade		
10–11	Year 6				Fifth Grade		
11–12	Year 7	KS3[i]	Secondary		Sixth Grade	Middle School	
12–13	Year 8				Seventh Grade		
13–14	Year 9				Eighth Grade		
14–15	Year 10	KS4			Ninth Grade	Secondary / High School	
15–16	Year 11			GCSE[ii]	Tenth Grade		
16–17	Year 12	KS5	Sixth Form	AS level	Eleventh Grade		Preliminary Scholastic Aptitude Test (P-SAT)
17–18	Year 13		College[iii]	A level[iv]	Twelfth Grade		Scholastic Aptitude Test (SAT)

[i] Some schools only have a two-year KS3 in Years 7–8.

[ii] Students in some private schools take the International GCSE (IGCSE).

[iii] There is a variety of educational establishments at this stage, including Sixth Forms attached to secondary schools, stand-alone Sixth Form Colleges and Further Education Colleges often for vocational studies.

[iv] Students in some private schools take the Pre-U qualification. Some students take the International Baccalaureate examination.

Index